ENGLISH MEN OF LETTERS

JAMES THOMSON

MACMILLAN AND CO., Limited
LONDON · BOMBAY · CALCUTTA
MELBOURNE

THE MACMILLAN COMPANY
NEW YORK · BOSTON · CHICAGO
ATLANTA · SAN FRANCISCO

THE MACMILLAN CO. OF CANADA, Ltd.
TORONTO

JAMES THOMSON

BY

G. C. MACAULAY

LATE FELLOW OF TRINITY COLLEGE, CAMBRIDGE

MACMILLAN AND CO., LIMITED
ST. MARTIN'S STREET, LONDON
1908

x°

PREFATORY NOTE

In this book an attempt is made to present the subject as a chapter of the history of English Literature, and to bring out the part played by Thomson in the development of the poetry of the eighteenth century. Partly with a view to this, a distinct line has been drawn between biography and literary criticism, though the relation between the life and the writings has not been ignored.

For the biography of Thomson fairly good materials are available, thanks to the labours of a series of investigators devoted to the memory of the poet. The present writer gladly acknowledges obligation to those by whom these materials have been contributed or elucidated. After the first biographers, Shiels, Murdoch and Johnson, we are indebted in the eighteenth century especially to the eleventh Earl of Buchan, by whose enthusiasm many memorials were preserved, which would otherwise have perished, and in the first half of the nineteenth century to Harris Nicolas, Bolton Corney and Peter Cunningham. In more recent times useful work has been done especially by M. Léon Morel, whose book on Thomson is a monument of praiseworthy industry, by Mr. Tovey, as editor of the new Aldine edition of Thomson, by Mr. Seccombe in the *Dictionary of National Biography*, and by Dr. Birkbeck Hill in his notes on Johnson's *Lives of the Poets*. The present writer has contributed some facts, especially with regard to the production of Thomson's plays, his relations with Lyttelton, and the tenure of his posts, which have not appeared in any previous biography.

The due estimation of Thomson's literary work involves a careful collation of the early editions of *The Seasons*, since there is as yet no full information published with regard to their important variations of text. Mr. Tovey's critical notes are useful, but incomplete; and, moreover, he takes no account of any edition earlier than 1730. In general it may be said that all information given in this book about variations is derived from original sources.

With regard to other parts of the work, acknowledgments are especially due to Mr. J. L. Robertson, whose excellent annotated edition of *The Seasons* and *The Castle of Indolence* has been frequently useful, to M. Morel again, and (with reference to the influence of other poets upon *Winter*) to Dr. Otto Zippel, from whom a complete critical edition of *The Seasons* is to be expected.

The discussion on the revision of the text of *The Seasons* has been, with some hesitation, relegated to an appendix, not because the subject is unimportant or uninteresting, but because it is of a somewhat controversial character.

I am unwilling to pass over without notice the useful reprint, by Judge Willis, of the very rare first edition of *Winter*, with a preface in which the mistakes of editors and biographers are faithfully pointed out. I did not make acquaintance with this book until my own was already finished; but I hope that by a careful following of original texts I have been preserved from such errors as are there denounced.

CONTENTS

JAMES THOMSON

CHAPTER I

EARLY CAREER

JAMES THOMSON was the fourth child of Thomas Thomson, minister of Ednam, in the north-eastern corner of the county of Roxburgh, and was baptized on the 15th of September, 1700. In spite of the doubts raised by some of his biographers, there seems every reason to accept the statement of his friend Murdoch, that he was born on September 11th (22nd by the new style), which was certainly regarded by his family as his birthday. His father, a native of Ednam, was the son of Andrew Thomson, a gardener in the service of a Mr. Edmonston of that place, and several other members of the poet's family followed this vocation. The Rev. Thomas Thomson had married Beatrix, daughter of Alexander Trotter of Widehope, whose wife Margaret was descended apparently from a branch of the noble family of Home. Thomas Thomson was a minister of good repute, and devoted to his spiritual charge: his wife is described for us, by one who knew her, as a person of uncommon natural endowments, "with an imagination for vivacity and warmth scarce inferior to her son's, and which raised her devotional exercises to a pitch bordering on enthusiasm."

It is of some interest to note what the scenery and

surroundings were, in which the future poet of *The Seasons* grew up. These, however, are not to be sought for at Ednam; for within two months of James Thomson's birth his father accepted a call from the more important parish of Southdean, situated close to the Cheviots, on the upper stream of the "sylvan Jed," a locality which combines bleak mountain scenery with the charm of prettily wooded valleys; and it was here that the first impressions of external nature were received by the growing boy. Thomson is not very apt to describe particular localities, but it is partly on the scenery of Southdean that the descriptions are based which appeared in the first-published poem of *The Seasons*, and the poem is introduced by a passage which refers to his early experiences :—

> " Welcome, kindred glooms !
> Cogenial [1] horrors, hail ! with frequent foot
> Pleas'd have I, in my cheerful morn of life,
> When nurs'd by careless solitude I liv'd,
> And sung of Nature with unceasing joy,
> Pleas'd have I wander'd thro' your rough domain,
> Trod the pure virgin snows, myself as pure,
> Heard the winds roar, and the big torrents burst,
> Or seen the deep-fermenting tempest brew'd
> In the grim evening sky."

The manse is described as a straw-thatched house, "clinging with a nestling snugness to the base of Southdean Law," and commanding a view of the valley. The river Jed sweeps round its garden, and in the distance is seen "the clear-cut sky-line of Carter Fell, . . . whose heathland slopes retain the eye of the spectator above surrounding objects, as the storm-drift

---

[1] "Cogenial" is Thomson's word, though it has been altered in all modern editions. He meant, of course, "familiar from birth."

careers along them, or as the sunbeam reddens their purple beauty."[1] Carter Fell rises in fact to a height of about 1800 feet, and there are other considerable hills in the immediate neighbourhood.

Young Thomson was sent to school at Jedburgh, where the classes were held in an aisle or chapel of the partly ruined Abbey ; and as the distance from South-dean is about eight miles, he probably resided in the town during the week. He made no very brilliant impression on his schoolmaster : an early biographer says that he was considered stupid, "really without a common share of parts." He was probably judged by his progress in Latin grammar, while he was chiefly devoting his attention, even at this early age, to English poetry. He very soon attracted the attention of some persons who were competent to judge of his literary ability, and were ready to give help and encourage-ment. It is generally agreed by Thomson's biographers, and gratefully acknowledged by Thomson himself, that a very important influence was exercised upon him by Robert Riccaltoun, a resident in the neighbourhood of Southdean, afterwards minister of the adjoining parish of Hobkirk. Riccaltoun was nine years older than James Thomson, and is described as a man of excellent literary taste and some original talent. He seems to have supplied the boy with books, and to have directed his early reading and his first essays in poetry ; and Thomson, at the time when he was engaged on his own poem of *Winter*, wrote thus : "Mr. Riccaltoun's poem on Winter, which I still have, first put the design into my head ; in it are some masterly strokes which awakened me." The poem referred to is generally assumed to be that entitled *A Winter's Day*, published in Savage's

[1] Description communicated in 1891 to Mr. J. Logie Robert-son by Dr. John Mair, minister of Southdean.

Miscellany, 1726, and there attributed to the author of
William and Margaret, that is, Mallet, but reprinted in
the *Gentleman's Magazine*, 1740, as "written by a Scotch
clergyman: corrected by an eminent hand." The
"eminent hand" was probably Mallet, who may well
have obtained the copy in the first instance from
Thomson, and who was quite capable of publishing it
in his own name on the strength of his corrections.
We hear, however, of another poem by Riccaltoun,
which possibly may have been that referred to in
Thomson's letter. Dr. Somerville, minister of Jedburgh, writing in 1814, describes Riccaltoun as the
most distinguished member of the Presbytery of Jedburgh about the year 1767, combining original genius
with facetious manners and an ample store of observation and anecdote, and then adds: "He modestly
acknowledged to me that he had considerable influence
in discovering and prompting the poetical genius of
Thomson, who in his youthful days had been his frequent visitor. . . . He also mentioned that a poem
of his own composition, the subject of which was the
description of a storm, or the effects of an extraordinary
fall of snow on the hill of Ruberslaw, suggested to
Thomson the idea of expatiating on the same theme,
and produced his divine poem of *Winter*, the first
and best of his compositions." The description of
this poem does not apply to *A Winter's Day* as we
have it.

Others besides Riccaltoun took an interest in James
Thomson's boyish verse, among whom were Sir Gilbert
Eliot of Minto, in whose service two of the young poet's
relatives were, and Sir William Bennett of Grubbat;
and he was invited sometimes to stay in his summer
vacations, while at school or at the University, with one
of these, at Minto, or at Marlefield. His friend and

biographer, Murdoch, declares, with reference to this
period, that it was his practice every New Year to
destroy the pieces of verse which he had composed in
the past year, committing them to the flames in their
due order, "and crowning the solemnity with a copy
of verses, in which were humorously recited the several
grounds of their condemnation." A certain number of
juvenile poems survive nevertheless, having been
written out by Thomson afterwards, at the request
of Lord George Graham. Of these the only piece
which has much merit is *Lisy's Parting with her Cat*,
a rather clever exercise in mock-heroic blank verse.
Lisy (or Lizzie) was his favourite sister. Of his other
pursuits at this period we have no record, but from
the early poems, as well as from *The Seasons*, we may
conjecture that mountain walks, bathing,[1] and trout-
fishing were among his favourite occupations.

From Jedburgh school he passed at the age of fifteen
to the University of Edinburgh, being intended for the
ministry. There is a tradition that he was sent to
Edinburgh seated behind his father's man on horseback, and that being arrived there, he returned
promptly on foot, declaring that he could study as well
"on the braes of Sou'den" as at Edinburgh. His father
naturally did not take that view, and he was forced
to exchange a country life for the town. Soon after
his admission his father died, under rather remarkable
circumstances, which throw some light on the customs
and religious beliefs of the time. While endeavouring
to exorcise an evil spirit, which haunted a house in the
parish, the minister was seized with a fit (of apoplexy,
probably), from the effects of which he died, his death
being generally ascribed to diabolical agency.

[1] Savage's remark, recorded by Johnson, is of course no
evidence against this.

After the death of her husband, Mrs. Thomson, who had a family of nine children to provide for, with a very moderate income, removed her home, with the assistance of her friends, to Edinburgh, where her son continued his studies for a good many years. Ramsay of Ochtertyre, writing about fifty years later, speaks thus of the conditions which prevailed at this time in Edinburgh : "Soon after the extinction of the rebellion of 1715 a number of promising young men began to distinguish themselves in science and polite literature. In order to improve themselves and counteract conceit, . . . societies were instituted, wherein at stated times literary subjects were discussed with freedom and impartiality. . . . There the members used to submit their first essays in composition to the friendly censure of their associates, which helped to lop away luxuriances and check presumption. . . . These juvenile adventurers and their counsellors would soon see the impossibility of making a distinguished figure in the republic of letters without a proper attention to the graces of composition. Latin was by this time out of fashion except in Colleges; and for more than a century nothing of character had appeared in the dialect usually called 'broad Scots.' To render it polished and corrected would have been a herculean labour, not likely to procure them much renown. Nothing therefore remained but to write classical English, which, though exceedingly difficult to men who spoke their mother-tongue without disguise, was greatly facilitated by the enthusiastic ardour with which they studied the best English authors. In all their essays at composition it behoved them to avoid everything that could be called a Scotticism or solecism, while they endeavoured to catch the manner of their favourite writers. In this generous but unpromising attempt our countrymen at length succeeded to the conviction of the world." [1]

It was under these literary influences that the young student found himself at Edinburgh. He became a member of more than one of the literary clubs which have been referred to—the "Grotesques" and the "Athenian Society" are both mentioned—but it seems that he did not make any great figure in them, being perhaps a little deficient in smartness of repartee, and apt to be silent except in congenial society, so that he was by some regarded as a dull fellow; and the exuberance of his literary style laid him open to criticism. Murdoch, who was one of his contemporaries at Edinburgh, implies that the productions of Thomson were somewhat unfairly dealt with by his companions; and after the publication of *Winter*, Mallet in a letter to a friend expressed regret for the injustice of which he had himself been guilty, in joining with his companions "to ridicule the first imperfect essays of an excellent genius." He contributed several poems to the *Edinburgh Miscellany*, a magazine published by the "Athenian Society" in 1720, and one of these, "Of a Country Life," in rhyming couplets, contains a review of the seasons of the year, with some passages which may be recognised in altered forms in the young poet's later work, *e.g* :—

> "Anon black winter, from the frozen north,
> Its treasuries of snow and hail pours forth ;
> Then stormy winds blow through the hazy sky,
> In desolation nature seems to lie ;
>   .   .   .   .   .
> In maiden white the glittering fields do shine ;
> Then bleating flocks for want of food repine,
> With wither'd eyes they see all snow around,
> And with their fore feet paw and scrape the ground."

---

[1] *Scotland and Scotsmen in the Eighteenth Century*, pp. 8, 9.

Angling and bathing are also mentioned, and field-sports take their place as reasonable diversions, with no more than a slight and conventional note of sympathy for the hunted animals. Already, we may note, "the dear image of a charming she" has taken its place in his mental vision. On the whole, these poems are essentially schoolboy exercises, with some happy images here and there, but full of awkward inversions and tasteless puerilities of expression.

Thomson completed the Arts course and was entered as a student of Divinity in 1719, neglecting the form of graduation, as most of his contemporaries also did, the degree having fallen into disregard. Mallet, for example, in 1724, writes, "I never took any degree at Edinburgh, nor ever asked for any." One of Thomson's exercises in the Divinity Hall, apparently towards the end of his course, created some sensation, but the accounts of it differ a good deal as regards details. Hamilton, the Professor of Divinity, had prescribed to him a discourse on a certain Psalm (one authority says the tenth portion of the 119th), and his composition was in so ornate and poetical a style that the Professor, while complimenting the young student on his performance, told him that if he thought of being useful in the ministry, he must express himself in language more intelligible to an ordinary congregation. We are told that some of his fellow-students could not be persuaded that he was capable of composing such a declamation, and endeavoured to convict him of plagiarism, but without success. Either this incident, or the advice of friends who were acquainted with his poems, seems to have determined Thomson to try his fortune in London, without, however, giving up the idea of the ministry. In particular he was encouraged by "a lady of quality," then in London, who was

acquainted with his mother, and who is supposed to
have been Lady Grizel Baillie.[1] He made his journey
to London by sea, in the latter part of February, 1725,
and almost immediately after his arrival, "as he
wandered admiring through the streets," he had his
pocket picked, and lost the letters of introduction
which he had brought with him, an incident, says
one of his biographers, which would have been morti-
fying to a man less philosophical than Thomson, "but
he was of a temper never to be agitated; he then
smiled at it, and frequently made his companions
laugh at the relation." Similarly in later life, when he
was robbed of his watch on the road between London
and Richmond, he only remarked, "I am glad they took
it. It was never good for anything." In this instance
the inconvenience was probably soon remedied. By a
letter dated April 3rd, to his friend Dr. Cranston, a
young doctor of medicine, son of the minister of
Ancrum, we learn that he had already obtained a
renewal of one of the lost letters, and had called upon
the person to whom it was addressed. In the meantime he had visited Mallet, who was acting as tutor to
the young Duke of Montrose and his brother, Lord
George Graham, and from him he obtained a good deal
of information as to the conditions of the literary
world in London, a subject about which Thomson was
not likely to be very well informed. Mallet, who is
noted by Johnson as "the only Scot whom Scotchmen
did not commend," was of great assistance both now
and afterwards to his countryman and fellow-student,
whom he had formerly joined in ridiculing, and the
friendship between them lasted without interruption

[1] She was the daughter of Sir Patrick Home, and may therefore have been distantly related to Thomson's maternal grand-
mother.

till Thomson's death.   Mallet was received in good
society, where he made himself very agreeable by the
ease and elegance of his conversation, having altogether "cleared his tongue from his native pronunciation," a thing which Thomson certainly never did ; and
by his *savoir vivre* he was able, when the time came, to
assist his friend very materially in his first dealings
with publishers, as well as to introduce him to several
of the leading literary men of the day.   At the same
time, Thomson was very kindly received by Duncan
Forbes of Culloden, afterwards Lord President of the
Court of Session, who had been interested in his poetry
in Scotland, and who recommended him to some of his
influential friends, and made him acquainted also with
Aikman the painter, between whom and Thomson a
sincere friendship sprang up.

On the whole, we may say that, when he first arrived
in London, Thomson found himself fairly well provided
with friends and well-wishers.   The creditable manner
in which natives of Scotland are apt to recognise and
support one another in a foreign country had evidently
much to do with this fact, and his future relations with
publishers were probably determined to some extent
by considerations of nationality.   How he spent his
time during his first days in London, we learn partly
from the letter which has already been referred to,
where he narrates particularly his experiences at the
theatre, highly praising the performance of Booth,
Mrs. Oldfield, and Mrs. Porter, and remarking that he
has paid five visits already to Drury Lane, but has not
yet been at the New House, his purse not keeping
pace with his inclinations in the matter.   The plays
which he mentions or refers to are *Oroonoko, Hamlet, A
Trip to the Jubilee,* and *Cato,* all of which were acted at
Drury Lane near the beginning of March, 1726.   From

the same letter we learn that, whatever may have
been his literary aspirations, he had not yet given up
the idea of the ministry. After referring darkly to
his prospects of success in some other design, he
continues : " Succeed or not, I firmly resolve to pursue
divinity, as the only thing now I am fit for"; and
though his friend may laugh, he adds with deep
seriousness, that the more he sees of the vanity and
wickedness of the world, the more he is inclined to
the sacred office. He proposes, if he cannot accomplish the design for which he came up, to pass his
trials for the ministry in London, so that if he is
obliged soon to return to Scotland, he may at least
have made some progress in his course. This is
plainly inconsistent with the idea that he came up
to London merely as a literary adventurer, though
the design to which he refers may have had something
to do with literature.

In May of this year he lost his mother, to whom he
was tenderly attached. In a poem written on this
occasion, but first published in 1792, he refers in
a touching manner to the details of his last parting
from her :—

> " When on the margin of the briny flood,
>   Chill'd with a sad presaging damp, I stood,
>   Took the last look, ne'er to behold her more,
>   And mix'd our murmurs with the wavy roar :
>   Heard the last words fall from her pious tongue,
>   Then wild into the bulging vessel flung,
>   Which soon, too soon, convey'd me from her sight,
>   Dearer than life and liberty and light ! "

A letter to Mallet, dated July 10, 1725, but without note of place, shows us the friends engaged in
mutual criticism and appreciation :—

" If you knew the satisfaction the sight of your hand gives

me, you would not spare me frequent letters. . . . You may
take what liberties you please with my poem, and I will
thank you for it.   Your own celebrated performance is a
shining instance of your being able to enter into the very
spirit of a piece where nature reigns.   The six lines you
favour me with raise my expectation vastly of the whole.
The character expressed in them is lovely, natural, and finely
touched. ' Sweetness is hers,' etc., is both easy and pathetic.
. . . To fill up this letter I shall give you a few loose lines I
composed in my last evening walk ; they may be once worth
the reading, but no more."

Accordingly there follows a *Hymn on Solitude*, beginning "Hail, ever pleasing Solitude!" which was
published in an improved form in 1729.   The previously mentioned poem, which the writer abandons
to Mallet's criticism, may have been a first draught of
Winter, or more probably some smaller piece, which
was afterwards incorporated in that work.   Spence in
fact says, apparently on the authority of Mallet, that
at first Thomson wrote single winter pieces, and they
(*i.e.* the author and Mallet) at last thought it might
make a poem.   In any case *Winter* was still in embryo
in the autumn of this year, as we shall shortly see.
As to Mallet's poems which are referred to here, "your
celebrated performance" must be the ballad of *William
and Margaret*, which had come out in the preceding
year, and which was the only work by which Mallet
was as yet known.   The later reference is to the poem
To Mira from the Country, which appeared in Savage's
Miscellany, 1726.

A letter to Cranston gives us more definite information.   It is dated "East Barnet, July 20," and it
tells us that he was there installed as tutor in the
family of Lord Binning (eldest son of the Earl of
Haddington), who, we may observe, was the son-in-
law of Lady Grizel Baillie.   The post had probably

been obtained by means of that lady, though, according
to Spence, Mallet claimed to have recommended him
for it. He had, in fact, undertaken to teach Lord
Binning's son, a child of five years old, to read—not
an occupation which he very much cared for, but one
which he accepted for want of a better, resolving to
pursue his own studies in the meantime. He professes
inability to give his correspondent much London news,
but he hears that it is a very dead season there as regards literature, and especially that poetry has "lost all
her flame, life, and spirit." The year 1725 had not, in
fact, much to boast of in the way of poetry. Pope
had lately been engaged on his edition of Shakespeare,
which came out in that year, and had not yet bestowed
his energy upon the Dunces; Gay's Fables were not
published till 1727. Young's satires, *The Universal
Passion*, began to appear in 1725, and these were the
best poetical productions of the year in London; but
we know that Thomson did not very highly appreciate
Young as a poet, at least at this time. In Scotland,
meanwhile, the most interesting literary event of the
year was the publication at Edinburgh of Allan
Ramsay's *Gentle Shepherd*.

The next letter to Cranston[1] was written from
Barnet, evidently in the autumn of the same year.
This contains the first mention of his designed poem
on Winter. After speaking of money difficulties, and
asking for a loan of twelve pounds, to be repaid when
his mother's inheritance at Widehope should be sold,
the writer casts aside the necessary but unwelcome
subject of business, and proceeds to a matter which
interests him much more, namely the feelings which

[1] First published in the *European Magazine* of May, 1797,
having been used to wrap up a parcel, and rescued from destruction by an intelligent tradesman of Dumfries.

autumn may be expected to inspire, especially in the places where his correspondent has the happiness to be.

"Now I figure you wandering, philosophical and pensive, amidst the brown withered groves, while the leaves rustle under your feet, the sun gives a farewell, parting gleam, and the birds

> 'Stir the faint note and but attempt to sing.'

Then again, when the heavens wear a more gloomy aspect, . . . I see you in the well-known cleugh, beneath the solemn arch of the tall, thick, embowering trees, listening to the amusing lull of the many steep, moss-grown cascades, while deep, divine Contemplation, the genius of the place, prompts each swelling, awful thought. I'm sure you would not resign your part in that scene at an easy rate. None e'er enjoyed it to the height you do, and you're worthy of it. There I walk in spirit and disport in its beloved gloom."

We are reminded by these descriptions of the fact that at Ancrum is situated "Thomson's Cave," a recess high up in the rock, near the cascades which are referred to in the letter, where he is traditionally reported to have composed some of his youthful poetry. The writer then proceeds to speak of his own actual surroundings and of the poetical work upon which he is engaged.

"This country I am in is not very entertaining; no variety but that of woods, and them we have in abundance; but where is the living stream, the airy mountain, and the hanging rock? . . . Nature delights me in every form; I am just now painting her in her most lugubrious dress; for my own amusement describing Winter as it presents itself. After my first proposal of the subject,

> 'I sing of Winter and his gelid reign,
>   Nor let a ryming insect of the Spring
>   Deem it a barren theme. To me 'tis full
>   Of manly charms; to me who court the shade,

Whom the gay seasons suit not, and who shun
The glare of Summer, welcome, kindred glooms !
Drear, awful, Wintry horrors, welcome all ! ' etc.

After this introduction, I say, which insists for a few lines
further, I prosecute the purport of the following ones :—

' Nor can I, O departing Summer, choose
But consecrate one pitying line to you ;
Sing your last temper'd days and sunny calms,
That cheer the spirits and serene the soul.'

Then terrible floods, and high winds, that usually happen
about this time of the year, and have already happened here
(I wish you have not felt them too dreadfully) ; the first
produced the enclosed lines, the last are not completed.   Mr.
Rickleton's poem on Winter, which I still have, first put the
design into my head : in it are some masterly strokes that
awakened me.   Being only a present amusement, it is ten to
one but I drop it, whene'er another fancy comes cross."

This account is sufficient to refute the statement of
Johnson, that the young poet came up to London with
his *Winter* already written and ready to be offered to
the publishers.   It is pretty evident that it was not
even begun till he had been several months in England.
The lines cited in the letter, as forming the introduction to *Winter*, are not actually reproduced at the
beginning of the poem as published, except the expression " Welcome, kindred glooms ! "   The line

" Of thy last temper'd days and sunny calms,"

which occurs in the first editions of *Winter*, is there
applied to autumn.   The " enclosed lines " which are
mentioned must have been a passage descriptive of
winter floods, corresponding to ll. 94-105 of *Winter* as
we have it ; the other passage, which is spoken of as
unfinished, would correspond to the highly elabo-
rated description of a storm of wind, which follows
(ll. 111-201).

The poem upon which he had been engaged in the autumn of 1725 was published by John Millan in March, 1726. It is said to have been offered to several booksellers without success, and to have been at length accepted by Millan owing to Mallet's influence. The publisher advanced a small sum to the author on accepting the manuscript, one account says three guineas; but it is clear that Thomson retained the copyright, for he was able to dispose of it in 1729.

The poem came out in a thin folio of sixteen pages, and was sold for a shilling. It was dedicated, apparently without permission, to Sir Spencer Compton, Speaker of the House of Commons. As first published it consisted of 405 lines only, a number which (in spite of the transference to *Autumn* of a passage of some length near the beginning) had grown to 781, when the first collected edition of *The Seasons* was published, in 1730, and was increased finally to 1069. On the whole, it may be said that hardly any poem in literature has been more completely altered from its original form than Thomson's *Winter*, so that readers of the later editions only are hardly in a position to judge of the impression which it might be expected to produce upon its first publication.[1]

The circumstances of its reception by the public are variously reported, but its success was not long in doubt. Shiels says that very few copies were sold at

---

[1] In a general way it may be noted that the following passages are wanting in the first edition, viz. ll. 17-71 (including the address to Lord Wilmington, formerly Sir Spencer Compton, in place of the original prose dedication), 126-152, 158-174, 245-256, 276-423, nearly all the passage 440-526, 546-692 (except one line), most of the passage 695-793 (represented by 23 lines only), 794-987; and the concluding portion was very different. On the other hand, 95 lines, which occurred originally after l. 16, were removed in 1730.

first, "till Mr. Whatley, a man of some taste and enthusiasm in appreciation, happened to see it, and went round the coffee-houses praising it," and Johnson accepts this statement. Others say that Rundle was the person who first recommended the poem; and Warton tells us that "it lay neglected till Mr. Spence made honourable mention of it in his Essay on the *Odyssey*," adding that Thomson always acknowledged the use of this recommendation. Spence's notice, however, is very slight, and, moreover, his essay was not published until *Winter* had attained to a certain degree of success. It is certain, in any case, that the attention of the public was drawn to the new poem before very long, for the first edition was apparently sold out in about three months. One of the first to express appreciation to the author himself was Aaron Hill, a man highly esteemed in the world of letters. He was no great literary genius certainly, and on this account he has been made an object of ridicule by some modern editors of Thomson; but his position was a highly respectable one. Born of a good family, he had travelled to an unusual extent in his youth, having seen Asia Minor, Egypt, and Palestine, and visited most of the courts of Europe in company with his relative Lord Paget, ambassador at Constantinople, and later with Sir William Wentworth. He had been manager of Drury Lane Theatre in 1709, and of the Haymarket Opera-house in 1710; he himself wrote for the stage, and was praised both by Voltaire and Lessing. But, as a contemporary remarks, "he was one of those enterprising spirits that attempt everything, and for want of discerning their proper province, bring nothing to perfection." His versatility was really remarkable, and with regard to one, at least, of his projects, that for bringing timber from the

Highlands of Scotland for the use of the navy, he
showed much energy and spirit.[1] With some degree
of literary talent, he combined a certain dignified
independence of demeanour, a great deal of what
Johnson calls "humanity and politeness," and much
readiness to appreciate the literary work of others,
especially of young authors. "With a warm and
benevolent mind," says Davies, "he had the delicate
address and polite manners of a complete gentleman."
He actually induced Pope to make something like an
apology for including him among the "Dunces"; and
his remonstrance, which is said to have given Pope
serious uneasiness, is both gentlemanly and reasonable,
a protest against the unfairness of accepting praise
without repaying it :—

> "Tuneful Alexis on the Thames' fair side,
>   The ladies' plaything and the Muses' pride,
>
> .   .   .   .   .   .
>
>   Desiring and deserving others' praise,
>   Poorly accepts a fame he ne'er repays."

This was by no means in accordance with Hill's ideas.
If he praised generously, he expected generous praise
in return, and he usually obtained it. Very soon after
the publication of *Winter*, he wrote a letter of appreciation to Mallet, which rejoiced the soul of the author.
Thomson replied with apologies for approaching "so

[1] A letter from Richard Savage to Mallet, dated Aug. 15,
1726, gives us a glimpse of him as he was in the year when
Winter was published. "Mr. Hill has finished his affair,
and by disposing of it to a company, has secured a hundred
thousand pounds for himself. On Friday was se'nnight he set
out in his own coach-and-six to Scotland, with his wife, and
his mother-in-law accompanied him in her chariot. The gold
medal he has been presented with from the Czarina has
doubtless been related to you by Mr. Thomson and by the
newspapers."

supreme a genius" without an introduction, and
expressing transports of joy at his praise. "How
rare, how happy is it to find a judge whose discerning
goodness overlooks the faults of what is well meant,
at the same time that his fine enthusiastic taste improves the beauties. To you alone it belongs to write
so inimitably, and to read so indulgently." It would
be ill-nature to criticise severely so natural an effusion
of pleasure and gratitude. The result of this letter
was some further correspondence, which doubtless
gave satisfaction on both sides, and finally a visit to
Hill's house, the delights of which overflowed afterwards in a letter of very exaggerated adulation from
Thomson. We must remember, however, that the
game of give and take was fully understood in this
circle, and the tone of the correspondence, which had
been first set by the extravagant praises of Hill himself, could hardly be lowered by the young aspirant
without risk of incivility.

A somewhat curious episode followed upon this,
which illustrates the manners of this last age of dedication and patronage. Sir Spencer Compton, to whom
Winter had been dedicated, took no notice of the compliment, apparently not thinking himself bound to
acknowledge an unauthorised dedication. Hill then
addressed some verses to Thomson, which were published in the newspapers, wherein, besides highly
praising the poet, he censured the great for their
neglect of men of genius ; and upon this the Speaker
sent for Thomson on June 4th, and made him a present
of twenty guineas, which the young author thought
generous. This produced something of a difficulty,
because it had been intended to print Hill's lines, together with some to the same effect by Mallet, in the
second edition of *Winter*, which was just being pre-

pared. Thomson was very unwilling to sacrifice the
praise contained in these copies of verse, and yet it
was not possible any longer to reflect upon the
Speaker. His desire was, therefore, to get the lines
altered in such a way as to fit them for publication
under the altered circumstances. The point was thus
put by Thomson in a letter to Hill dated June 7th :—

"As the case now is, one of your infinite delicacy will
be the best judge, whether it will be proper to print
these two inimitable copies of verses I have from you and
Mr. Mallet, without such little alterations as shall clear Sir
Spencer of the best satire I ever read. I shall say no more
on that head ; for if there be any reasons for such alterations,
you will of necessity at one glance see them in the strongest
and finest light. Only this let me add, should you find that
the case required some small alterations, and yet not indulge
me with them, I shall reckon what my patron gave me a
fatal present. 'Tis a thought too shocking to be borne, to
lose the applause of the great genius of the age, my charter
of fame, for——I will not name it ! But you are too good to
plague me so severely. I expect this favour from Mr. Mallet
next post."

Mallet made some difficulty, and at first found it
"absolutely out of his power" to alter the verses, but
eventually the affair was accomplished, though not
without much negotiation and several letters. The
last, dated June 17th, informs Hill that the poem is
to be printed off on the next Monday, but that the press
can wait till the revised copy of verses is ready.

The second, third, and fourth editions of *Winter*, all
published before the end of the year, do not very
materially differ from the first, though some fifty or
sixty lines in all are added (including the well-known
passage on the robin-redbreast, now ll. 245-256), but
they have an interesting preface on the present state
of Poetry, containing a protest against low and trifling

themes, and a plea for elevated subjects, among which none, according to the author, is more inspiring than the works of Nature. This proposition is further enforced by a reference to the later chapters of the Book of Job, and a quotation from Virgil's *Georgics*. The author concludes by expressing his intention to treat of the various appearances of Nature in the other seasons of the year.

Meanwhile, as we learn from his correspondence, he has quitted the household of Lord Binning, and resides at "Mr. Watt's Academy in Little Tower Street," as tutor to a young gentleman there. Not long afterwards he was living at Lancaster Court in the Strand. He was engaged at the same time on the composition of *Summer*; and both in June and in August he was sending passages of that poem to Mallet, and receiving in return portions of Mallet's *Excursion*. The correspondence between them seems to have been of the kind which was usual in Hill's circle. We have only Thomson's letters, but from them we can easily picture to ourselves the style of Mallet's, and it is probable that there was the most fulsome flattery on both sides. It was clearly a case such as that described by Pope :—

> "'My dear Tibullus,'—if that will not do,
> Let me be Horace and be Ovid you :
> Or I'm content, allow me Dryden's strains,
> And you shall rise up Otway for your pains."

As regards the structure of his poem, the author says that he has resolved in this case to represent the season by the course of a day, a scheme which is suitable to "the uniform appearances of Nature in summer."

Summer was published in the following year. The author had intended to dedicate the poem to Lord Binning, in whose family he had been for some months, in acknowledgment of his kindness; but Bubb Dodington, then a member of the Government, sent a message about this time through Young, that he would like to make the young poet's acquaintance, and Lord Binning advised him to make use of the opportunity. Accordingly the dedication was transferred to Dodington, who was addressed as one "in whom the Virtues, the Graces, and the Muses join their influence." It must be remembered with reference to these and other praises that Dodington was a man of considerable wit and geniality, with a genuine interest in literature, and there was no reason, at least at this time, to suppose that he was more unprincipled in politics than his fellows. Later we shall find Thomson staying at Eastbury, Dodington's seat in Dorsetshire, and writing letters to him from France and Italy.

When first published, *Summer* had 1146 lines, but it was finally increased to 1805, among the additions being the lines addressed to Dodington in place of the original prose dedication, the descriptions of haymaking, sheep-washing and shearing, the address to Miss Stanley, most of the scenes of tropical climates as they stand at present, the episode of Damon and Musidora, the walk with Amanda, and the view from Richmond Hill. As to the reception of the poem, we have no very exact account, but it must certainly have tended to increase the credit of the author. Two editions of it were published in the year 1727.

The *Seasons*, however, did not occupy all Thomson's literary energies. The death of Sir Isaac Newton, March 20, 1727, called forth from him a poem, published in the following June, which is not wholly unworthy of the subject, and is a rather remarkable example of scientific accuracy combined with poetical feeling. For the former the author is said to have

been indebted "to his friend Mr. Gray, a gentleman
well versed in the Newtonian philosophy, who on that
occasion gave him a very exact, though general,
abstract of its principles." This was John Gray,
afterwards Rector of Marischal College, Aberdeen.
Thomson himself, however, was always interested in
the operation of the laws of nature, and he had gone
through a course of scientific study at Edinburgh. The
poem was dedicated to Sir Robert Walpole, addressed as
the country's "most illustrious patriot," who by the wise
choice of "the best of kings" is engaged in balancing the
power of Europe, in looking after the common welfare,
and, "like Heaven, dispensing happiness to the discon-
tented and ungrateful." These sentiments are at variance, no doubt, with those that Thomson held later,
but there is no reason to suppose that the expressions
were more insincere than was usual in dedications. It
seems probable, in any case, that the poem of *Britannia*,
in which they are supposed to be contradicted, was
composed later than this year.

In the meantime Thomson had been invited to stay
during a part of the summer of 1727 at Marlborough
Castle, the seat of the Earl of Hertford. It was the
practice of the Countess of Hertford, says Johnson,
"to invite every summer some poet into the country,
to hear her verses and assist her studies." He proceeds
to tell us that Thomson took more delight on this
occasion in carousing with Lord Hertford and his
friends than in "assisting her ladyship's poetical
operations," and therefore never received another
invitation. It may be so ; but Lady Hertford did not
lose her interest in him, for a letter of a later date is
extant, in which she enthusiastically praises his work.
Thomson probably wrote a considerable portion of
Spring at Marlborough Castle, and the poem was pub-

lished in the succeeding year, with a dedication to the
Countess, in which he speaks of it as having grown up
under her encouragement.   She was, in fact, a woman
of some poetical taste and of a feeling heart.   Her sense
of justice and pity for misfortune led her in the early
part of 1728 to use her influence with the Queen in
favour of Richard Savage, then under sentence of
death for homicide committed in a tavern brawl, and
he seems to have owed his life to her intercession.
Her genuine love of the country is testified not only
by Thomson, but by her own letters to Lady Pomfret,
in one of which she gives a pleasing account in verse
of the occupations of a day in a well-ordered English
country-house.

The poem of *Spring* was not very much increased in
bulk after its first publication ; but the description of
trout-fishing and of the noonday rest was added later,
and also, of course, the address to Lyttelton and the
description of Hagley Park.   The additions, however,
were to some extent balanced by omissions, and the
total increase amounted to less than a hundred lines.
The author is said to have received £50 (or fifty
guineas) for the poem from Andrew Millar.   *Spring*
was, in fact, published by Andrew Millar and G.
Strahan, and sold at eighteenpence.

In September of the next year, 1729, we find
Thomson at Eastbury, staying with Dodington, whence
he writes to Mallet that he is "far from that divine
freedom, that independent life, which the Muses love;
but it shall not be long thus."   He expresses at some
length his disgust at the attitude of the public towards
poets, and concludes : "Evil is their good.   Damn
their corruption, their low taste, and their stupid
expense."   Then he turns to a softer theme : "I am
really touched with a fair neighbour of yours,—you

know who. . . . Lay your hand upon a kindred heart, and despise me not. I know not what it is, but she dwells upon my thought in a mingled sentiment, which is the sweetest, the most intimately pleasing the soul can receive, and which I would wish never to want towards some dear object or other." Who the "dear object" in this case was, Mallet doubtless knew, but we do not.

In the course of the year 1729 some transactions took place between Thomson and his publishers with regard to the copyright of his poems. Our information about these is derived from law reports, for the law of copyright was subsequently determined by means of suits connected with this very matter. The best information is to be obtained from the report of the case of Donaldson *v.* Beckett on an appeal against a perpetual injunction, which was decided in favour of the appellants in 1774.[1] According to this the tragedy of *Sophonisba* and the poem *Spring* were sold to Andrew Millar in January, 1729, for £137, 10s.,[2] and the copyright of the remaining poems, including that in memory of Sir Isaac Newton and *Britannia*, was disposed of in July of the same year to John Millan for £105, and sold by him to Millar in 1738 for the same sum. This statement agrees with the facts of publication. Millan was the publisher of all the editions of the separate poems, with the exception of *Spring*, and also of the collected editions of the *Seasons* (in association with Millar as the proprietor of *Spring*)

[1] Brown's *Parliamentary Cases*, vol. vii. p. 88. The statement by the editor of a report of Millar *v.* Taylor, that the copyright of the *Seasons* was sold to Millar in 1729 for £160, must be inaccurate.

[2] This was probably made up of fifty guineas paid for *Spring*, and £85 for *Sophonisba*.

till the year 1738, and thenceforth the name of Millar
alone appears.

Millar regularly published Thomson's later works,
and he proved a good friend as well as an honest
publisher, notwithstanding a certain outward roughness
of manner. Johnson says of him that he " raised the
price of literature "; and he certainly seems to have
introduced a more liberal scale of payment to authors
for copyright. He gave Fielding £600 for *Tom Jones*
and £1000 for *Amelia*, and was especially helpful to
his brother Scots, to Thomson now, and afterwards to
Hume. When Thomson established himself at Richmond, Millar took a house near him, and on Thomson's
death he expressed his sorrow in a heartfelt manner.
One who knew both him and Thomson says, " Andrew
was a good-natured man and not an unpleasant companion ; but he was a little contracted in his mind by
his business, and had the dross of a bookseller about
him." However this may be, he was not so contracted
in mind by his business as to fail in justice and
generosity towards authors.

During the year 1729 Thomson was engaged not
only with the completion of the *Seasons*, of which a
collected edition had been announced, to be published
by subscription, but also with a tragedy, which was to
be produced at Drury Lane in the ensuing winter.
However, he found time to contribute several small
pieces to Ralph's Miscellany, including the *Hymn on
Solitude*, *The Happy Man*, addressed to Dodington, and
a poetical paraphrase of part of the sixth chapter
of St. Matthew's Gospel. A poem of some three
hundred lines came out also without his name, but was
acknowledged in the succeeding year. This was
Britannia, a patriotic lamentation over the supposed
decay of national spirit, and the want of sufficient

protection of British trade against the rivalry of foreign nations, especially Spain—in short, an attack upon the peace policy of Walpole. The fact that the author had so highly eulogised Walpole as a statesman only two years before, in the dedication of the poem in memory of Sir Isaac Newton, was perhaps regarded as a rather awkward circumstance, not to mention the fact that Dodington was a member of the Government ; and hence perhaps the absence of the author's name, and a note which stated that the poem was written in the year 1719. In later editions this date was altered to 1727, but the piece as we have it evidently belongs to the year in which it was published, for it has a reference to the coming over of the Prince of Wales to England in 1728. The poem is full of Thomson's characteristic patriotism—a patriotism always of the "Rule Britannia" type ; and its sentiments, which are vigorously expressed in high-sounding blank verse, might naturally cause him to be welcomed by the Opposition as a literary supporter : but he was not prepared to go all the way with them yet, and his tragedy of *Sophonisba* at the beginning of the next year was dedicated to the Queen in terms of high compliment.

Sophonisba was brought out at Drury Lane on the 28th of February, 1730, and the reputation of the author was now so well established that the occasion was looked forward to with great expectation, and very distinguished companies attended the rehearsals. The prologue is said, on the authority of Savage, to have been written partly by Pope.[1] The play was "acted with applause," but the success of it was largely due to the admirable performance of Mrs.

[1] See, however, Pope's letter to Hill, dated September 3, 1731.

Oldfield in the character of the heroine. This popular
actress died in the course of the year, and Sophonisba
was her last new tragic part. Davies records especially
the effect of one passage. "In reply to some degrad-
ing expression of Masinissa relating to Carthage, she
uttered the following line :

> 'Not one base word of Carthage, for thy soul !'

with such grandeur in her action and look, and in a
voice so powerful, that it is said she even astonished
Wilks, her Masinissa : it is certain the audience was
struck, and expressed their feelings by the most
uncommon applause."[1] To the same authority we
owe a story about Cibber, whom the public were
resolved not to tolerate as a tragic actor. "When
Thomson's *Sophonisba* was read to the actors, Cibber
laid his hand upon Scipio, a character which, though
it appears only in the last act, is of great dignity and
importance. For two nights Cibber was hissed, and
then the part was taken by Williams, who was mistaken for Cibber, and received with hisses and cat-
calls ; but as soon as they found out, they converted
their hisses into applause."

There is extant a contemporary attack upon the play
and its author, which was published as a pamphlet
under the title *A Criticism on the New Sophonisba*. This
was provoked apparently by the comparative neglect of
the tragedy of *Timoleon* by Benjamin Martyn, acted at
Drury Lane about a month before *Sophonisba*. The
critic states that Thomson was present at the performance of *Timoleon*, "and could not stifle his envy,
which burst into expressions very unbecoming a
brother adventurer." With regard to the success
of *Sophonisba*, he says : "The tragedy has been re-

---

[1] *Dramatic Miscellanies*, iii. p. 465.

commended to the world by a crowded patronage.
. . . 'Tis true, the thing seemed to please some
persons: there was a numerous party in the house.
Scotchmen with tuneful hands and merry feet attested
it to be a true-born of wit." It may be remarked that
Timoleon is at least as good a drama as *Sophonisba*, and
was fairly successful; but the author and his friends
seem to have had a grievance against the managers for
neglecting its interests in some way not easily dis-
coverable now.

Sophonisba is perhaps chiefly remembered for the
absurd line in Act III. Scene 2,

> "O, Sophonisba, Sophonisba, O!"

which was eventually altered into

> "O, Sophonisba, I am wholly thine."

According to Shiels, who must probably have
known the facts, the well-known parody of this line,

> "O, Jemmy Thomson, Jemmy Thomson, O!"

was uttered by "a smart from the pit," on the first
night, and Johnson seems to imply that the credit of
the play suffered a good deal in consequence of this
being "echoed through the town." The parody was
first printed in the pamphlet to which we have just
now referred, but it is much more likely to have been
"echoed through the town" from the theatre than
from an obscure performance of that kind. Fielding
also produced a parody of this line in the next year,
in his *Tom Thumb the Great*,

> "O, Huncamunca, Huncamunca, O!"[1]

but after all, it is not very clear that the absurdity in

---

[1] This and the other references to *Sophonisba* in *Tom Thumb
the Great* do not appear in the first edition of that "tragedy of
tragedies," produced in 1730.

question injured the credit of the play, which was considered a success on the stage, and seems to have sold well when published. The line was not altered in consequence of these parodies; for it remained still without change in the edition of 1738.

An incident is recorded in connection with the performance of this play, which illustrates the author's simplicity of character. Wishing to sit in some obscure corner of the house, he went to the upper gallery, and "such was the power of nature in him, that he could not help repeating the parts along with the players, . . . by which he was soon discovered to be the author by some gentlemen who could not on account of the great crowd be situated in any other part of the house."[1]

This year, 1730, was that of the first collected edition of *The Seasons*, in which *Autumn* and the *Hymn*, with which the whole work is concluded, appeared for the first time. This edition contained also the poem *To the Memory of Sir Isaac Newton*, and *Britannia*. The book was published by subscription, a method which had somewhat fallen out of favour, as we may gather both from the Advertisement prefixed to *Spring*, and from a passage in Thomson's letter to Mallet of September, 1729: "I have heard of an agreement among some of our modern Goths, . . . by which they bind themselves not to encourage any subscription whatever, under a certain penalty." Considering the abuses to which the system was liable, the "modern Goths," of whom our author speaks, may not have been far wrong in their resolution; but the subscription for this edition of *The Seasons* was a fairly successful one, and it is probable

---

[1] Cibber's *Lives of the Poets*. The story is sometimes told in connection with the production of *Agamemnon*.

that the profits belonged to the author, whatever
arrangements may have been made for the disposal of
the copyright generally. The number of copies
subscribed for was 454, at a guinea a piece, and the
list of subscribers is a highly distinguished one,
including Mr. Aikman, Dr. Arbuthnot, the Duke
of Argyll, Sir Wm. Bennett of Grubbat, Mrs. Martha
Blount, the Earl of Bute, Lord Bathurst, Lord
Bolingbroke, the Earl of Burlington (five copies),
the Earl of Chesterfield, Mr. Conduitt (ten copies),
Mr. Dodington (twenty copies), Mr. Elliot, Mr.
Duncan Forbes, the Duke of Gordon, the Duke of
Hamilton, the Countess of Hertford, the Lord Provost
of Edinburgh (ten copies), Simon Lord Lovat, Mr.
A. Mitchell, Mr. Wortley Montague, the Duke of
Montrose, the Duke of Norfolk, Mr. Arthur Onslow,
Speaker of the House of Commons (to whom *Autumn*
was dedicated), Mr. Oglethorpe, the Earl of Peter-
borough, Mr. Pope (three copies), Mr. Pulteney, Mr.
Allan Ramsay, Dr. Rundle, Mr. Richard Savage, Mr.
William Somerville, Mr. Spence, Mr. Charles Talbot,
junior, Sir Robert Walpole, the Earl of Wilmington,
Mr. Whatley, Dr. Edward Young.

The volume is a handsome quarto, with four engravings by Kent. Besides *Autumn* and the *Hymn*,
there was an increase of 318 lines in *Winter*, as compared with the fourth edition of the poem, and if we
take into account the removal of the passage near the
beginning, which referred to Autumn, we shall see that
the total number of new lines in this poem was above
four hundred. *Summer* was increased by sixty lines,
which contained the episode of Damon and Musidora,
in a form rather different from that which it finally
received. The poems had been subjected to a careful
revision throughout, and a good many verbal altera-

tions had been made. It may be noted that an " Essay
on Descriptive Poetry" had been promised in the
advertisements, but never appeared. A popular
edition of *The Seasons* in octavo, with different engravings, was issued in the same year.

From a statement made by Pope in a letter to Hill
of September 1731, we gather that Thomson had
already been at work on a new tragedy, but we have
no means of knowing what the subject of this was, or
whether it was ever completed. Other prospects had
opened to him meanwhile. On the recommendation
of Dr Rundle, who had shown great appreciation of
the merits of Thomson's work, he was selected as
travelling tutor to the young Charles Talbot, son
of Sir Charles Talbot, then Solicitor-General and soon
afterwards Lord Chancellor. Rundle was on intimate
terms with the Talbot family, having been for many
years domestic chaplain to Dr. William Talbot,
Bishop successively of Oxford, Salisbury, and Durham,
and he was afterwards associated with the Lord
Chancellor Talbot in Thomson's memorial poem. The
young man is described as intelligent and accomplished, and Thomson gladly accepted the opportunity
which this position offered him, of travelling abroad
under the most favourable circumstances. During
his absence from England he kept up a correspondence
with Dodington, and some of his letters have been
preserved. From Paris he writes in December, 1730,
that Voltaire's *Brutus* is being acted with applause,
and that the author has no mercy upon the English
custom of ending the act with a simile. It has been
pointed out that Voltaire did not publish this criticism
till some years later, in the second dedicatory letter
to Falkener, prefixed to the tragedy of *Zaïre* in 1736,
and that consequently Thomson must have gathered

it from Voltaire's own mouth. Voltaire, in fact, had made acquaintance with Thomson during his stay in England, as we know from his letter to Lyttelton of May, 1750; and it is highly probable that Thomson called upon him in Paris. We may notice that while the first three acts of *Sophonisba* end regularly with the expected simile, the custom was entirely dropped by Thomson from this time forward.

At the time when this letter from Paris was written, Thomson had the idea before his mind of presenting in a poetical form a series of descriptions of the countries through which he should pass.

"It seems to me that such a poetical landscape of countries, mixed with moral observations on their government and people, would not be an ill-judged undertaking. But then the description of the different face of Nature in different countries must be particularly marked and characteristic, — the portrait-painting of Nature."

About ten months later, in October, 1731, he writes again from Paris; but if Murdoch's statement is correct, that he "visited most of the courts and capital cities of Europe," he must have travelled extensively in the interval.[1] He is now looking forward to seeing Italy :—

---

[1] There seems to be no reason to doubt the statement made by Johnson, that Pope once expressed his regard for Thomson in a poetical epistle sent to him while he was abroad; but it is not at all likely, as suggested by Mr. Courthope, that the lines which were transferred from it to the Epistle to Arbuthnot were those quoted in Pope's letter to Hill, dated September 3, 1731. The "successful youth," who is there addressed and coupled with Bolingbroke, can hardly be Thomson. Warton has a note on l. 15 of the Epistle to Arbuthnot, which seems to suggest that the passage to which the note is attached contained the lines in question, and this is not unlikely. He adds that Thomson was somewhat displeased by the transference.

"Travelling has long been my fondest wish, for the very purpose you recommend, the storing one's imagination with ideas of all-beautiful, all-great, and all-perfect Nature. These are the true *materia poetica*, the light and colours, with which fancy kindles up her whole creation, paints a sentiment, and even embodies an abstracted thought. I long to see the fields where Virgil gathered his immortal honey, and tread the same ground where men have thought and acted so greatly."

He adds, however, that he has in his mind the idea of another tragedy, on a theme "more addressed to common passions than *Sophonisba*," and then refers to the possibility even of "an epic performance," in the idea of which Dodington seems recklessly to have encouraged him. "My heart both trembles with diffidence and burns with ardour at the thought." The subject of Timoleon, with which his rival's tragedy had dealt, occurs to him now for his epic; but he rejects it for various reasons—among others because such a subject would admit of no "machinery" (a necessary part of an epic, of course) except that of the heathen gods. In fact, we may say that our poet was on a dangerous course, and very far from following the true bent of his genius, towards what he had happily called "the portrait-painting of Nature." We cannot be in the least surprised at the state of things which is revealed in the next letter, written about a month later from Rome :—

"That enthusiasm which I had upon me with regard to travelling goes off, I find, very fast. One may imagine fine things in reading ancient authors, but to travel is to dissipate that vision."

He proceeds to reflect how easily one may do without Greek statues and Italian paintings, how simple a matter it would be to produce equally valu-

able works of art in England ; and even if in the fine
arts, "the gracefully superfluous," we should be found
wanting, "yet I hope we shall never lose the sub-
stantial, necessary, and vital arts of life, such as depend
on labour, liberty, and all-commanding trade."

After this patriotic utterance on art, he proceeds to
speak of poetry :—

"Should you inquire after my Muse, all that I can answer
is, that I believe she did not cross the Channel with me.   I
know not whether your gardener at Eastbury has heard anything of her among the woods there ; she has not thought fit
to visit me while I have been in this once poetic land, nor do
I feel the least presage that she will." [1]

This indicates for the moment a tolerably clear
perception of the truth ; and it is strange that after
this he should have convinced himself that his Muse
could be profitably set to work upon Greece and
Rome.   Yet so it was.   He returned to England in
December, and he probably very soon set his pen to
the poem of *Liberty*.

On the return of the travellers they went to stay at
Ashdown Park, the seat of Sir Charles Talbot, where
their arrival is reported by Rundle before the end of
the year.   It is probable that Thomson spent a considerable portion of the next year in the country, perhaps
residing with his young friend at Ashdown, which is
described by Rundle as a "little solitary island, in the
midst of a vast verdant ocean, secured from the
intrusion of chance company and the interruption of
business."   We hear of him very little during the

---

[1] In fact, the only poem which we can point to as probably
belonging to this year, is one which was not published in his
lifetime, that on the death of his friend Aikman, which took
place in June 1731, an expression of sincere feeling, of which
the concluding lines are touching and beautiful.

next two years, in the course of which, however,
several events occurred which seriously affected him.
The young Charles Talbot died in September 1733,
his father became Lord Chancellor in November of the
same year, and soon after this Thomson was appointed
by him to the post of Secretary of Briefs in the Court
of Chancery, "a place of little attendance, suiting his
retired, indolent way of life, and equal to all his
wants," a sinecure, in fact, which produced an income
of about £300.   His indolence, however, was not
such as to make him neglect the claims of those who
were less fortunate.   He exerted himself vigorously
in favour of the aged Dennis, for whom a benefit
performance at the Haymarket took place on December 18th, 1733.   Some lines appeared in the *Gentleman's Magazine* signed "J. D.," and inscribed "To
Mr. Thomson on his generous concern for Mr. Dennis's
last benefit," but they were not written by Dennis
himself.   "They could be no one's but that fool
Savage's," is said to have been his remark on seeing
them.   A letter from Thomson to Hill, of December,
1733, contains some highly-spiced compliments on the
translation of *Zaïre*, which in some points he considers
superior to the original : "Allow me to say that in
these respects I deeply feel the difference between Mr.
Voltaire and Mr. Hill."   He proposes soon "to fix in
town for the winter," and hopes to pass several happy
evenings in his correspondent's company, adding,
"Mr. Pope earnestly wishes the same."

With regard to the poem of *Liberty*, which must
have been occupying his attention in the meantime,
Murdoch says :—

"Mr. Thomson . . returned with his views greatly
enlarged, not of exterior nature only and the works of art,
but of human life and manners, of the constitution and policy

of the several states, their connections and their religious
institutions. How particular and judicious his observations
were, we see in his poem of *Liberty*, begun soon after his
return to England. We see at the same time to what high
pitch his love of his country was raised, by the comparisons
he had all along been making of our happy, well-poised
government with those of other nations. To inspire his
fellow-subjects with the like sentiments, and to show them
by what means the precious freedom we enjoy may be preserved, and how it may be abused or lost, he employed two
years of his life in composing that noble work ; upon which,
conscious of the importance and dignity of the subject, he
valued himself more than upon all his other writings."

Johnson expresses the same thing rather differ-
ently :—

"At this time a long course of opposition to Sir Robert
Walpole had filled the nation with clamours for liberty, of
which no man felt the want, and with care for liberty, which
was not in danger. Thomson, in his travels on the Continent,
found or fancied so many evils arising from the tyranny of
other Governments, that he resolved to write a very long
poem, in five parts, upon Liberty."

In whatever way we may choose to express it, the
result is the same. The poet was attempting something which he was quite unfitted to achieve, and
instead of producing, as he had at first proposed, a
poetical landscape of various countries, mixed with
moral observations on their government, taking care
that the description of the different aspects of nature
should be " particularly marked and characteristic," he
presented the public with a series of moral and
political treatises in blank verse, in which the aspects
of nature were almost wholly neglected. He had
been persuaded, in fact, by his own ambition and by
his friends' encouragement that his genius was fitted
for something higher than landscape-painting in verse,

and he had to some extent lost sight of the true objects
of his art.

Liberty was a failure with the public.   It was brought
out in separate parts in the years 1735 and 1736, and
the gradual reduction in the number of copies printed,
as each successive part was published, tells an unmistakable story.   Of the first part, three thousand
ordinary copies were printed ; of the second and third,
two thousand ; while of the fourth and fifth, one thousand
proved enough, and apparently more than enough, to
satisfy the public.[1]   It was evidently a very unprofit-
able affair for Millar, who had paid money for the
copyright, and though Thomson writes to Hill in
May, 1736, "I think . . . of annulling the bargain I
made with [my publisher], who would else be a considerable loser by the paper, printing, and publication
of *Liberty*," we have no evidence that he actually did
so.   Hill, of course, had praised with his usual taste
and judgment "this inimitable masterpiece both of
language and genius," and in his reply to the letter
above cited he endeavours to dissuade his correspondent from carrying out his intention, oddly arguing
that the beauty of the action would prevent its being
forgotten, and that the national reputation would
permanently suffer, if it were recorded that such a
poem, in such a nation as Great Britain, had failed to
enrich its publisher.

A letter which Thomson wrote to Dr. Cranston in
August, 1735, allows us to see something of his position
and expectations.   The immediate occasion of it was
the illness of his brother John, who had been with
him as an amanuensis, but had been attacked by
consumption and was returning to his native country.

[1] Woodfall's ledger : see *Notes and Queries*, first series, xi.
418.

In this letter, after recommending his brother to
Dr. Cranston's care, he says :—

"Should you inquire into my circumstances, they blossomed
pretty well of late, the Chancellor having given me the office
of Secretary of Briefs under him : but the blight of an idle
inquiry into the fees and offices of the Courts of Justice,
which arose of late, seems to threaten its destruction. In
that case I am made to hope amends : to be reduced, however,
from enjoyment to hope will be but an awkward affair."

He is sending his correspondent, besides the first
three parts of *Liberty*, some of the best things that
have recently been published, Pope's *Essay on Man*, the
Persian Letters, and Hoadly's book on the Sacrament.
"One Mr. Lyttelton, a young gentleman and member
of Parliament, wrote the *Persian Letters*. They are
reckoned prettily done."

In October he writes to the same correspondent
again, on hearing news of his brother's death, and
among other things he expresses that belief in a future
life, consisting of a never-ending succession of states,
each rising higher than the last, which we find suggested also in the later editions of the *Seasons* and in
the *Castle of Indolence*.

With reference to the "idle inquiry into the fees
and offices of the Courts of Justice," of which mention
is made in the former of these letters, we have an
interesting statement, published in the *Critical Review*
of 1765, which seems to have escaped the attention of
Thomson's biographers. It is there stated that
"Thomson's place fell under the cognisance of a
Commission of the great Officers of State for inquiring
into the public offices. He made a speech explaining
the duty, etc., of his place, in terms that, though very
concise, were so perspicuous and elegant, that Lord
Chancellor Talbot publicly said he preferred that

single speech to the best of his poetical compositions.
The income of the place was by the Commissioners
reduced from about £300 to £100 a year; but Mr.
Thomson offered to resign it, nor did he ever receive a
shilling from it during its reduced state. We have
his own authority for saying that it was not optional
to him whether he should remain in the place after his
patron's death." [1]

[1] Quoted by Dr. Birkbeck Hill in his edition of Johnson's
Lives of the Poets, vol. iii. p. 290.

CHAPTER II

LATER LIFE

IN the early part of 1736 Thomson took up his abode at a house in Kew Lane, Richmond, where he lived till his death. The letter to Hill already mentioned, which suggests the idea of securing Millar from loss, was written in May of that year, and gives his correspondent the new address, inviting him at the same time to spend an evening there, and suggesting that Pope and Savage might both be engaged to meet him, though as to Savage, "how to find him requires more intelligence than is allotted to mortals." The house to which he had now removed, some portions of which still exist, forming a part of the Royal Richmond Hospital, was on the right-hand side of the foot-lane leading from Richmond towards Kew. It was about a mile from Twickenham, and a real intimacy soon sprang up between Thomson and Pope, who had been fairly well acquainted even before this. Pope was jealous of all rivalry in his own province, but from Thomson he had nothing to fear in this respect; and he seems to have appreciated Thomson's genius, and to have been attracted by his simplicity and enthusiasm. He is said to have admitted him at all hours, and often to have walked back with him late at night as far as the bottom of Kew foot-lane. At the same time we may note the occurrence of Thomson's name in distinguished company on the

Committee of the Society for the Encouragement of
Learning, formed in 1736, as an indication that he was
now regarded as a leading personage in literature.

For the time he was at his ease as regards money
matters, and he showed an affectionate regard for the
welfare of his family in Scotland. He writes thus to
his friend Ross, under date November 6th, 1736 :—

"My sisters have been advised by their friends to set up
at Edinburgh a little milliner's shop ; and if you can conveniently advance to them twelve pounds on my account, it
will be a particular favour. That will set them a-going, and
I design from time to time to send them goods from hence.
I will not draw upon you, in case you be not prepared to
defend yourself ; but if your purse be valiant, please to
inquire for Jean or Elizabeth Thomson, at the Reverend Mr.
Gusthart's ; and if this letter be not sufficient testimony of
the debt, I will send you whatever you shall desire.

"It is late, and I would not lose this post. Like a laconic
man of business, therefore, I must stop short ; though I have
several things to impart to you, and through your canal to the
dearest, truest, heartiest youth that treads on Scottish ground.
The next letter I write you shall be washed clean from business in the Castalian fountain.

"I am whipping and spurring to finish a tragedy for you
this winter, but am still at some distance from the goal,
which makes me fear being distanced. Remember me to all
friends, and above them all to Mr. Forbes. Though my
affection to him is not favoured by letters, yet it is as high as
when I was his brother in the virtu, and played at chess with
him in a post-chaise."

This Mr. Forbes is John Forbes, the son of the
Lord President, the "joyous youth" of the *Castle of
Indolence,* and no doubt the same who is referred to
above as the "dearest, truest, heartiest youth that
treads on Scottish ground."

In February of the next year, 1737, Lord Chancellor

Talbot died, and thereby Thomson's place as Secretary of Briefs was vacated. He published in June a poem to the memory of his patron, which is a fairly good specimen of the panegyric elegy, and though too diffuse, has some happy passages. The praise of Lord Talbot is gracefully combined with a tribute to Rundle, who, being suspected of insufficient orthodoxy, had been put off with an Irish bishopric, after his appointment to the see of Gloucester had been publicly announced.[1] As for his post, it is said that the new Chancellor, Lord Hardwicke, kept it open for a time, expecting that Thomson would apply for it, which either from "bashfulness or pride, or some other motive perhaps not more laudable," as Johnson characteristically expresses it, he failed to do. It is quite possible that, while not averse to accepting a place from Lord Talbot, with whom he had had personal relations, he was unwilling to solicit a member of the Walpole cabinet, to whom he was a stranger, after having by his writings and personal connections identified himself with the Opposition. Murdoch says that "he was so dispirited, and so listless to every concern of that kind," that he took no steps in the matter, "a neglect which his friends greatly blamed in him"; but he may well have had reasons which seemed sufficient to himself, and if we accept the account quoted at the end of the preceding chapter from the *Critical Review*, we shall have no difficulty in understanding the position.

Johnson says that after the publication of *Liberty*, he "seems for a while to have suspended his poetry," because he was at ease as regards money matters, and that when he "relapsed to his former indigence" by the loss of his post, being compelled to write, he

[1] *Gentleman's Magazine*, January 1734.

produced the tragedy of *Agamemnon*. This representation is not in accordance with the facts of the
case. There is no evidence that he suspended his
work. He was engaged already on the *Agamemnon*
in the autumn of 1736, as we have seen, and "whipping
and spurring" to complete it, and by a letter from
Rundle, evidently written in December 1736, we learn
that he had been planning a drama on a subject
suggested by Mrs. Sandys, but had deferred this in
favour of the story of "another untoward heroine,"
namely, Clytemnestra. The subject alluded to was
probably the death of Socrates; for it is stated elsewhere that Rundle urged him to write a play on that
theme, and in this letter reference is made to "the
delicacy of the subject and the judgment required in
saying bold truths, whose boldness should not degenerate into offensiveness." We are told also that
the whole scheme of the play had been drawn out
into acts and scenes; and it is impossible not to
connect this statement with what Voltaire says of his
drama *Socrate*, produced in 1759, namely, that it was
founded upon a drama in prose by the late Mr.
Thomson, which had been communicated by Mr.
Lyttelton. It is true that the preface in which these
statements are made is a piece of mystification; but it
does not follow that all the statements made in it are
untrue, and we know that Voltaire was in correspondence with Lyttelton shortly after Thomson's
death.

For a time Thomson may have been in some straits
for money, but these can hardly have been serious. It
has been usual to refer to this period a legend about
his acquaintance with Quin, which (as regards its details
at least) does not rest on very good evidence. He is
said to have been arrested for a debt of £70, and to

have been visited by Quin, who announced that he had come for the purpose of "settling accounts" with him, an expression which at first rather alarmed Thomson. But the famous actor proceeded to say that he felt himself indebted in a considerable sum to the poet for the pleasure which he had derived from his work, and producing a note for £100, left it on the table and departed. Thomson was careless in money matters, but we have no other record than this of his having been arrested for debt, and Murdoch gives us to understand that he was provided with friends who would not have allowed matters to come to this extremity: "Millar was always at hand to answer, or even to prevent, his demands."

It was probably at this time that Lyttelton, not yet personally acquainted with Thomson, recommended him to the favour of the Prince of Wales, to whom *Liberty* had been dedicated, and who, having now finally broken with the Court, had accepted the notion that he might gain influence by becoming a patron of literature. Being interrogated about the state of his worldly affairs, Thomson replied that they were "in a more poetical posture than formerly," and was allowed a pension of £100 a year. Mallet and West were in the same position, these also apparently being recommended by Lyttelton. In September Thomson published in the *Gentleman's Magazine* an ode addressed to the Prince of Wales on the birth of his first child, the Princess Augusta. The only other record of this autumn is that on September 13th he and Armstrong were admitted Free Masons at Old Man's Coffee-house, Charing Cross, Savage officiating as Master.

In a letter to Ross, dated January 12, 1737, he tells his friend that his tragedy is finished, and has been accepted at Drury Lane :—

"May we hope to see you this winter, and to have the assistance of your hands in case it is asked? What will become of you if you don't come up? I am afraid the *Creepy* and you will become acquainted. Forbes, I hope, is cheerful and in good health. . . . I long to see him in order to play out that game of chess which we left unfinished."

He then refers to the recent "parsonification" of Murdoch :—

"How a gown and cassock will become him ; and with what a holy leer he will edify the devout females ! There is no doubt of his having a call, for he is immediately to enter upon a tolerable living. . . . It rejoices me to see one worthy, honest, excellent man raised at least to any independency."

In February again he writes to Mr. Gavin Hamilton, making arrangements for the payment of £16 a year to his sisters, and informing him that his tragedy is to be represented in three weeks' time. It was actually produced in April.

It is recorded that when the author undertook to read his play to the actors before the rehearsals, he pronounced his lines with such a broad Scottish accent, that they could not restrain themselves from laughter. Upon this he good-naturedly said to the manager, "Do you, sir, take my play and go on with it, for though I can write a tragedy, I find I cannot read one." Glover, on a somewhat similar occasion, was less unruffled, and abruptly refused Garrick's offer to read his play. Thomson seems to have taken much interest in the arrangement of the cast, and especially insisted that the part of Melisander should be given to Theophilus Cibber. The part of Agamemnon was played by Quin, with becoming dignity, no doubt, and Mrs. Porter is said to have made a very good Clytemnestra. At the performance Pope was present, and so rare were his visits to the theatre, that the audience honoured him with a general round of applause.

The success of the play at its first performance was more than doubtful. The account given by Victor is rather curious, and has not hitherto been noticed by Thomson's biographers :—

"I take the first three acts to be equal to anything that ever was written : they were excellently performed, and with the loudest and most universal applause. After this (such is the uncertainty of human affairs) the two following acts (particularly the last) were as deservedly hissed and cat-called, and the reason of all this proceeded from a palpable defect in the plan. The hero, Agamemnon, dies in the fourth act, and in the fifth . . . you are chiefly entertained with the prophetic strains of Cassandra . . . and the distress of young lovers, children to the departed heroes. . . . But a club of wits, with Mr. Pope at the head of them, met at the theatre next morning, and cut and slashed like dexterous surgeons— the lovers are no more—and they have brought a fine scene that finished the fourth act, into the fifth."

The author suffered great anxiety during the first performance, and perspired so freely that his wig had to be dressed by a barber before he could join the friends with whom he was engaged for supper. He was unfortunate both in the prologue and in the epilogue : the first, which was written by Mallet, had been curtailed by the censor of its last six lines, because of a political allusion which they contained ; and the epilogue was so much disapproved of by the audience, for reasons which cannot now be known, that it was replaced by an almost completely new one after the first night. All that we know is, that in the altered form the author admits that the censure was just, and by the language which is used we gather that there had been some offence against decency ; but as the original began by condemning the "mean mirth"

of the modern epilogue, it is rather surprising that
such an offence should have been committed.

The play was published by Millar, and the sale was
very successful. Woodfall printed three thousand copies
of the first edition on the 24th of April, and only four
days later a second edition of fifteen hundred. It was
dedicated to the Princess of Wales, and the interest
taken in it by the public was probably to a great
extent due to the political allusions which it contains.
The references to the corruption of Sir Robert Walpole's
government and to the absences of the King from England are unmistakable :—

> " Curse on the coward or perfidious tongue,
> That dares not, even to kings, avow the truth !
> Let traitors wrap them in delusive incense,
> On flattery flattery heap, on falsehood falsehood :
> Truth is the living liberal breath of heaven,
> That sweeps these fogs away, with all their vermin.
> And, on my soul, I think that Agamemnon
> Deserves some touch of blame. To put the power,
> The power of blessing or oppressing *millions*,
> Of doing or great good or equal mischief,
> Even into doubtful hands, is worse than careless."

This applies much more aptly to the situation in
England, where Sir Robert Walpole was supposed to
depend for his power chiefly on the influence of the
Queen, than to the case of Egisthus and Clytemnestra
in the play ; for Agamemnon had not left power in the
hands of Egisthus. Again, the following has an unmistakable reference to the King's frequent absences
from the country during the ten years which had
elapsed since his accession, and to Sir Robert Walpole's
system of parliamentary corruption :—

> " Hence ten loosely-govern'd years
> Have wrought such strange events, that you no more
> Behold your ancient Argos and Mycenæ.

These cities now with slaves and villains swarm.
At first Egisthus, popular and fair,
All smiles and softness, as if each man's friend,
By hidden ways proceeded, mining virtue :
He pride, he pomp, he luxury diffus'd,
He taught them wants beyond their private means ;
And straight in bounty's pleasing chains involv'd
They grew his slaves.   Who cannot live on little,
Or as his various fortunes shall permit,
Stands in the market ready to be sold."

This kind of thing was becoming the fashion in the current drama, and in the course of the year 1738 a new Act was passed for the licensing of stage-plays, which took effect in the prohibition of plays containing reflections such as these.   It was probably with special reference to this that Millar published in 1738 a new edition of Milton's *Areopagitica*, and the preface to this is said to have been written by Thomson.   It is a creditable piece of prose, and pleads with some eloquence for the free expression of every kind of opinion.

Thomson himself was one of the first to suffer from the new Licensing Act.   He was engaged in the winter of 1738-39 on a new tragedy, *Edward and Eleonora*.   On the 8th of December, Pope informs Hill that two acts only have been completed, and on the 12th of February he writes again, that "after many shameful tricks from the manager" of Drury Lane, Thomson is determined to bring out his play at Covent Garden, "where the advantage lies as to the women."   It was, in fact, put in rehearsal at Covent Garden with Delane as Edward and Mrs. Horton as Eleonora ; but its representation, which had been announced for March 29th, was prohibited by the censorship.

The first victim of the new regulations had been Henry Brooke's *Gustavus Vasa*, which was to have been

D

acted at Drury Lane, but was prohibited, "after being
in rehearsal for five weeks and after many tickets had
been sold." It is easy to see why *Gustavus Vasa* was
prohibited. There may be nothing in it which does
not naturally arise out of the plot of the play, and the
politics are those of Sweden and not of Great Britain;
but the glorification of liberty which it contains was
"very inconsistent with the ends for which the power
of licensing was given," and there are several passages
which evidently refer to the abuses against which the
Opposition was constantly inveighing.[1]

The second play to which a licence was refused was
Thomson's, and though his early biographers profess
to be unable to find anything in the text of the play
which could account for the prohibition, it is not very
difficult to discover the reasons. The partisan utter-
ances are in fact extremely obvious, and if the refusal
of a licence on political grounds was justifiable in any
case, it might be justified here. The Prince Edward
of the play is clearly intended to represent the exist-
ing "illustrious heir of England's throne," and the
Eleonora of the play undisguisedly stands for the
Princess of Wales, to whom the play was dedicated.
There are several very marked references to the evil
and corruption from which the Prince is to deliver his
country, and to

> " The soothing slave, the traitor in the bosom,"

who has been tempting his royal father to subvert the
freedom of the nation :—

> " Has not the royal heir a juster claim
>   To share his father's inmost heart and counsels,

---

[1] Johnson's *Complete Vindication of the Licensers of the Stage*,
published on this occasion, is an ironical defence of the prohibition, which deserves to be better known.

> Than aliens to his interest, those who make
> A property, a market of his honour ? "

And again :—

> " O save our country, Edward, save a nation,
> The chosen land, the last retreat of freedom,
> Amidst a world enslav'd ! . . .
> In this important, this decisive hour,
> On thee, on thee alone, our weeping country
> Turns her distressful eye ; to thee she calls,
> And with a helpless parent's piercing voice."

Even if particular passages like these had been cancelled, the general intention of exalting the characters of the Prince and Princess of Wales, under the idealised forms of Edward and Eleonora, would still have been easily visible, and in the political circumstances of the day the prohibition was almost inevitable. The play was published with a dedication in which its political purpose was plainly avowed. The number of copies printed was 4500, and the sale no doubt brought in some profit to the author.[1] The play was brought on the stage at last at Covent Garden Theatre in 1775, with an epilogue by Sheridan, and seems to have been well received.

In the next year Thomson received a commission from the Prince of Wales to produce, in conjunction with Mallet, a dramatic entertainment to be performed in the gardens at Clifden. The result was *Alfred : a Masque*, performed before a brilliant audience on the

---

[1] Johnson says that the public recompensed Brooke for the prohibition of his play " by a very liberal subscription," and that Thomson also "endeavoured to repair his loss by subscription." *Edward and Eleonora* was not published by subscription, but the fact that of the 4500 copies printed, 1000 were "fine," a much larger number than usual, probably indicates that the author's friends purchased a good many copies at a special price.

first of August, 1740, and published in the same year.
This piece, naturally, has political tendencies, and in
particular passages there are definite and direct references to the Prince of Wales and his position, but on
the whole it displays more of patriotism than of party
spirit, and the prevailing tone is finely echoed in the
celebrated song which is introduced towards the conclusion. The question of the authorship of "Rule
Britannia," has been much discussed, but we need not
have much hesitation in assigning it to Thomson.

We know little of his life during the next two years
except that he was living at Richmond, and had there
made acquaintance, apparently as early as 1736,[1] with
a person to whom he became more deeply attached
than to any other of the "dear objects" for whom he
felt the most pleasing sentiment which the soul can
receive. This was a Miss Elizabeth Young, originally
of Goolie Hill, Dumfriesshire, who is addressed in *The
Seasons* and in other poems under the name of Amanda.
She frequently resided at Richmond in the house of
her sister, married to a surgeon named Robertson, to
whom we owe some interesting reminiscences of
Thomson. We are told that she was not exactly
beautiful, but gentle-mannered and sensible; and from
the descriptions of her which are given by her lover,
it would appear that there was a certain pensive
seriousness in her air and expression, which gave
evidence of some depth of feeling:—

> "O thou, whose tender, serious eyes
>   Expressive speak the mind I love,
> The gentle azure of the skies,
>   The pensive shadows of the grove."

---

[1] A poem referring to Amanda, "Come, gentle god of soft
desire," was published by Thomson in the *Gentleman's Magazine*,
Feb. 1736.

And in the later editions of *Spring* :—

> " And thou, Amanda, come, pride of my song !
> Formed by the graces, loveliness itself !
> Come with those downcast eyes, sedate and sweet,
> Those looks demure, that deeply pierce the soul—
> Where, with the light of thoughtful reason mixed,
> Shines lively fancy and the feeling heart."

Her mother, Mrs. Young, is described as a coarse, vulgar woman, who discouraged the match because the lover had no very satisfactory worldly prospects. "What!" she exclaimed to her daughter, "would you marry Thomson? He will make ballads and you will sing them?" Her brother-in-law, Robertson, observes that Thomson was never rich enough to marry; but it is clear that he would have married Miss Young, if he could have obtained her mother's consent. She afterwards became the wife of an Admiral Campbell, a much more advantageous match, no doubt.

There are some letters extant addressed by Thomson to Mrs. Robertson, when she and her sister were absent at Bath in 1742, and one written in 1743 to Miss Young herself, which throw light upon the progress of his suit.

On Christmas Day, 1742, he writes thus to the sister of his beloved object :—

> "Madam,—I believe I am in love with some one or all of you ; for though you will not favour me with a scrap of a pen, yet I cannot forbear writing to you again. Is it not, however, barbarous not to send me a few soft characters, one pretty name to cheer my eyes withal? How easily some people might make others happy, if they would! But it is no small comfort to me, since you will not write, that I shall soon have the pleasure of being in your company."

He then proceeds to relate a pleasing incident, no

other than the fact that he has encountered Mrs.
Robertson's baby and kissed it :—

"I took the liberty to touch him with unhallowed lips,
which restored me to the good opinion of the nurse, who had
neither forgot nor forgiven my having slighted that favour
once."

After quoting Milton's lines on marriage, "Hail,
wedded love," etc., he goes on :—

"Now that I have been transcribing some lines of poetry,
I think I once engaged myself, while walking in Kew-lane,
to write two or three songs. The following is one of them,
which I have stolen from the Song of Solomon, from that
beautiful expression of love, 'Turn away thine eyes from me,
for they have overcome me,'"

and then follow the stanzas beginning,

"O thou, whose tender, serious eyes."

The letter ends :—

"My best respects attend Miss Young and Miss Berry,
who I hope are heartily tired of Bath, and will leave it without
the least regret, whomsoever they leave pining behind them.
I wish you all a much happier and merrier Christmas than
we can have without you. But in amends you will bring us
along with you a gay and happy New Year."

In August of the next year he is writing to Miss
Young from Hagley, and it would seem that his suit
is advancing favourably :—

"After a disagreeable stage-coach journey, disagreeable in
itself, and infinitely so as it carried me from you, I am come
to the most agreeable place and company in the world. The
park, where we pass a great part of our time, is thoroughly
delightful, quite enchanting. It consists of several little hills,
finely tufted with wood, and rising softly one above another ; from which one sees a great variety of at once beautiful
and grand, extensive prospects : but I am most charmed with
its sweet, embowered retirements, and particularly with a

winding dale that runs through the middle of it. This dale is
overhung with deep woods, and enlivened by a stream, that
now gushing from mossy rocks, now falling in cascades, and
now spreading into a calm length of water, forms the most
natural and pleasing scene imaginable. At the source of this
water, composed of some pretty rills, that purl from beneath
the roots of oaks, there is as fine a retired seat as lover's heart
can wish. There I often sit, and with a dear exquisite mixture of pleasure and pain, of all that love can boast of excellent
and tender, think of you. But what do I talk of sitting and
thinking of you there? Wherever I am and however employed, I never cease to think of my loveliest Miss Young.
You are part of my being; you mix with all my thoughts,
even the most studious, and instead of disturbing give them
greater harmony and spirit. Ah! tell me, do I now and then
steal a tender thought from you? I may claim that distinction from the merit of my love. . . .

"Nor is the society here inferior to the scene. It is gentle,
animated, pleasing. Nothing passes but what either tends
to amuse the imagination, improve the head, or better the
heart. This is the truly happy life, the union of retirement and choice society; it gives an idea of that which
the patriarchal or golden age is supposed to have been, when
every family was a little state of itself, governed by the
mild laws of reason, benevolence, and love. Don't, however, imagine me so madly rural, as not to think those who
have the powers of happiness in their own minds happy
everywhere. The mind is its own place, the genuine source
of its own happiness; and amidst all my raptures with regard
to the country, I would rather live in the most London corner
of London with you, than in the finest country retirement,
and that too enlivened by the best society, without you. You
so fill my mind with all ideas of beauty, so satisfy my soul
with the purest and most sincere delight, I should feel the
want of little else. Yet still, the country life with you,
diversified now and then by the contrast of the town, is the
wish of my heart. . . .

"Let me now, my dearest Miss Young, bespeak your goodness. I shall soon, I am afraid, have occasion for all your

friendship; and I would fain flatter myself that you will
generously in my absence speak of me more than you ever
owned to me. If I am so happy as to have your heart, I
know you have spirit to maintain your choice; and it shall
be the most earnest study and purpose of my life, not only to
justify but to do you credit by it. . . . I will not be so extravagant as to hope to hear from you, but I will hope to hear of
you, or rather from you by the means of our friend. Think
with friendship and tenderness of him who is with friendship
and tenderness inexpressible all yours,

"JAMES THOMSON."

It seems from this letter that the writer was an
accepted lover, so far as Miss Young was concerned,
but had reason to fear difficulties in another quarter;
and this confirms the statement, made independently,
that the marriage was prevented by the opposition
of Miss Young's mother, who desired a better match
for her daughter. Thomson's song, "To Fortune,"
may well serve to illustrate the situation.

The letter which we have just quoted was written
during his first visit to Hagley; but it is evident that
for some time past he had been living in considerable
intimacy with Lyttelton. George Lyttelton was, in
fact, rather a friend than a patron to Thomson. He
was a man whom such people as Lord Hervey were
apt to ridicule, on the score of a certain gaunt awk-
wardness of demeanour; and Lord Chesterfield, who
was Lyttelton's friend, and expresses appreciation of his
virtue and learning, nevertheless holds him up to his
son as an awful example of absent-minded blundering.
But whatever his manners may have been, he had taste
and culture as well as high principle. In public life
he was as transparently honest, as he was simple and
affectionate in private; and his speeches in the House
of Commons were highly esteemed, though he had a
bad delivery and was not very ready in debate. His

political position was due chiefly to the family connections which allied him with Pitt and the Grenvilles;
and as one of the "Cobham cousins" he eventually
became Chancellor of the Exchequer, a very inappropriate place for an absent-minded idealist like Lyttelton.
Horace Walpole, who, as Sir Robert's son, was apt to
be critical of his successors in financial management,
says of him that he "never knew prices from duties,
nor drawbacks from premiums."   But as a friend he
was eminent; and that his literary taste was catholic,
we may gather from the fact that Thomson and Fielding were almost equally indebted to him, so that his
name is inseparably connected both with *The Seasons*
and with *Tom Jones*.   In early life he was one of the
rising hopes of the Opposition, and Bolingbroke's *Idea
of a Patriot King* was originally in the form of a letter
addressed to him.   He was on terms of friendship with
Pope, who takes him as a type of youthful freshness
and enthusiasm,—

> "Free as young Lyttelton, her cause pursue;
>   Still true to Virtue, and as warm as true."

His own literary talent was by no means contemptible.
The *Dialogues of the Dead* are quite worth reading, the
monody on the death of his wife is graceful and touching, and he produced a historical work which, on
account of its accuracy and original research, is still
a standard authority for the period with which it deals.
At one time he was reputed to be something of a
freethinker in matters of religion; but he is said to have
been converted to orthodoxy by Gilbert West, and he
then set himself to convert others.   He was in regular
correspondence with Dr. Doddridge, to whom he re-
commends *Tom Jones* as a remedy for depression.   In
the year 1743 he was thirty-four years old, and his

father, Sir Thomas, was still alive; but the Lyttel-
tons were a united family, and the eldest son, who
had lately been married to Lucy Fortescue, the "lov'd
Lucinda" of *The Seasons*, brought his wife home to
Hagley Hall. He became Sir George Lyttelton by the
death of his father in 1750, and was created a peer
in 1757.

In July, 1743, Thomson had written to him thus, in
anticipation of his visit :—

"Hagley is the place in all England I most desire to see ;
I imagine it to be greatly delightful in itself, and I know it
to be so in the highest degree by the company it is animated
with. Some reasons prevent my waiting upon you immediately, but if you will be so good as let me know how long you
design to stay in the country, nothing shall hinder me from
passing three weeks or a month with you before you leave it.
As this will fall in autumn, I shall like it the better, for I
think that season of the year the most poetical. . . . In the
meantime I will go on with correcting *The Seasons*, and hope
to carry down more than one of them with me. The Muses,
whom you obligingly say I shall bring along with me, I shall
find with you,—the Muses of the great simple country, not
the little fine-lady Muses of Richmond Hill. . . . My compliments attend all at Hagley, and in particular her who gives
it charms to you it never had before."

The revision of *The Seasons*, to which Thomson refers
in this letter, was in preparation for the new edition
to be published in the next year, and involved not only
a complete revision, but numerous additions, which
brought the poem practically to its final form. In the
process of correction Lyttelton took a great interest,
and contributed to it many suggestions, his classical
taste being inclined to a far simpler style than that
which was natural to Thomson. There exists an interleaved copy of *The Seasons*, which was evidently used
in this work of revision, full of manuscript corrections

and additions, most of which are reproduced in the issue of 1744. These are written chiefly in Thomson's own handwriting, but partly also in that of Lyttelton. Lyttelton's hand, which hardly appears in the early part of the book, is found most frequently and regularly in *Autumn*, which we must assume was worked through in this volume by the two friends together, probably during Thomson's visit to Hagley in 1743. The corrections and suggestions are here given in such a manner as to make it probable that they were the immediate result of critical discussion.

In 1744 the new edition of *The Seasons* was published, with very considerable enlargement of the poems. Altogether they were increased by rather more than a thousand lines, nearly six hundred being added to *Summer*, and nearly three hundred to *Winter*. The new passages contain several interesting personal and local references. There were added, for example, in *Spring*, the address to Lyttelton and the description of Hagley Park; in *Summer*, the lines on Miss Stanley, the description of the pestilence among the crews of the British ships under Vernon at Carthagena, the walk with Amanda and the view from Richmond Hill; in *Autumn*, the description of Stowe; and in *Winter*, the reference to Hammond and the address to Chesterfield. In this edition the book very nearly assumed its final form; another was called for in 1746, but it was almost a reproduction of this, and had hardly any new matter, one passage of seven lines in *Summer* (669-675) being the only addition of any consequence. Altogether, comparing the extent of the work in its final form with that of the poems as first published, we find that it had grown from 4023 to 5541 lines.

At the end of the year 1744 Lyttelton came into office, and appointed Thomson to the post of Surveyor-

General of the Leeward Islands, an office of which he
performed the duties by deputy, and from which he
received, after paying his deputy, the sum of £300 a
year. The deputy was his friend William Paterson,
who succeeded him in the post little more than a year
later, May 29, 1746. Probably Thomson, who never
was grasping in the matter of money, found that he
had enough to live upon, and resigned the post in
favour of his friend, who was performing the duties
of it. Paterson had acted for a time as Thomson's
amanuensis, and there is a story, told by Murdoch,
that the refusal of *Edward and Eleonora* by the licenser
was followed by the similar rejection of a tragedy by
Paterson of a quite inoffensive character, merely because
it was written in the same hand as the other. Paterson's *Arminius*, as a matter of fact, does not seem to
contain any political allusions to which the Government could take exception.

In 1745 was produced at the Drury Lane Theatre
the tragedy of *Tancred and Sigismunda*, generally considered the best of Thomson's dramas, with Garrick in
the part of Tancred and Mrs. Cibber as Sigismunda.
Pitt and Lyttelton concerned themselves actively in the
success of the drama, and Victor was moved to a protest against their proceedings, in the *Daily Advertiser*.[1]
"We all plainly see by what interest the author of the
new tragedy of *Tancred and Sigismunda* was supported,
a very remarkable new Lord of the Treasury was proud
of appearing its foster-father at all the rehearsals, and
on the first night of the performance he and his friends
in the box with him (both very lately most flaming
patriots) were seen clapping their hands violently at
the following remarkable speeches," and then he quotes
some protests which occur in the play against party

[1] Benjamin Victor, *Letters*, p. 101.

passion, from which he considers that the "patriots" have no right to consider themselves exempt.   His indignation even moves him to make verses addressed to the author :—

> "Lull'd with the flat unanimated tale,
>   We sigh'd, we nodded, nay some snor'd aloud,
>   But claps suborn'd awak'd the sleepy crowd.
>
> .   .   .   .
>
> What tho' thy tedious scenes are void of fire,
>   They'll do if Pitt and Lyttelton admire ;
>   They lead the fashion, fashion governs all,
>   Attends their nod, or waits on Russel's call."

Davies confirms Victor's statement about Pitt and Lyttelton, telling us that they not only attended the rehearsals, but gave directions to the actors, who very readily listened to their instructions ; but he adds that the success of the play was due chiefly to the admirable acting of Garrick and Mrs. Cibber, "who were formed by nature for the illustration of each other's talents."[1] In publishing his drama the author remarks that it was considerably shortened in the performance.   It was dedicated to the Prince of Wales, with complimentary remarks upon the encouragement which he had extended to every art and science.   The edition was a large one, 5000 copies being printed.

The friendship with Mallet was still kept up, but its outward manifestations had become less frequent. We have a letter from Thomson to Mallet dated August, 1745, in which, replying apparently to some reproaches of his correspondent, he acknowledges himself to blame for neglecting the external forms of friendship.

"But I hope in time to amend in this instance, among the many other things we all have and ever will have to correct.

---

[1] *Life of Garrick*, i. 78.

. . . I shall be sincerely glad to sustain and cultivate our old friendship, and I think I dare engage for my heart, that it will not in this be deficient in fully answering to yours."

In another letter to the same, of March 31, 1747, in reply to a proposal that they should meet in a London tavern, in order that Thomson might read Mallet's latest poem (*Amyntor and Theodora*, no doubt) before publication, he asks for the favour of having it sent down to Richmond, alleging various pretexts : the evenings are too short now to read a poem of any length in a tavern, "and I am besides much of the humour of Sancho,—I love to munch a good morsel of that kind by myself in a corner." Moreover, Richmond is a more appropriate place to read poetry in, and "should you send me your song for a night or two, the nightingales will strike up at the same time." If this is inconvenient, he will endeavour to restrain his impatience, till he can see it in print. Meanwhile he would desire Mallet to make an opportunity of coming to read *Coriolanus* (Thomson's latest play) as soon as he is at leisure.

With Lyttelton the intimacy was considerably closer. Visits were paid to Hagley in the autumn of each year, and letters seem to have been frequently interchanged. There is one from Lyttelton dated May 21, 1747, which allows us to infer something about Thomson's religious opinions, and shows us the interest which his friend took in the subject. As regards the first paragraph, we must suppose that Lyttelton had given him the use of his key of the Richmond Park Gardens, and that objections had been raised to this transfer.

"Dear Thomson,—I entirely agree with you that you have the same natural right as the nightingales have to the Garden of Richmond ; but as those iniquitous gardeners will dispute it, and might overcomes right, I doubt you will not be able to keep the key ; nor can I refuse to give it up if demanded, therefore I have disposed of it to the Duchess of Bridgewater, who will be better able to maintain her possession than either I or you at this time. She is very desirous of it, and I could not deny it her, as she knows that I don't use it myself. Be so good as to send it back as soon as possible. I have enjoyed the spring tolerably well in Kensington Gardens and in some little excursions I have made out of town, but propose to do it more agreeably on this day se'nnight at Mrs. Stanley's in your company. Meet me at Hounslow by 12 o'clock, and we will go on together in a post-chaise. I intend staying till Monday afternoon. I have sent you a small present of claret in return for your rum, of which my father will send me back a good part, having more than he has occasion for. . . .

"I wish you joy of Anson's success, an action that does him great honour, and of great benefit to his country ; but the joy of it is palled to our family by the loss of poor Captain Grenville, one of the most promising young men in the navy, and who, had he lived, would have been an honour, not to his family only, but to his country. I never saw in any man a finer mixture of spirit, temper, and judgment. He fought and died with the gallantry of Sir Philip Sidney.

"How grievously has our family felt within these few months the condition of mortality and uncertainty of our happiness ! Who was happier than I, who so fortunate as the Grenvilles, at the beginning of the year ? I will say no more on this subject ; your mind will supply the rest. My refuge and consolation is in philosophy,—Christian philosophy, —which I heartily wish you may be a disciple of, as well as myself. Indeed, my dear friend, it is far above the Platonic. I have sent you a pamphlet upon a subject relative to it, which we have formerly talked of. I writ it in Kew Lane last year, and I writ it with a particular view to your satisfaction. You have therefore a double right to it, and I wish to God it may appear to you as convincing as it does to me, and bring you to add the faith to the heart of a Christian. Adieu. I long for the pleasure of seeing you.—Yours affectionately,

"G. LYTTELTON."

The pamphlet of which Lyttelton speaks in this letter is that on the Conversion of St. Paul, which is afterwards referred to as having had a serious influence upon Thomson's mind. Lyttelton's own sorrow was occasioned by the death of his wife in the early part of this year.

In September Thomson was at Hagley, and visited Shenstone at the Leasowes. In a letter of September 20th Shenstone says :—

"As I was returning from church on Sunday last, whom should I meet in a chaise, with two horses lengthways, but that right friendly bard Mr. Thomson. I complimented him upon his arrival in this country, and asked him to accompany Mr. Lyttelton to the Leasowes, which he said he would with abundance of pleasure, and so we parted."

Shenstone afterwards placed an inscription in honour of Thomson on a seat in his grounds, "prope fontes illi non fastiditos."

In October Thomson wrote from Hagley to one of his sisters, Mrs. Thomson of Lanark. This is one of the letters which Boswell communicated to Johnson as a proof of the writer's goodness of heart and attachment to his family. The letter, in fact, is an affectionate one. After apologising for the irregularity of his correspondence, the writer refers at some length to the affairs of the family, and especially to the death of his sister Lizzie, which had taken place some time before this. Her husband, a Mr. Bell, intends to marry again, and his design is approved by the family. This leads to some remarks which have a bearing on Thomson's own circumstances :—

"I esteem you for your sensible and disinterested advice to Mr. Bell, as you will see by my letter to him ; as I approve entirely of his marrying again, you may readily ask me why I don't marry at all. My circumstances have hitherto been so variable and uncertain in this fluctuating world, as induce to keep me from engaging in such a state ; and now, though they are more settled, and of late (which you will be glad to hear) considerably improved, I begin to think myself too far advanced in life for such youthful undertakings, not to mention some other petty reasons that are apt to startle the delicacy of difficult old bachelors. I am, however, not a little suspicious that, was I to pay a visit to Scotland (which I have some thoughts of doing soon), I might possibly be tempted to think of a thing not easily repaired if done amiss. . . . Pray let me hear of you now and then ; and though I am not a regular correspondent, yet perhaps I may mend in that respect."

The question of Thomson's possible marriage was discussed by some of his friends in the autumn of this year, as we see by a letter from him to Lyttelton, apparently in reply to a very definite suggestion on the subject. He writes from Kew Lane, December 14, 1747 :—

" Dear Sir,—I should have answered your kind and truly friendly letter some time ago. My not having answered it hitherto proceeded from my giving it mature and deep consideration. I have considered it in all lights and in all humours, by night, by day, and even during these long evenings. But the result of my consideration is not such as you would wish. My judgment agrees with you, and you know I first impressed yours in her favour. She deserves a better than me, and has as many good and worthy qualities as any woman : nay, to others, and I hope too men of taste, she has charming and piquant ones : but every man has a singular and uncontrollable imagination of his own : now, as I told you before, she does not pique mine. I wonder you should treat that objection so lightly as you seem to do in your last. To strike one's fancy is the same in love that charity is in religion. Though a woman had the form and spoke with the tongue of angels, though all divine gifts and graces were hers, yet without striking the fancy she does nothing. I am too much advanced in life to venture to marry, without feeling

myself invigorated, and made, as it were, young again, with a
great flame of imagination.   But we shall discuss this matter
more fully when I have the happiness of seeing you at full
leisure.   What betwixt judgment and fancy, I shall run a
great risk of never entering into the holy state : in the mean
time I wish to see you once more happy in it.   Forgive me if
I say, it would be an ungrateful frowardness to refuse the
bounty of providence, because you have been deprived of
former enjoyments.   If you cannot again love so exquisitely
as you have done, so much the better ; you will not then risk
being so miserable.   To say that one cannot love twice is
utterly unphilosophical, and give me leave to say, contrary to
my own experience."

We may note here that the story, repeated by some
recent biographers, that Thomson had been actually
married, and that his wife had lived in his house at Richmond under the disguise of a domestic, until her death
shortly before this time, rests on no evidence worth
mentioning, and is inconsistent with what we know of
his frankness of character, as well as with the history
of his attachment to Miss Young.

Since the production of *Tancred and Sigismunda* he
had been engaged partly on the completion of the
Castle of Indolence, which had been in hand for many
years, and was at last published in May, 1748, and
partly on the tragedy of *Coriolanus*, which, as we have
seen, was nearly finished in March, 1747.   This play
was offered for the stage at the beginning of 1748,
but was delayed (as Thomson says) by jealousies between Garrick and Quin, and was not acted until after
the author's death.   His pension of £100 a year from
the Prince of Wales was discontinued about this time,
owing to the displeasure of the Prince with Lyttelton,
which he showed by striking all Lyttelton's friends,
including Thomson and Mallet, off his pension list.
These and other details we learn by a letter from

Thomson to Paterson, which is sufficiently interesting to be worth citing almost at length. The date of the letter must be the latter part of April, 1748.

"Dear Paterson,—In the first place, and previous to my letter, I must recommend to your favour and protection Mr. James Smith, searcher in St. Christopher's; and I beg you, as occasion shall serve, and as you find he merits it, to advance him in the business of the Customs. He is warmly recommended to me by Sargent, who in verity turns out one of the best men of our youthful acquaintance, honest, honourable, friendly and generous. If we are not to oblige one another, life becomes a paltry, selfish affair, a pitiful morsel in a corner. Sargent is so happily married, that I could almost say, the same case happen to us all. That I have not answered several letters of yours, is not owing to the want of friendship and the sincerest regard for you; but you know me well enough to account for my silence without my saying any more upon that head; besides, I have very little to say that is worthy to be transmitted over the great ocean. The world either futilises so much, or we grow so dead to it, that its transactions make but feeble impressions on us. Retirement and Nature are more and more my passion every day; and now, even now, the charming time comes on: Heaven is just on the point, or rather in the very act, of giving earth a green gown. The voice of the nightingale is heard in our lane.

"You must know that I have enlarged my rural domain much to the same dimensions you have done yours. The two fields next to me, from the first of which I have walled,—no, no,—paled in, about as much as my garden consisted of before, so that the walk runs round the hedge, where you may figure *me* walking any time of the day, and sometimes of the night. For *you*, I imagine you reclining under cedars, and there enjoying more magnificent slumbers than are known to the pale climates of the north, slumbers rendered awful and divine by the solemn stillness and deep fervours of the torrid noon. At other times I image you drinking punch in groves of lime or orange trees, gathering pine-apples from hedges, as commonly as we may blackberries; poetising under lofty

laurels, or making love under full-spread myrtles. But, to
lower my style a little, as I am such a genuine lover of
gardening, why do you not remember me in that instance,
and send me some seeds of things that might succeed here
during the summer, though they cannot perfect their seed
sufficiently in this to them uncongenial climate, to propagate ?
in which case is the caliloo, which from the seed it bore here
came up puny, rickety, and good for nothing. There are other
things certainly with you, not yet brought over hither, that
might flourish here in the summer-time, and live tolerably
well, provided they be sheltered in a hospitable stove or
green-house during the winter. You will give me no small
pleasure by sending me from time to time some of these
seeds, if it were no more but to amuse me in making the
trial. . . .

"As to more important business, I have nothing to write to
you. You know best. Be, as you always must be, just and
honest ; but if you are, unhappily, romantic, you shall come
home without money and write a tragedy on yourself. Mr.
Lyttelton told me that the Grenvilles and he had strongly
recommended the person the governor and you proposed, for
that considerable office lately fallen vacant in your department,
and that there was good hopes of succeeding. He told me also
that Mr. Pitt had said that it was not to be expected that
offices such as that is, for which the greatest interest is made
here at home, could be accorded to your recommendation, but
that as to the middling or inferior offices, if there was not
some particular reason to the contrary, regard would be had
thereto. This is all that can be reasonably desired ; and if you
are not infected with a certain Creolian distemper, whereof
I am persuaded your soul will utterly resist the contagion, as
I hope your body will that of the natural ones, there are few
men so capable of that unperishable happiness, that peace and
satisfaction of mind at least, that proceeds from being reasonable and moderate in our desires, as you. These are the
treasures dug from an inexhaustible mine in our own breasts,
which, like those in the kingdom of heaven, the rust of time
cannot corrupt, nor thieves break through and steal. I must
learn to work this mine a little more, being struck off from a

certain hundred pounds a year which you know I had. West, Mallet, and I were all routed in one day ; if you would know why,—out of resentment to our friend in Argyll Street. Yet I have hopes of having it restored with interest some time or other. Oh, that "some time or other" is a great deceiver.

"*Coriolanus* has not yet appeared on the stage, from the little, dirty jealousy of Tullus towards him who alone can act Coriolanus. Indeed the first has entirely jockeyed the last off the stage for this season, like a giant in his wrath. Let us have a little more patience, Paterson ; nay, let us be cheerful : at last all will be well, at least all will be over—here I mean : God forbid it should be so hereafter ! But as sure as there is a God, that will not be so.

"Now that I am prating of myself, know that after fourteen or fifteen years the *Castle of Indolence* comes abroad in a fortnight. It will certainly travel as far as Barbadoes. You have an apartment in it as a night pensioner, which you may remember I filled up for you during our delightful party at North Ham. Will ever those days return again ? Do not you remember eating the raw fish that were never caught ? All our friends are pretty much *in statu quo*, except it be poor Mr. Lyttelton. He has had the severest trial a human tender heart can have ; but the old physician, time, will at last close up his wounds, though there must always remain an inward smarting. Mitchell is in the House for Aberdeenshire, and has spoke modestly well ; I hope he will be something else soon ; none deserves better : true friendship and humanity dwell in his heart. . . .

"Symmer is at last tired of gaiety, and is going to take a semi-country house at Hammersmith. I am sorry that honest, sensible Warrender, who is in town, seems to be stunted in church preferment. He ought to be a tall cedar in the house of the Lord. . . . Peter Murdoch is in town, tutor to Admiral Vernon's son, and is in good hope of another living in Suffolk, that country of tranquillity, where he will then burrow himself in a wife and be happy. Good-natured, obliging Millar is as usual. Though the Doctor increases in business, he does not decrease in spleen ; but there is a certain kind of spleen that is both humane and agreeable,

like Jacques in the play : I sometimes too have a touch
of it. . . .

"May your health, which never failed you yet, still continue,
till you have scraped together enough to return home and live
in some snug corner, as happy as the 'Corycius senex' in
Virgil's fourth Georgic, whom I recommend both to you and
myself as a perfect model of the truest happy life. Believe
me to be ever most sincerely and affectionately yours,
                                        "JAMES THOMSON."

Mitchell, who is mentioned in this letter, was one
of Thomson's most faithful friends.   He afterwards
played a very important and honourable part in
public events as English Minister at Berlin ; for he is
the Sir Andrew Mitchell whom Carlyle praises as by
far the best of English excellencies at that Court, and
whose able despatches, dealing both with political and
with military matters, are one of the principal sources
of the *History of Frederick the Great*.   The 'Doctor' is
Armstrong.

The *Castle of Indolence*, which is referred to in this
letter as on the point of publication, came out in May ;
and several of Thomson's friends, as well as the author
himself, had apartments in it.   The origin of the poem
is thus described by Murdoch :—

"It was at first little more than a few detached stanzas, in
the way of raillery on himself and on some of his friends, who
would reproach him with indolence, while he thought them at
least as indolent as himself.   But he saw very soon that the
subject deserved to be treated more seriously, and in a form
fitted to convey one of the most important moral lessons."

The friends referred to contributed something to the
poem, for we know that the last four stanzas of the
first canto, a description of the diseases arising from
indolence, were written by Armstrong, and we are told
that the stanza which describes Thomson himself was

composed, except the first line, by "a friend of the author," who may, or may not, have been Lyttelton.

We have no means of knowing how many copies of the *Castle of Indolence* were printed, nor can we say very definitely how far it was successful with the public ; but a second edition was called for within the same year.   In later times, though not the most popular, it has been held to be the most finished and exquisite of Thomson's works, and Wordsworth's addition to the personal stanzas, written on the fly-leaf of his pocket copy of the poem, and intended to be a description of himself and Coleridge, bears testimony to the appreciation in which he held it.

The tragedy of *Coriolanus* still hung fire, for one reason or another, and was not actually produced until after the death of the author, which took place at the end of this summer.

"He had always been a timorous horseman, and more so in a road where numbers of giddy or unskilful riders are continually passing ; so that when the weather did not invite him to go by water, he would commonly walk the distance between London and Richmond, with any acquaintance that offered, with whom he might chat and rest himself, or perhaps dine, by the way.   One summer evening, being alone, in his walk from town to Hammersmith he had overheated himself, and in that condition imprudently took a boat to carry him to Kew, apprehending no bad consequence from the chill air on the river, which his walk to his house, at the upper end of Kew Lane, had always hitherto prevented.   But now the cold had so seized him, that next day he found himself in a high fever, so much the more to be dreaded, that he was of a full habit.   This, however, by the use of proper medicines was removed, so that he was thought to be out of danger ; till the fine weather having tempted him to expose himself once more to the evening dews, his fever returned with violence, and with such symptoms as left no hopes of a cure.   Two days had passed before his relapse was known in town : at last, Mr.

Mitchell and Mr. Reid, with Dr. Armstrong, being informed of it, posted out at midnight to his assistance ; but alas ! came only to endure a sight of all others the most shocking to nature, the last agonies of their beloved friend. This lamented death happened on the 27th day of August, 1748."

So Murdoch relates it. From the letters written on the occasion we get the impression that Thomson's death was a cause of very real grief to his friends: the expressions used have reference more to his personal qualities than to his genius, and are not those of mere conventional mourning. "Nothing in life has ever more shocked and affected me," writes Murdoch to Forbes. "We have lost our old, tried, amiable, open and honest-hearted Thomson . . . whom we found ever the same delightful companion, the most faithful depository of our inmost thoughts, and the same sensible, sympathising adviser." To the same person Andrew Millar writes as follows, having received the news of Thomson's death on his arrival in London from Scotland :—

"I thank God we all arrived safe here, after a most agreeable journey. But ever since I have never been able to act or think, for that very evening our dear friend Thomson was buried. How it damped all my joy, you who knew him well and how I loved him, can best feel. . . . Mr. Mitchell spent the evening with me : we remembered you kindly and all surviving friends. Poor Mr. Lyttelton is in great grief, as indeed are all his friends, and even those that did not know him."

Lyttelton's letters to Dr. Doddridge testify to the feeling of which Millar speaks :—

"But God's will be done ! It has pleased his providence to afflict me lately with a new stroke in the sudden death of poor Mr. Thomson, one of the best and most beloved of my friends. He loved my Lucy, too, and was loved by her ;

I hope and trust in the Divine Goodness that they are now
together in a much happier state : that is my consolation, that
is my support."

In another letter of about a month later he refers
thus to Thomson's religious belief :—

"Thomson, I hope and believe, died a Christian. Had he
lived longer, I don't doubt but he would have openly professed
his faith ; for he wanted no courage in what he thought right,
but his mind had been much perplexed with doubts, which
I have the pleasure to think my book on St. Paul had almost
entirely removed. He told me so himself, and in his sickness
declared so to others. This is my best consolation in the loss
of him, for as to the heart of a Christian, he always had that,
in a degree of perfection beyond most men I have known."

Mitchell undertook the charge of the funeral, and
wrote to Mr. Gusthart at Edinburgh, acquainting him
with the event, and offering to undertake the management of all business matters on behalf of the poet's
sisters. He was also the first to inform Murdoch, in
a few lines which concluded : "I am almost sunk with
this last stroke."

Thomson was buried in Richmond churchyard, his
funeral being attended, among others, by Quin, Mallet,
and Andrew Millar. Murdoch seems to complain that
Thomson suffered from some neglect on the part of his
"brother poets," who failed to exert themselves on
this occasion "as they had lately done for one who
had been the terror of poets all his lifetime"; that is
to say, Pope. "Only one gentleman, Mr. Collins, who
had lived some time at Richmond, but forsook it when
Mr. Thomson died, wrote an Ode to his memory."
The many poems which the death of Pope called forth
have all been forgotten, but the beautiful Ode on the
death of Thomson by Collins is a lasting memorial.

Thomson apparently died intestate, and Mitchell

joined with Lyttelton in administering his effects for the benefit of his sisters in Scotland. The contents of his house were sold by auction in May, 1749, and the sale catalogue still exists. There were some five or six hundred books, including Harrington's *Oceana*, Raleigh's *History of the World*, and the works of the chief Italian classic poets, Dante, Ariosto, and Tasso. No less than eighty-three pictures were hung on the walls, and there was also a large portfolio of prints and drawings, containing a considerable number of engravings after Old Masters, Raphael, Guido, Correggio, Carlo Maratti, Poussin, etc., and a series of drawings by Castelli of famous antique statues, the Venus de' Medici, the Fighting and the Dying Gladiator, Meleager, Laocoön, etc. The cellar had six or seven dozen bottles of wine, Burgundy, port, Madeira, and Rhenish, and about thirteen dozen of Scotch ale.

The tragedy of *Coriolanus* was produced in January, 1749. Lyttelton wrote the prologue, in which it was claimed that Thomson's Muse had inspired

> " Not one immoral, one corrupted thought,
> No line, which dying he could wish to blot."

The part of Coriolanus was taken by Quin, who also spoke the prologue, and displayed more than merely feigned emotion, when he came to the line,

> " Alas ! I feel I am no actor here."

The performance was successful, though the drama cannot be said to be a good one ; and a fair sum was realised altogether for the benefit of the author's relations.

Lyttelton assumed the position of literary executor, and it must be said that he took a very extraordinary view of his duties in that capacity. He had taken part with the author in the revision of his work, and he now claimed authority to revise it further without

the author's assistance. Accordingly, in 1750, he
brought out an edition of his friend's poetical works,
in which they were very freely dealt with, the editor
assuring the public that it had been the intention of
the author to make the alterations which were thus
introduced. In sending a copy of this edition to
Dr. Doddridge, he writes as follows :—

"You will find this edition much preferable to any of the
former. . . . Great corrections have been made in the diction,
and many redundancies have been cut off, which hurt the
spirit and weakened the force of the more sublime and nervous
parts, so that upon the whole I am persuaded that you will
think Mr. Thomson a much better poet, if you take the trouble
to read over his works in their present form, than you ever
thought him before."

The most important alterations are the transference
to an appendix of the description of the fox-chase and
the drinking-bout which follows it, in *Autumn*, 470 ff.,
on the ground that the burlesque tone was unsuitable
to the general style of the work, the complete recasting of *Liberty*, so as to shorten the poem by about
1400 lines, and to present it in three parts instead of
five, and the omission of two stanzas in the *Castle of
Indolence*. Johnson had not been able to read *Liberty*
through in its original form, but he protests against
this manner of treating it. "I wish to see it exhibited
as its author left it," is his very reasonable remark.

But the editor was not satisfied with this performance. He designed a complete revision of the
text of *The Seasons*, in which all the most characteristic
features of the style should be improved away, and
the concluding *Hymn* altogether omitted ; and there is
extant a copy of the numerous alterations which he
proposed to introduce into the text of a poet, who
more strongly than most had professed his inability

to write by the judgment of another. For these it is impossible that Lyttelton can have had any authority, however it may have been with some of the previous changes ; and, so far as the text of *The Seasons* was concerned, he met with a firm resistance from Murdoch, who, in an admirable letter to Millar, refused to have any hand in the projected edition of 1762, if these alterations were insisted upon.

> "A detail of my reasons would be needless, it being agreed that an author's works should be presented genuine and entire. If he has written well, well ; if not, the sin lieth, and ought to lie, at his door. It is a pity, indeed, that Mr. Thomson, aided by my Lord Lyttelton, did not correct and alter many things himself, but as that went no further than a bare intention, 'tis too late to think of it now, and we can only say, 'emendaturus, si licuisset, erat.' And my Lord Lyttelton, notwithstanding the generosity and the purity of his friendly design, can never make more of it without hurting the author and himself."

After referring to the fact that Thomson had himself revised his work "with so much deliberation and care that his printers were tired to death, as you well remember," he argues for the restitution of the fox-chase, and against the exclusion of the *Hymn* ("the theology of it, allowance made for poetical expression, is orthodox"); and concludes thus :—

> "As to Mr. Thomson's diction, of which my Lord's acquaintances so much complain, I would recommend to these gentlemen to read Milton with care, and the greatest part of their objections would vanish. For the rest Thomson himself is answerable, and I believe could answer tolerably well, if he were alive to speak for himself. Certain it is, that Thomson's language has been well received by the public, excepting perhaps those my Lord speaks of, who are more disposed to find blemishes than capable of feeling beauties, and who, I think, do not much deserve his Lordship's regard. His numbers

and manner have been adopted by good authors, and since he began to write, our poetry is become more nervous and rich.

"Grammars and dictionaries will always have their due place; but no man of genius ever found himself distressed or fettered by them. He could always use the liberty that belonged to and became him, without falling into solecisms or into obscurity; and indeed without this liberty no language could be enriched or improved, but must soon be reduced to a dead stand, like the style of law-writings."[1]

This sensible protest prevailed, so far as concerned *The Seasons*, but Murdoch did not feel called upon to exert himself in favour of *Liberty*, and this accordingly was reproduced in its abridged form. The edition of 1762, published by subscription, was in two volumes quarto, finely printed. The proceeds were devoted chiefly to the erection of the monument to the author, which stands in Westminster Abbey.

Thomson was in his person above the middle height, and rather robust than graceful. Johnson charges him with "a dull countenance, and a gross, unanimated, uninviting appearance," adding that he was "silent in mingled company, but cheerful among select friends, and by his friends very tenderly and warmly beloved." His personal friend Murdoch says: "His worst appearance was when you saw him walking alone in a thoughtful mood; but let a friend accost him and enter into conversation, he would instantly brighten in a most amiable aspect, his features no longer the same, and his eye darting a peculiar animated fire. The case was much alike in company; where, if it was mixed,

[1] Letter published in Wooll's *Memoirs of Joseph Warton*, p. 252.

or very numerous, he made but an indifferent figure,
but with a few select friends he was open, sprightly,
and entertaining."

With regard to his personal appearance we have
the evidence of several portraits. One of these, by
Aikman, taken when Thomson was a young man, is
pleasing enough, but not very characteristic: in that
of Paton, now in the National Portrait Gallery, which
was painted in 1746-7, the lower part of the face is
rather heavy, but the forehead and eyes are good.
His manners were never very polished. Shenstone
notes in connection with a visit which he paid to the
Leasowes: "He had nothing of the gentleman in his
person or address; but he made amends for this
deficiency by his refined sense, spirited expressions,
and manner of speaking not unlike his friend Quin."
And from Robertson we have the statement: "He
was neither a *petit-maître* nor a boor; he had
simplicity without rudeness, and a cultivated manner
without being courtly." He certainly never "cleared
his tongue from his native pronunciation," as Mallet
had successfully done; and that he continued to use
the Scots dialect in conversation with his countrymen,
is proved by an anecdote recorded by Shiels as an
illustration of his warmth of heart. A son of
Mr. Gusthart of Edinburgh, who had been a very
helpful friend of his family, paid him a visit in Kew
Lane during the last year of his life, and asked the
servant to say that an old acquaintance desired to see
Mr. Thomson. Thomson came forward to receive him,
and looking steadfastly at him said: "Troth, sir, I
cannot say I ken your countenance well. Let me
therefore crave your name." When he heard the
reply, he could not restrain his emotion, and exclaim-
ing, "Good God! are you the son of my old bene-

factor ?" he embraced him with the greatest tenderness, everjoyed at the unexpected meeting.

Willam Taylor, the barber who shaved him for many years, and whom Thomson called "Wull," deposes that he was very negligent in his dress and wore his clothes remarkably plain, but was extravagant with his wigs. His head was remarkably large, so that he wore a larger size than any one else, and his habit of taking long walks, in which he often heated himself overmuch, was very detrimental to their condition. "I have known him spoil a new wig only in walking to London. . . . He used to walk from Malloch's at Strand-on-the-Green and from London at all hours of the night : he seldom liked to go into a carriage, and I never saw him on horseback."

A love of gardening was one of his characteristics, and we note his interest in this pursuit especially in the letter to Paterson, which has already been quoted. Much has been made of his indolence, a fault which he himself admitted in a good-humoured manner, while retorting the charge playfully upon his friends. But the fact is, it was more apparent than real. Men of business, like Cave the publisher, were scandalised to find him hardly out of bed at noon ; but this was not necessarily the result of indolence. The night, we are told, was his favourite time for composition. "He would often be heard walking in his library till near morning, humming over in his way what he was to correct and write out next day ;" and Robertson says that he was often up at dawn, but this was because he had not been to bed. He was, in fact, in the habit of "Turning the night to day, and day to night." In his youth he must certainly have been physically active ; and the habit of taking long walks was continued, as we have seen, to the end of his life. As to the general charge of indolence, it is clear that a man who produced so considerable an amount of literary work, and revised it so carefully and constantly, cannot be said to have led an idle life.

He loved the society of his friends, and in their company he was "sometimes tempted to an excessive indulgence." His decent housekeeper, Mrs. Hobart, dreaded the appearance of Quin at Richmond, and "often wished him dead," because he made her master drink too much; and William Taylor, the barber, had seen him and Quin "coming from the Castle at four o'clock in the morning, and not over sober, you may be sure." Another account says that "he used to associate with Parson Cromer and some other con-vivials at the Old Orange Tree in Kew Lane." At the same time he lived on easy terms of friendship with Pope, who was too careful of his health to take part in any such revelry. "Pope courted Thomson," says Robertson, "and Thomson was always admitted to Pope, whether he had company or not." Probably Thomson's goodness of heart and evenness of temper served to calm the irritation which Pope so often felt. Of Thomson it is said :—

"He took no part in the poetical squabbles which happened in his time, and was respected and left undisturbed by both sides. He would even refuse to take offence when he justly might, by interrupting any personal story that was brought him, with some jest or some humorous apology for the offender. Nor was he ever ruffled or discomposed, but when he read or heard of some flagrant instance of injustice, oppression, or cruelty." [1]

In a few instances he showed irritation under criti-cism, as, for example, in the case of Joseph Mitchell, who found fault too freely with *Winter*, but here

[1] Murdoch's *Life of Thomson.*

there seems to have been some personal cause of dislike.

He was of an open, generous disposition, and never forgot those who had done him service. The humanitarian sentiment which was characteristic of the time found a ready echo in Thomson's heart. Human suffering always moved his sympathy, and he was ever ready to do what lay in his power to relieve it. The well-known passage in *Winter* on the sufferings of the poor, concluding with enthusiastic praise of those who were endeavouring to reform the prison system, expresses genuine feeling; and his dislike of cruelty to animals leads him to condemn almost all field-sports.

"Although he performed on no instrument," says his biographer, "he was passionately fond of music," and when abroad he took great delight in the Italian musical drama. He was also much interested in painting and sculpture, which he studied enthusiastically while on his travels, and he showed his taste in the collection of prints and drawings which he left behind him. In *Liberty* some of the most celebrated ancient statues are described; in the additions to *The Seasons* which were made after the author's visit to Italy we have a reference to the Venus de' Medici (*Summer*, 1347), and apparently also to Guido's 'Aurora' (*Summer*, 120 ff.); while in the *Castle of Indolence* mention is made of the landscapes of Claude, Poussin, and Salvator Rosa. It must be remembered that the English school of landscape-painting was at that time entirely undeveloped. Of his taste in reading we are especially told that he was interested in history and in the relations of travellers, "the most authentic he could procure."

His style of elocution in reading aloud is noted by

his biographers as peculiarly bad, partly owing to his
Scottish accent, and partly to his emotional temperament.

"Such was his extreme sensibility," says Murdoch, "so
perfect the harmony of his organs with the sentiments of his
mind, that his looks always announced, and half expressed,
what he was about to say, and his voice corresponded exactly
to the manner and degree in which he was affected. This
sensibility had one inconvenience attending it, that it rendered
him the very worst reader of good poetry ; . . . a passage of
Virgil, Milton, or Shakespeare would sometimes quite oppress
him, that you could hear little else than some ill-articulated
sounds, rising as from the bottom of his breast."

This is to the same effect as Johnson's less sym-
pathetic remark :—

"Among his peculiarities was a very unskilful and in-
articulate manner of pronouncing any lofty or solemn composition. He was once reading to Dodington, who, being
himself a reader eminently elegant, was so much provoked by
his odd utterance, that he snatched the paper from his hands,
and told him that he did not understand his own verses."

In the matter of religion Thomson was inclined by
temperament to a cheerful optimism, and he dwelt by
preference upon the evidences of love and wisdom in
Creation, upon which he founded the idea of an all-
powerful and benevolent Creator. His religion, therefore, was based upon the cultivation of his emotional
sensibility by enthusiastic contemplation of the works
of Nature. There is no evidence of an acceptance of
revealed Christianity, except Lyttelton's impressions
of the last months of his life ; but he certainly believed
in a future state of individual existence, and in several
places he gives expression to a theory about the
progress of the soul, through successive stages of being,
to ultimate perfection :—

> " Heirs of eternity ! yborn to rise
>   Through endless states of being, still more near
>   To bliss approaching and perfection clear."

And this was conceived as part of a law of evolution
which embraced the whole of Creation :—

> " From seeming evil still educing good,
>   And better thence again, and better still,
>   In infinite progression."

CHAPTER III

THOMSON AND THE POETRY OF NATURE

THOMSON'S friend Patrick Murdoch, in concluding that biography to which we have frequently referred, makes the remark that "to judge from the imitations of his manner, which have been following him close from the very first publication of *Winter*, he seems to have fixed no inconsiderable era of English poetry." This is a very just observation, but it must be accepted with due reserves. It has sometimes been assumed that the true feeling for external nature was altogether dead in the age of Queen Anne and George I., and that Thomson created the taste by which he was appreciated. Wordsworth, as is well known, remarks that, "excepting the *Nocturnal Reverie* of Lady Winchilsea and a passage or two in the *Windsor Forest* of Pope, the poetry of the period intervening between the publication of *Paradise Lost* and *The Seasons* does not contain a single new image of external nature, and scarcely presents a familiar one from which it can be inferred that the eye of the poet had been steadily fixed upon his object, much less that his feelings had urged him to work upon it in the spirit of genuine imagination," and he proceeds to illustrate this absence of true observation from the description of night in Dryden's *Indian Emperor*, and from the celebrated moonlight scene in the eighth book of Pope's *Iliad*. In the main this criticism of the literature of the period which preceded the publication of *The Seasons* is fairly sound, though the list of exceptions ought certainly to be extended. The conclusion, however, which Wordsworth endeavours to draw, namely, that there existed no true popular taste for the poetry of external nature, is by no means a necessary one, and it is contradicted by the fact, admitted by Wordsworth himself, of the immediate popularity of *The Seasons*, a fact which he endeavours to dispose of by a somewhat quibbling distinction between wonder and legitimate admiration. But indeed the passage of Thomson's biography in which this fact is stated supplies qualifications which may serve to suggest a sounder view. The writer says :—

"The poem of *Winter*, published in March 1726, was no sooner read than universally admired, those only excepted who had not been used to feel or to look for anything in poetry beyond a *point* of satirical or epigrammatic wit, a smart *antithesis* richly trimmed with rhyme, or the softness of an elegiac complaint. To such his manly, classical spirit could not readily recommend itself, till after a more attentive perusal they had got the better of their prejudices and either acquired or affected a truer taste. A few others stood aloof, merely because they had long before fixed the articles of their poetical creed, and resigned themselves to an absolute despair of ever seeing anything new and original. These were somewhat mortified to find their notions disturbed by the appearance of a poet, who seemed to owe nothing but to nature and his own genius. But in a short time the applause became unanimous, every one wondering how so many pictures, and pictures so familiar, should have moved them but faintly to what they felt in his descriptions." [1]

This passage seems to point to the true state of things, namely, that there existed a certain divergence on some important matters between the taste of the

[1] Murdoch's *Life of Thomson*.

reading public generally and that of the literary
circles to which the poets and the critics of the day
alike belonged.

The causes of this divergence need not here be
discussed in any detail, but it will hardly be denied
that circumstances had been singularly favourable to
its development. The origin of it goes back to a
somewhat earlier time, and depends primarily upon
those political and religious influences which estranged
the main body of the nation from literature, in the
second quarter of the seventeenth century, and owing
to which poetry was for a time almost confined within
the limits of a Court circle. The result had been a
great loss of the power of true imaginative expression,
shown first in the exaggerated fashion of overstrained
conceits and far-fetched comparisons, and then in the
reign of what the authors of the *Rehearsal* call "Prose
and Sense," which followed as a reaction from this,
and was accompanied by a great narrowing of the
range of poetical interest. This reform of literary
taste had been carried out under conditions which
tended definitely towards centralisation. The literary
influence of the Court had been strong in the reign of
Charles II., who was himself a man of good judgment
in literary matters, and made his personal tastes distinctly felt, and the functions of an Academy had
been exercised to some extent by the Royal Society,
of which in its early days Dryden and other distinguished men of letters were members. We have
the evidence of its historian for the fact that the
Royal Society made it one of its principal objects to
promote the use of a simple and lucid English style,
as far as possible free from ornament and superfluity.

Meanwhile the position of authors, not yet able to
appeal to a large reading public through publishers

who were willing to risk something upon their ventures, was usually one of dependence. Unless they had private means, they were compelled to solicit the patronage either of individual persons of rank and wealth or of a political party. Even Dryden for the greater part of his career was unable to make a reasonable income out of the profession of literature, except on condition of writing for the theatres; and when the translation of Virgil was published, in 1697, though he declined to ask for royal patronage, he fortified his venture with as many dedications as possible. Both political and social conditions had been favourable to the concentration of literary production and literary criticism in the hands of a comparatively small circle of wits, who wrote primarily for fashionable society; and conditions, partly political and partly literary, had determined that the accepted principles of criticism and the established models of literature should be primarily French rather than English.

Hence arose the divergence which we have noted between the popular feeling and the taste of the literary coteries, and hence also that narrowing of the range of interest which is observable in the literature of this age, from which those subjects were for the most part excluded which did not interest the town. That the popular appreciation of literature was by no means confined within these limits, is sufficiently evident from the decisive recognition during this period of the superiority in genius of Milton and Shakespeare.

Milton had achieved his great reputation by direct appeal to the reading public, without any of the usual aids of patronage or influence, and without making the smallest concession to the literary fashions of the day, the year being 1667 and the poem a religious epic of considerable extent, in a style of versification "new to all

and disgusting to many," by an author who had previously been chiefly known for his hostility to the pre-
latical government of the Church and his defence before
Europe of the conduct of the Regicides. This was in
truth, what Johnson calls it, an uncommon example of
the prevalence of genius. The fact that the poems of
fashionable writers, like Waller and Cleveland, went
through many more editions than *Paradise Lost* is no
indication that *Paradise Lost* was not appreciated.
When Addison wrote his well-known papers on
Paradise Lost, which are sometimes supposed to have
been the foundation of its fame, he was evidently
not so much concerned to introduce his readers
to the merits of an unrecognised work of genius,
as to show that its acknowledged merits would
square with the rules of criticism accepted in literary
circles. "I shall examine it by the rules of epic poetry,
and see whether it falls short of the *Iliad* or *Æneid* in
the beauties which are essential to that kind of writing." Less than forty years after the author's death
he takes it as admitted by the best judges that *Paradise
Lost* is "the noblest work of genius in our language,"
and in the motto of the first paper, "Cedite, Romani
scriptores, cedite Graii," he seems to imply a still
higher claim.

With regard to Shakespeare, the successive critical
editions of Rowe, Pope, and Theobald, from 1709 to
1733, supply evidence enough, even if there were no
other, of the extent to which he found appreciation
apart from the stage.

There is reason therefore to assert that the taste
of the reading public was not confined within the limits
prescribed by the literary coteries ; and it is certain
that the average Englishman's love of outdoor life and
of outdoor sports had not been repressed in deference

to any new French fashion. Nor is it the case that the natural beauty of fields, woods, streams, and hills was altogether unappreciated by the poets of the period. John Philips, in his Miltonic poem called *Cider*, published in 1706, shows himself very sensible of the beauties of nature, though he regards it chiefly from a practical point of view. The following lines on the apple orchard in autumn are characteristic :—

> " O let me now, when the kind, early dew
> Unlocks th' embosom'd odours, walk among
> The well-rang'd files of trees, whose full-ag'd store
> Diffuse ambrosial steams, than myrrh or nard
> More grateful, or perfuming flowery bean.
> Soft whispering airs, and the lark's matin song
> Then woo to musing, and becalm the mind
> Perplex'd with irksome thoughts.   Thrice happy time,
> Best portion of the various year, in which
> Nature rejoiceth, smiling on her works,
> Lovely, to full perfection wrought."

It is usual to speak of the juvenile Pastorals of Pope, published in 1708, as entirely imitative, but they contain lines which prove that the author was by no means without appreciation of the beauty of external nature. True observation is shown in the couplet,

> " Where dancing sunbeams on the waters play'd,
> And verdant alders form'd a quivering shade,"

in the lines which speak of the smoke curling upward from the village roofs at evening, while the shade rapidly spreads over the darkening green, and in the description of the stillness of night, broken only by the song of the nightingale, while the whispering wind dies away among the trees.

The Pastorals of Ambrose Philips, published in 1709, are no doubt conventional ; yet here too, and still more in his Epistle to the Earl of Dorset, dated from Copen-

hagen in the same year, there are passages which show
that the author was capable of observing and appreciating natural beauty.   Gay's "Georgic" under the title
of *Rural Sports*, which came out in 1713, has both independent observation and truth to nature, though
the form of expression is artificial.   The following
description of sunset over the sea, presumably in
Devonshire, may serve as an example :—

> " Or when the ploughman leaves the task of day,
>   And trudging homeward, whistles on the way,
> When the big-udder'd cows with patience stand,
> Waiting the strokings of the damsel's hand,
> .   .   .   .   .
> When no rude gale disturbs the sleeping trees,
> Nor aspen leaves confess the gentlest breeze,
> Engag'd in thought to Neptune's bounds I stray,
> To take my farewell of the parting day.
> Far in the deep the Sun his glory hides,
> A streak of gold the sea and sky divides ;
> The purple clouds their amber linings show,
> And edg'd with flame rolls every wave below :
> Here pensive I behold the fading light,
> And o'er the distant billow lose my sight."

In Pope's *Windsor Forest*, published in the same year,
the author gives us some vivid colouring both in the
landscape and in the account of the various forms of
sport; but it is true that the descriptions are sometimes such as to suggest the game-dealer's or fish-
monger's shop rather than the woods and streams.
The best line in the original poem,

> " Lead me thro' arching bowers and glimmering glades,"

was omitted in the later editions.   What was wanting
in the case of Pope was not so much power of observation as enthusiasm for the subject.

But apart from the indications afforded by the
generally current poetry of the day, we have to note

that during these apparently rather barren years there had in fact been growing up, partly by way of reaction against the social and literary conditions of the town, but partly also in the course of a natural development, a completely new school of nature-poetry. The descriptions of external nature by Lady Winchilsea, by Thomson and by Dyer, are of a different character altogether from those which we have from the earlier poets. Poetical "nature-study" in the modern sense of the term had its origin, paradoxical as the assertion may seem, in the first half of the eighteenth century; for it was then for the first time that the phenomena of external nature came to be regarded as objects of poetry in and for themselves. The term is not one which can be properly applied to such representations of nature as we have, for example, ordinarily in Shakespeare or Milton; and the question is not one of comparative truth or beauty, but of method and point of view. It is true that Shakespeare in his first poem, *Venus and Adonis*, shows a distinct tendency to describe natural objects for their own sake, but in his maturer work nature description is entirely subordinated to emotion, as in the Sonnets, or to dramatic effect, as in the plays. The most striking example of minute description which we have in the dramas is the cliff scene in *King Lear*, and the particularity here is evidently necessary for the dramatic purpose. In *L'Allegro* and *Il Penseroso* the appearances of external nature are harmonised with the moods of the speaker. One of the earliest distinct manifestations of the new movement is to be found in the country and garden poems of Marvell, but for its development we have to wait till the eighteenth century has been well begun. The *Nocturnal Reverie*, published in 1714, is a most characteristic example of the school:—

" In such a night, when passing clouds give place,
    Or thinly veil the heaven's mysterious face ;
    When in some river overhung with green,
    The waving moon and trembling leaves are seen ;
    When freshen'd grass now bears itself upright,
    And makes cool banks to pleasing rest invite,
    Whence springs the woodbine and the bramble-rose,
    And where the sleepy cowslip shelter'd grows ;
    Whilst now a paler hue the foxglove takes,
    Yet chequers still with red the dusky brakes ;

    When the loos'd horse now, as his pasture leads,
    Comes slowly grazing through the adjoining meads,
    Whose stealing pace and lengthen'd shade we fear,
    Till torn-up forage in his teeth we hear ;

    In such a night let me abroad remain,
    Till morning breaks, and all's confus'd again."

Thomson, it cannot be denied, was an original poet,
but he did not create the taste by which he was appreciated ; and the very artificiality of the London literary
society had been preparing the way for some such
assertion as his of the claims of the country.

There was indeed nothing in the task which Thomson
undertook, which was necessarily at variance with the
principles of the so-called classical school. "Nature"
was the watchword of that school, and there was no
reason why the term should be restricted to the application made of it by Boileau or Pope. The idea of truth
to nature in its widest sense is one which pervades the
literary criticism of the age, and this idea suggests something quite definite and intelligible. It suggests primarily the representation of things as they really are, or
rather as they naturally present themselves to the
imagination, and the abandonment of what is fantastic,
far-fetched, or allegorical. In this there was nothing
which in the least precluded the new poetry of nature.

Indeed, the very word "Nature," and the suggestion
which it conveyed of the value of truth to nature in
poetry, pleaded in favour of true and vivid representation
of every kind. Some literary critics insist on regarding
Thomson chiefly as a herald of the romantic revival;
but this is wholly to misconceive his position. He was
essentially a representative of his own age, and that
was also the age of Pope. He was, in fact, in a
certain sense the complement of Pope, applying to
country scenes something of the same power of true
observation and vivid portraiture which Pope used
upon the town. It is hardly necessary to say that
there is nothing necessarily "romantic" about the
scenes and operations of external nature. No doubt,
in the infinite variety of its forms and influences, and
in the awful character of some of its aspects, there are
suggestions of mystery and terror, which are congenial
to the romantic temper. Thomson has distinct touches
of true romance, as will afterwards be seen; and he
repeatedly uses the word "romantic" quite in the
modern sense, as when he says of the lover,

> "Sudden he starts,
> Shook from his tender trance, and restless runs
> To glimmering shades and sympathetic glooms;
> Where the dun umbrage o'er the falling stream
> Romantic hangs."

But for all that, Thomson is not on the whole a
romantic poet; his representations are broadly objective, not lyrical or personal, and he does not by
preference select for treatment that which is wild or
awful in nature: he is led by the love of nature to a
cheerful and practical religion, rather than to a sense
of the inexplicable mystery of the universe. When
he expresses the mood of pensive melancholy, which is
suggested in the lines just quoted, he is dealing with

what he regards as a morbid or exceptional state of
mind. Every age has its share of the romantic as of
the classical spirit, and the evidences of this which we
find in Thomson (and it may be added in Pope also)
are characteristic of that time and not of the next
generation but one. In imitating Milton he was
following one who had been established as a model
worthy of general imitation, and in the *Castle of
Indolence* he was not endeavouring to revolutionise
English poetry, but merely following a fashion of
Spenserianism, which had by that time set in with
considerable violence.

The philosophy and religion of Thomson, as it
appears in his poetry, is an optimistic Deism, and this
in effect was also the philosophy and religion of Pope.
His optimism, however, was not, like that of Pope, a
theory adopted for the purposes of poetical argument,
but the result of a deep feeling of the perfection and
beauty of the created world and of the adaptation of
external nature to the needs of living creatures. He
had exceptionally keen and delicate sense perceptions,
and he was naturally disposed to enjoyment of the
more refined pleasures which the exercise of his senses
afforded. An essentially healthy and cheerful temperament produced in him a happy and hopeful view,
both of this life and of the next. But the sentimental
melancholy which was already a note of the times is
also occasionally expressed in Thomson's work, and
pity for the sufferings of the poor and of the lower
animals was a feeling congenial to his kindly disposition.

With all this it is true, of course, as has been
already suggested, that Thomson's poetry represented
something of a reaction against the one-sided view
of life which had been presented in very much

of the poetry of the age; and this reaction, like most movements of the kind, had itself a somewhat one-sided character. Thus, while Pope, for example, dealt almost exclusively with the interests of an artificial town society, Thomson is led by his enthusiasm to conceive of what he calls "the works of Nature," as almost the only subject worthy of poetical treatment. "Where can we meet with such variety, such beauty, such magnificence, all that enlarges and transports the soul?" By his genius indeed he was peculiarly qualified to supply the element which was, to some extent at least, wanting in the poetry of the period. But he does not really transcend the limits imposed by the artificial division between nature and man. It is true that there are numerous passages in his poetry, where the labour of man is represented as dependent upon or co-operating with the conditions of the seasons, or where the influences of nature upon the human spirit are in some measure represented. But the human element in *The Seasons* is to a great extent a matter of embroidery; it is not wrought into the fabric of the poem. These episodes and digressions do not really belong to the subject, but are a concession to the spirit of the age. The *Castle of Indolence*, again, in which the aspects of external nature are up to a certain point successfully harmonised with the theme, is partly spoilt by the author's determination to extract a conventional moral from his work. The important difference between Pope and Thomson in the matter of poetical development is that the former realised his own powers more completely. He did not long wander "in Fancy's maze," but early chose the path which was most suitable to his genius, and hardly left it except when he was decoyed by Bolingbroke into the mazes of philosophy. He seldom failed in perception of the bent of his own genius. Thomson, on the other hand, partly because he had a high ideal of the functions of poetry, and partly from the influence of the prevailing literary fashions, failed to estimate correctly the limits of his own powers, and was constantly attempting tasks for which he was unfitted. *Liberty* is an admitted failure, and the dramas, though admired at the time, must on the whole be given up. Apart from a few songs, for he had also a lyrical gift, which might with advantage have been more fully developed, his reputation must rest upon the poetry of natural description which is to be found in *The Seasons* and in *The Castle of Indolence*. To represent him as primarily a "philosophical poet" is a strange aberration of criticism which has been reserved for our own times.[1]

The question arises therefore more especially in the case of Thomson: What rank can properly be assigned to poetry of this kind? Landscape-painting has successfully asserted its right to a distinct and honourable place in modern art, and the question is whether the poetry of natural description can claim an analogous position as compared with other poetry. It is idle to maintain as a general maxim that, as regards poetry, "The proper study of mankind is man." The operations of Nature generally are as much a legitimate field of poetical study as the doings of man, and may properly be treated objectively, and not merely as subordinate to human actions and emotions. The artistic success or failure will depend upon the method of treatment, and in some degree Thomson justly illustrates by the treatment of his subjects the true principles of distinction between the methods of painting and poetry.

[1] See Courthope's *History of English Poetry*, v. 305 ff.

Lessing wrote the *Laokoon* chiefly as a criticism upon the "picturesque" school of poetry, a school which took its rise in Germany quite independently of Thomson, though it was afterwards profoundly influenced by him; indeed it may be said that descriptive poetry in Germany underwent a complete change of style owing to Thomson's influence. Haller's poem *Die Alpen*, which seems to be particularly the object of Lessing's attack, was published in 1729, and the author does not seem to have been acquainted at that time with Thomson's *Seasons*, of which three out of the four parts had then been published. Lessing himself had a great regard for Thomson as a poet, and speaks of him with an affectionate admiration. He must therefore have seen reason to distinguish him, to some extent at least, from those descriptive poets whose method he altogether condemns, and we can without difficulty perceive on what lines he might have justified Thomson, while still condemning the picturesque school.

He would have adopted the line of defence which he follows in dealing with Homer's descriptions of the chariot of Hera or of the shield of Achilles. In these cases what we have is not the mere description of an object with successive enumeration of characteristics which exist simultaneously, but an account of the successive acts of fitting together the parts of the chariot, the axle, the seat, the pole, the traces, the straps, or again of the successive operations of the divine craftsman, as he works one after another the figures which are the ornament of the shield. It would be hard if he could not have demonstrated that Thomson presents us not with landscape pictures, but with a succession of descriptive strokes, each representing a definite development of action or natural

G

movement. We should have had another of those specimens of special pleading of which Lessing has given us so many masterly examples, and the descriptions which violate the rules, as for example those of the view from Richmond Hill or from Hagley Park, would have been dismissed as lightly as the wheels of the chariot of Hera. He has himself suggested the line that might have been taken, in his remarks upon Kleist's *Frühling*: "Had he lived longer, he would have thrown it into an entirely different form. He was intending to introduce a plan into the poem, and was devising a method by which the multitude of pictures which he had taken apparently at random, now here and now there, . . . might be made to appear before his eyes in a natural order and to follow one after another."

After all, in the case of Thomson this line of defence would not be altogether unreasonable. It is true that the poems of *The Seasons* are too diffuse and too loosely constructed; but if from criticism of the structure of the poems we turn our attention to the particular parts of which they are composed, we shall see that Thomson's method of description is by no means disorderly, and that it is, properly speaking, that of the poet and not of the painter : the points of his description arise in a certain natural order of succession; he describes, in fact, for the most part, not the several parts of a scene as it lies at rest before him, but the appearances which are successively developed, the changes caused by the action of the elements, of the lower animals, or of human beings. This is the character of Thomson's best work in description. Let us take for example the snow-storm :—

"Through the hush'd air the whitening shower descends,
At first thin-wavering ; till at last the flakes

> Fall broad and wide and fast, dimming the day
> With a continual flow.   The cherish'd fields
> Put on their winter robe of purest white.
> 'Tis brightness all ; save where the new snow melts
> Along the mazy current.   Low the woods
> Bow their hoar head," etc.

(Winter, 229 ff.)

Or again the delicately worked out *genre* picture of the
redbreast, which follows shortly after :—

> "Half-afraid, he first
> Against the window beats ; then brisk alights
> On the warm hearth ; then, hopping o'er the floor,
> Eyes all the smiling family askance,
> And pecks, and starts, and wonders where he is ;
> Till, more familiar grown, the table-crumbs
> Attract his slender feet."

These passages give details in each case which serve
to build up a picture, but under the form of a succession of events ; and this will be found to be the usual
character of Thomson's descriptions, and an essential
part of their poetical effectiveness.

The second of the passages above quoted, however, is
less characteristic of Thomson than the first, and in its
delicate minuteness of detail reminds us rather of the
style of Cowper.   Thomson had a certain largeness of
view, a power of presenting his scene in masses and in
a generalised form, which Cowper does not attain to.
He seems to have hesitated with regard to the pro-
priety of this particular passage : it appeared first in
the second edition of *Winter*, published in June, 1726,
but it was omitted in the quarto of 1730, though it
remained in the more popular octavo, and appeared
again in 1738.   It does, in fact, by its indoor details
somewhat injure the general effect of the description,
which in the first edition passed directly from—

> " The fowls of heaven,
> Tam'd by the cruel season, crowd around
> The winnowing store, and claim the little boon
> That Providence assigns "

to

> " The foodless wilds
> Pour forth their brown inhabitants."

Probably he was persuaded, against his better judgment, that the passage was too good to be omitted. In any case, Thomson's effects depend usually upon the power of creating a vivid impression by a few rapid touches, while Cowper builds up his delicate and beautiful pictures by patiently adding one detail after another.

Neither Thomson nor Cowper can be said to have arrived at a quite satisfactory view of the relations of man with external nature ; and a question naturally arises as to the value which such poetry as theirs may have with a view to the attainment of a more complete conception. That it gives pleasure is undoubted, but how far does it tend towards the highest poetical truth ? The answer is, that such poetry represents a preliminary stage, which must necessarily be traversed before the ultimate synthesis can be reached. Wordsworth's descriptions have great beauty and truth to nature, yet Wordsworth is not properly a descriptive poet, because his imagination constantly transforms the sense perceptions into symbols of spiritual truth. Wordsworth, however, himself went through the preliminary stage of which we are speaking, and it was this to which he referred when he wrote of his earlier years :—

> " The sounding cataract
> Haunted me like a passion : the tall rock,
> The mountain, and the deep and gloomy wood,

> Their colours and their forms, were then to me
> An appetite, a feeling, and a love,
> That had no need of a remoter charm
> Unborrow'd from the eye.   That time is past."

Of that past time he has left memorials in his early poems. Nature indeed must first be deeply loved for herself alone, her sounds and her sights must haunt the poet like a passion, the colours and forms which she presents must be to him "An appetite, a feeling, and a love," before he can rise to the higher sense of spiritual harmony. Thomson possessed what we may perhaps call the representative imagination : he was able to select the elements of his description in such a manner as to bring before his readers an impression nearly resembling that which he had experienced, and to communicate to them, in some degree at least, the emotions which it excited in himself. If we are ultimately to transcend the phenomena, and to realise the harmony between the aspects of external Nature and the spiritual needs of Man, we must first pass through the stage of poetical observation. It is this which is especially represented by Thomson, and however incomplete his work may seem to be, it is undeniable that the poetry of the eighteenth century has an appreciable obligation to his genius.

Thomson had, it may be admitted, an essentially poetical temperament; he saw things always with the eye of a poet, but "notwithstanding his high powers, he writes a vicious style." Such is Wordsworth's verdict, and it must to some extent be accepted. In Wordsworth's celebrated attack upon the poetic diction of the eighteenth century, Gray was selected as the special object of criticism, being at the head of those who, by their reasonings, had attempted to widen the space of separation between prose and metrical composition, and being also "more than any other man curiously elaborate in his own poetic diction." If the main attack had been made upon Thomson, it would probably have been more successful; for unquestionably the poetic diction of Thomson may with good reason be criticised, while at the same time it is more truly representative of the tendencies against which Wordsworth really desired to protest, than that of Gray. Thomson, equally with Gray, thought it right to maintain a wide space of separation between the language of prose and that of "metrical composition"; and so far he is not to be blamed. His fault was, not that he wrote in poetical language, but that he adopted a highly artificial kind of poetical language. Not satisfied with the poetry of his own day, which he justly criticised as wanting in elevation both of subject and of style, he chose to adopt Milton as his principal model of diction as well as verse. The Miltonic diction is a form of speech which was suitable to the genius of its original author, and to a great extent in harmony with the subjects of which he treated; but it was the source of most of that conventional unreality which characterises the poetical language of the eighteenth century. Even in the hands of Milton the results are not always happy; and when applied by an imitator to ordinary subjects, this style of diction is apt to produce the effect either of pompous artificiality or of unpleasant mannerism.

Thomson, however, was not a mere imitator in the matter of style. He was moved by a genuine impulse to restore to the language some of the richness and poetical colour of which it had been deprived by the writers of his own age in their endeavours after lucidity and common-sense. He instinctively felt that, for the subjects which stirred his imagination, a more truly

poetical diction was needed than that which was
current in the poetry of the day. He naturally looked
back to the last great example in English literature of
exalted poetical expression; and besides borrowing the
actual language of Milton, he endeavoured to advance
further in the spirit of his exemplar, and ventured
himself to make such additions to the poetical language
as he felt to be needed for the expression of his own
conceptions. He deserves the credit, as we shall see,
of having made an adventurous endeavour to vary and
enrich the forms of poetical expression in English, and
of having partially succeeded in his enterprise.

This general survey of Thomson's position as a poet
of nature may fitly be closed by a reference to some
noteworthy appreciations of his powers by critics of
very different schools. The first shall be that contained in Joseph Warton's *Essay on the Genius of Pope*,
which is quoted not because Warton was the first to
discover Thomson's true merits, as is suggested by
Wordsworth, who is determined to believe that Thomson was admired by his own generation, not for his
merits, but for his faults; but because it is a sound
and sober estimate of his position, and has been more
often talked of than read. It is true that Warton,
from his own love of romance, somewhat overvalues
the romantic element in Thomson; but in other
respects his appreciation is very just. The essay was
first published in 1756, eight years after the poet's
death.

" Thomson was blessed with a strong and copious fancy;
he hath enriched poetry with a variety of new and original
images, which he painted from nature itself and from his own
actual observations: his descriptions have therefore a distinct-
ness and truth which are utterly wanting in those of poets
who have only copied from each other, and have never looked

abroad on the objects themselves. . . . Though the diction of
The Seasons is sometimes harsh and inharmonious, and sometimes turgid and obscure, and though in many instances the
numbers are not sufficiently diversified by different pauses,
yet is this poem on the whole, from the numberless strokes of
nature in which it abounds, one of the most captivating and
amusing in our language. . . . The scenes of Thomson are
frequently as wild and romantic as those of Salvator Rosa,
varied with precipices and torrents and ' castled cliffs ' and
deep valleys, with piny mountains and the gloomiest caverns." [1]

In the second place we may quote the estimate of
Johnson, which is quite unexpectedly favourable :—

"As a writer he is entitled to one praise of the highest
kind : his mode of thinking and of expressing his thoughts is
original.   His blank verse is no more the blank verse of
Milton, or of any other poet, than the rhymes of Prior are the
rhymes of Cowley.   His numbers, his pauses, his diction are
of his own growth, without transcription, without imitation.
He thinks in a peculiar train, and he thinks always as a man
of genius : he looks round on Nature and on Life with the
eye which Nature bestows only on a poet, the eye that dis-
tinguishes, in everything presented to its view, whatever
there is on which imagination can delight to be detained ; and
with a mind that at once comprehends the vast and attends
to the minute." [2]

Finally, in our own day, Professor Saintsbury has
justly appreciated Thomson as follows :—

"He has the peculiar merit of choosing a subject which

---

[1] *Essay on the Genius and Writings of Pope*, vol. i. p. 41
(ed. 1772).   The statement of Wordsworth that most of the
passages of Thomson which were selected by Warton for admiration are absent from the early editions of *The Seasons*, is
quite without foundation.   Out of fifteen or sixteen passages
which Warton quotes or refers to, all but three (*Summer*,
976 ff., 1048 ff., and *Autumn*, 773 ff.) are to be found in the
edition of 1730, the first complete edition of *The Seasons*.

[2] *Lives of the Poets*.

appeals to and is comprehensible by everybody; which no one can scorn as trivial, and yet which no one can feel to be too fine or too esoteric for him. And though he treats this in the true poetical spirit of making the common as though it were uncommon, he does not make it too uncommon for the general taste to relish. . . . No degeneracy of education or of fashion, short of an absolute return to barbarism, can prevent *The Seasons* from attracting admiration as soon as they are read or heard. They are not perhaps in any single point possessed of the qualities of the highest poetry. But such poetry as they do possess is perfectly genuine and singularly suitable for its purpose."

And again :—

"It would hardly be too much to say that, making allowance for the time over which his influence has extended, no poet has given the special pleasure which poetry is capable of giving, to so large a number of persons, in so large a measure as Thomson."[1]

---

[1] *The English Poets*, ed. T. H. Ward, vol. iii. p. 169 f.

CHAPTER IV

THE SEASONS

OF the external history of *The Seasons*, that is to say, the circumstances of the publication of the separate poems, *Winter*, *Summer*, *Spring*, and *Autumn*, and of the main differences in extent and substance between the earlier and the later editions, something has already been said. The literary examination of this work remains to be undertaken, and as a preliminary to criticism we may properly set forth in the present chapter a summary of its contents, treating it now as a single complete poem, and following the text which was arrived at finally by the author.

"The great defect of *The Seasons*," says Johnson, "is want of method." It is true, no doubt, that the poems are of a somewhat rambling character, but it would be unjust to say that they are without plan. *Winter* describes the gradual progress of the season, from wind and rain to snow-storms, from snow to frost, and from frost to thaw; *Summer* sets before us the process of a day from sunrise to midnight; and *Spring* displays the influence of the season upon the natural world, in regular ascent from the lower to the higher spheres: *Autumn* alone can, with any justice, be said to be incoherent. But the advantage of regularity is to a great extent lost in all these poems by diffuseness and digressions; and in so far as each poem produces an impression of unity, this is chiefly by

virtue of the accumulation of scenes harmonised to a
particular tone, and representing in various forms the
same characteristics of external nature.　The total
impression would undoubtedly be more satisfactory, if
there were not an element of confusion and disorder
in the materials by which it is produced.

The unity of the whole work depends partly upon
the general similarity of subject and treatment in the
separate poems, and partly upon the thoughts and
feelings expressed in the concluding Hymn, beginning :—

> " These, as they change, Almighty Father, these
> 　　Are but the varied God.　The rolling year
> 　　Is full of Thee."

A strong religious sentiment is shown throughout *The
Seasons*, and here the religious idea is appropriately
set forth as the motive of the whole work.　That
Thomson believed in a personal God there can be
no doubt, however much some of his expressions
may seem to suggest Pantheism.　The following is
only one of many passages which might be quoted to
this effect :—

> " Mysterious round ! what skill, what force divine,
> 　Deep felt, in these appear ! a simple train,
> 　Yet so delightful, mix'd with such kind art,
> 　Such beauty and beneficence combin'd, . . .
> 　That as they still succeed, they ravish still.
> 　But wandering oft, with brute unconscious gaze,
> 　Man marks not Thee, marks not the mighty hand,
> 　That ever-busy wheels the silent spheres,
> 　Works in the secret deep, shoots steaming thence
> 　The fair profusion that o'erspreads the Spring ;
> 　Flings from the sun direct the flaming day ;
> 　Feeds every creature ; hurls the tempest forth :
> 　And as on earth this grateful change revolves,
> 　With transport touches all the springs of life.

> Nature, attend ! join every living soul,
> Beneath the spacious temple of the sky,
> In adoration join ; and ardent raise
> One general song ! "

Hymn, 21 ff.

The source of Thomson's enthusiasm for his subject
is to be found not only in his sense of the grandeur
and beauty of the "works of Nature," but also in his
religious convictions, and his belief in the existence
of a personal Creator and Sustainer of the Universe. It
is this which justifies his universality, and gives dignity
to the smallest details of his descriptions. We cannot
doubt the sincerity of the feeling, and it is expressed
repeatedly in every poem of *The Seasons*. We are in
presence here of a genuine religion of Nature, though
of a different kind from that of a later generation.

The opening poem, *Spring*, is not the best, but it is
at least happier than the others in its dedication.
The Countess of Hertford is a more interesting subject
of verse than Dodington, Onslow, or Wilmington, and
her praises are dealt out in a more discriminating
manner than theirs. The poem proceeds to a description of the wavering of the season between winter and
spring,—

> "so that scarce
> The bittern knows his time, with bill ingulf'd
> To shake the sounding marsh ; or from the shore
> The plovers when to scatter o'er the heath,
> And sing their wild notes to the listening waste."

Ploughing and sowing follow, and they are operations
with which Thomson was better acquainted than some
of his critics, who fail to understand the picturesque
epithet applied to the sower :—

> "White, through the neighbouring fields the sower stalks
> With measur'd step."

Then, after a tribute to the agriculture of his country,
the poet passes to the general plan which he proposes
to follow, a description of the effects of the season
upon the various parts of nature, "ascending from the
lower to the higher," a quasi-scientific arrangement
which is relieved by "digressions arising from the
subject." First comes the gathering of the clouds
"with vernal showers distent," and the expectant
pause before the rain :—

> "Gradual sinks the breeze
> Into a perfect calm ; that not a breath
> Is heard to quiver thro' the closing woods,
> Or rustling turn the many-twinkling leaves
> Of aspin tall.   Th' uncurling floods, diffus'd
> In glassy breadth, seem thro' delusive lapse
> Forgetful of their course.   'Tis silence all,
> And pleasing expectation."

Then :—

> "At last,
> The clouds consign their treasures to the fields ;
> And, softly shaking on the dimpled pool
> Prelusive drops, let all their moisture flow,
> In large effusion o'er the freshen'd world."

The fruitful rain is followed by a brilliant gleam,
when the setting sun looks out for a moment from
amid the clouds :—

> "The rapid radiance instantaneous strikes
> Th' illumin'd mountain, thro' the forest streams,
> Shakes on the floods, and in a yellow mist,
> Far smoking o'er th' interminable plain,
> In twinkling myriads lights the dewy gems.
> Moist, bright, and green, the landscape laughs around.
> Full swell the woods ; their every music wakes,
> Mix'd in wild concert with the warbling brooks
> Increas'd, the distant bleatings of the hills,
> The hollow lows responsive from the vales,
> Whence, blending all, the sweeten'd zephyr springs."

This passage owes something doubtless to Milton, but the brilliance of light and colour is Thomson's own.

The growth of plants suggests their uses to man, and this topic leads us back to the Golden Age, when man was as yet uncorrupted, and fed exclusively upon vegetable productions. Now, worse even than the wolf or the tiger, he slaughters the very animals to which he is indebted for milk or for wool, and who lend him their assistance in his labour. But pure vegetarianism is dismissed as a counsel of perfection :—

> "High Heaven forbids the bold presumptuous strain,
>   Whose wisest will has fixed us in a state,
>   That must not yet to pure perfection rise."

The orderly development of the poem is here rather seriously interrupted by a passage, inserted in the later editions, which describes some of the occupations of the morning and noon-day hours in spring. The passage in itself is valuable, but there is no proper connection here : it is, perhaps, the most glaring instance in *The Seasons* of this kind of interpolation of picturesque or poetical passages without sufficient regard to the general sequence. What we have here is a scene of fly-fishing for trout, described with an accuracy and a fulness of detail which betrays the enthusiastic angler. When the first flood has run down, and while the water is yet brown in the brooks, then is the time,

> "Then issuing cheerful to thy sport repair,"

and especially if there is a light west wind stirring the surface of the water, and carrying clouds across the sun. Then you should follow the brook down its "rocky-channelled maze" to the river, and

> "Just in the dubious point, where with the pool
>   Is mix'd the trembling stream, or where it boils

> Around the stone, or, from the hollow'd bank
> Reverted, plays in undulating flow,
> There throw nice-judging the delusive fly ;
> And as you lead it round in artful curve,
> With eye attentive mark the springing game.
> Straight as above the surface of the flood
> They wanton rise, or urg'd by hunger leap,
> Then fix, with gentle twitch, the barbed hook ;
> Some lightly tossing to the grassy bank,
> And to the shelving shore slow-dragging some,
> With various hand proportion'd to their force."

The description in the passage which follows of the contest with "the monarch of the brook," lured

> " From his dark haunt beneath the tangled roots
> Of pendent trees,"

is highly realistic, and a masterpiece in its kind. When we compare this angling scene with that which we find in Gay's *Rural Sports*, we are greatly impressed with the superiority of Thomson.

The lines which follow on the noon-day rest, also a part of the later interpolation, are not less admirable in a different way. When the clouds pass from the sky and the sport is abandoned,

> "Then seek the bank where flowering elders crowd,
> Where scatter'd wild the lily of the vale
> Its balmy essence breathes, where cowslips hang
> The dewy head, where purple violets lurk,
> With all the lowly children of the shade :
> Or lie reclin'd beneath yon spreading ash,
> Hung o'er the steep ; whence, borne on liquid wing,
> The sounding culver shoots ; or where the hawk
> High in the beetling cliff his aery builds."

The Virgilian reminiscence is here peculiarly happy.

Resuming the interrupted train of ideas, the author enlarges upon the varied beauty of flowers in spring,

both those that grow wild and those of the garden.
The list of garden flowers, reminding the reader too
much of a florist's catalogue, has sometimes been cited
as a characteristic of Thomson's style of description.
This, however, is likely to convey a false idea; for it is
in fact by no means typical, and except in the artificial confines of a garden, he hardly ever allows himself
to proceed by simple enumeration of details. Even here
it may be observed that he does not willingly confine
himself to the prescribed limits: his eye and imagination wander away from the green alleys and
bowery walks to the river, the lake, and the forest
beyond.   It is only with an effort that he recalls them
to the nearer scene of the garden.

From the vegetable world the poet passes to the
effects of the season upon birds, their song, their
courtship, and their breeding :—

> " Every copse
> Deep-tangled, tree irregular, and bush
> Bending with dewy moisture, o'er the heads
> Of the coy quiristers that lodge within,
> Are prodigal of harmony.   The thrush
> And woodlark, o'er the kind-contending throng
> Superior heard, run thro' the sweetest length
> Of notes ; . . .
> The blackbird whistles from the thorny brake ;
> The mellow bullfinch answers from the grove ;
> Nor are the linnets, o'er the flowering furze
> Pour'd out profusely, silent."

There is a pretty account of the courtship and
nesting of birds, of the hatching of the broods, and of
the first attempts of the young birds to fly, some of
which shows exact observation of their habits.   The
following passage is happy both in its description and
its tone of feeling, a genuinely classical combination :—

" This one glad office more, and then dissolves
  Parental love at once, now needless grown :
  Unlavish Wisdom never works in vain.
  'Tis on some evening, sunny, grateful, mild,
  When nought but balm is breathing thro' the woods,
  With yellow lustre bright, that the new tribes
  Visit the spacious heavens, and look abroad
  On Nature's common, far as they can see,
  Or wing, their range and pasture.   O'er the boughs
  Dancing about, still at the giddy verge
  Their resolution fails ; their pinions still,
  In loose libration stretch'd, to trust the void
  Trembling refuse : till down before them fly
  The parent-guides, and chide, exhort, command,
  Or push them off.   The surging air receives
  Its plumy burden ; and their self-taught wings
  Winnow the waving element.   On ground
  Alighted, bolder up again they lead,
  Farther and farther on, the lengthening flight ;
  Till vanish'd every fear, and every power
  Rous'd into life and action, light in air
  Th' acquitted parents see their soaring race,
  And, once rejoicing, never know them more."

The picture which follows of the eagle and his
brood on the summit of the craggy cliff,

        " such as amazing frowns
  On utmost Kilda's shore, whose lonely race
  Resign the setting sun to Indian worlds,"

is well contrasted with the homely English scene of
farm-yard and park,—the cawing rooks, the household
fowls, the swan jealously guarding his osier-isle, the
peacock spreading his glory to the sun and swimming
along in radiant majesty, and the doves cooing in
amorous chase.

We pass to the effects of the season upon the higher
animals, and finally upon man, whose soul, if he be
worthy, is raised to serene contemplation or warmed

to enthusiastic rapture. This introduces the mention of Lyttelton, the ideal friend, whose feelings and meditations vary thus, as he strays through Hagley Park, courting the Muse or occupied with plans for his country's welfare. Perhaps his walk is accompanied by that "loved Lucinda" with whom he is so happily united, and then all nature is transfigured for the lover, and he enjoys the inimitable happiness of soul to soul attuned, "which love Alone bestows, and on a favoured few." The view from the summit of the park is of a characteristically English landscape, and the truth of the description will be acknowledged by all who have seen the original of it. It is to be noticed that Thomson does not describe an extended view without first leading his reader to an elevation from which it may be seen.

> " Meantime you gain the height, from whose fair brow
>   The bursting prospect spreads immense around ;
>   And snatch'd o'er hill and dale, and wood and lawn,
>   And verdant field, and darkening heath between,
>   And villages embosom'd soft in trees,
>   And spiry towns by surging columns mark'd
>   Of household smoke, your eye excursive roams ;
>   Wide-stretching from the Hall, in whose kind haunt
>   The hospitable genius lingers still,
>   To where the broken landskip, by degrees
>   Ascending, roughens into rigid hills,
>   O'er which the Cambrian mountains, like far clouds
>   That skirt the blue horizon, dusky rise."

The whole concludes with "a dissuasive from the wild and irregular passion of love, opposed to that of a pure and happy kind."

In the poem which follows next, *Summer*, the author has succeeded better in conveying an impression of the characteristics of the season, perhaps because its appearances are more uniform. The plan proposed is to describe a summer's day from sunrise to midnight; but the digressions are so frequent and so considerable in extent, that we are in danger of losing sight of this design. On the whole, however, the general character of the poem is well preserved.

The summer sunrise,

> "At first faint-gleaming in the dappled east,
> Till far o'er ether spreads the widening glow,"

is portrayed as by one to whom it was familiar.

> "With quicken'd step
> Brown night retires : young day pours in apace,
> And opens all the lawny prospect wide.
> The dripping rock, the mountain's misty top,
> Swell on the sight, and brighten with the dawn.
> Blue thro' the dusk the smoking currents shine ;
> And from the bladed field the fearful hare
> Limps awkward."

But the well-known passage that follows must often have been turned against the author by his friends :—

> "Falsely luxurious, will not man awake,
> And springing from the bed of sloth, enjoy
> The cool, the fragrant and the silent hour,
> To meditation due and sacred song ?"

The actual entrance of the sun upon the scene is described with epic dignity, and the enthusiastic address which follows, rather happily blends scientific fact with poetical imagination. The day proceeds, numberless insects are wakened by the warmer rays, and the air resounds with a ceaseless hum, not undelightful to him who muses in the woods at noon, or to the drowsy shepherd lying by the brook, beneath the shade of the grey willows. The life of insects is described, and the wisdom of their Creator justified

in lines which need not detain us. Hay-making and
sheep-shearing, the last a lively scene which was added
in 1744, bring the day to full noon, and an impression
of intense heat is successfully produced by the succeeding passage :—

> "O'er heaven and earth, far as the ranging eye
> Can sweep, a dazzling deluge reigns ; and all,
> From pole to pole, is undistinguished blaze.
>
> .   .   .   .
>
> Echo no more returns the cheerful sound
> Of sharpening scythe : the mower sinking heaps
> O'er him the humid hay with flowers perfum'd ;
> And scarce a chirping grasshopper is heard
> Thro' the dumb mead."

With this is happily contrasted the delight of
coolness and shade :—

> "Thrice happy he, who on the sunless side
> Of a romantic mountain, forest-crown'd,
> Beneath the whole collected shade reclines ;
> Or in the gelid caverns, woodbine-wrought,
> And fresh bedew'd with ever-spouting streams,
> Sits coolly calm, while all the world without,
> Unsatisfied and sick, tosses in noon."

Our fastidious modern taste prefers to omit the
moralisation which follows,—

> "Emblem instructive of the virtuous man," etc.

It may be said, however, that as compared with the
other poets of his age, Dyer for example, Thomson
very seldom improves the occasion in this manner.

By the deep-embowered shades of the forest solemn
meditations are suggested, mysterious shapes seem to
"glide athwart the dusk," and a sacred terror creeps
through the mortal frame, with a feeling of the near
presence of the spirits of those who have passed away.
The charm is broken by the sound of falling water,

and the wanderer checks his steps to view the scene
of the cascade :—

> "At first an azure sheet it rushes broad ;
> Then whitening by degrees, as prone it falls,
> And from the loud-resounding rocks below
> Dash'd in a cloud of foam, it sends aloft
> A hoary mist, and forms a ceaseless shower.
> Nor can the tortur'd wave here find repose ;
> But raging still amid the shaggy rocks,
> Now flashes o'er the scatter'd fragments, now
> Aslant the hollow channel rapid darts,
> And falling fast from gradual slope to slope,
> With wild infracted course and lessen'd roar,
> It gains a safer bed, and steals at last
> Along the mazes of the quiet vale."

A moss-lined seat is found beside the stream, surrounded by the freshness of the humid air and over-
shaded by fragrant woodbine, and there, "While nature
lies around deep-lull'd in noon," the imagination takes
her flight, and views the wonders of the torrid zone.
There follow nearly five hundred lines descriptive of
tropical scenery in Africa, Asia, and America. The
author was not personally familiar with these scenes,
but he was an eager reader of books of travel, and he
often intuitively seized upon the characteristic features,
even in the case of such distant rivers as

> "Menam's orient stream, that nightly shines
> With insect-lamps."

He has been reading Lobo's *Voyage to Abyssinia*,
with its continuation, as translated by Johnson, and
speaks of "Gojam's sunny realm" and "the lucid
lake Of fair Dambea," through which the Blue Nile
flows not far from its sources. The destruction of a
caravan by a sand-storm of the African desert is well
described :—

> " Or from the black-red ether bursting broad
>   Sallies the sudden whirlwind.   Straight the sands,
>   Commov'd around, in gathering eddies play :
>   Nearer and nearer still they darkening come ;
>   Till, with the general all-involving storm
>   Swept up, the whole continuous wilds arise ;
>   And by their noon-day fount dejected thrown,
>   Or sunk at night, in sad, disastrous sleep,
>   Beneath descending hills the caravan
>   Is buried deep.   In Cairo's crowded streets
>   Th' impatient merchant, wondering, waits in vain,
>   And Mecca saddens at the long delay."

There is both reality and pathos in the picture of
the plague-stricken British squadron at Carthagena
in 1740 :—

> "You, gallant Vernon, saw
>   The miserable scene ;   .   .
>   .   .   .   you heard the groans
>   Of agonising ships from shore to shore ;
>   Heard, nightly plung'd amid the sullen waves,
>   The frequent corse ; while, on each other fix'd
>   In sad presage, the blank assistants seem'd
>   Silent to ask whom fate would next demand."

Returning to more familiar scenes, the poet vividly
describes a thunder-storm, introducing here the idyllic
story of Celadon and Amelia, to illustrate the proposition that "the fated flash" does not always descend
upon a guilty head :—

> "Young Celadon,
>   And his Amelia were a matchless pair ;
>   With equal virtue form'd and equal grace,
>   The same, distinguish'd by their sex alone :
>   Hers the mild lustre of the blooming morn,
>   And his the radiance of the risen day."

Each was a dearer self to the other : they lived through
the rural day in harmonious intercourse,

> "and talk'd the flowing heart,
> Or sigh'd and look'd unutterable things."

A thunder-storm surprises them in their walk. Amelia's terror cannot be concealed ; but Celadon is assured that no bolt from heaven can harm such innocence, and declares that it is safety for him to be near her. As he is about to clasp her to his bosom, she is struck to the ground a blackened corpse, while the lover stands speechless and hating life, fixed as the shape of a mourner upon a marble tomb,

> "For ever silent and for ever sad."

Returning to the aspects of nature, the poet describes the brightness which follows the storm :—

> "while, as if in sign
> Of danger past, a glittering robe of joy,
> Set off abundant by the yellow ray,
> Invests the fields, yet dropping from distress."

A scene of bathing follows, pictured by one who had evidently been himself in early life an enthusiastic swimmer, and apparently not in summer only :—

> "This is the purest exercise of health,
> The kind refresher of the summer heats ;
> Nor when cold Winter keens the brightening flood,
> Would I weak-shivering linger on the brink."

The subject of bathing introduces a second episode, the story of Damon and Musidora, of a lover who in the concealment afforded by a hazel copse near a stream, sees his mistress in the heat of the day unclothe herself and bathe, and then, "Check'd, at last, By love's respectful modesty," retires from his post, first throwing down on the bank a writing which indicates his identity. Startled by the sound of his retreat, she flies "to find those robes Which blissful Eden knew not," and arrays herself in them with haste ;

but when at length she reads the paper, and recognises
Damon's hand, her terrors vanish.   Finally she leaves
on an aged beech-tree an inscription which admits that
his feelings are returned, and urges him to be still
discreet as now : eventually perhaps the time may
come when such extreme delicacy as he has shown
may be unnecessary.

The story is worked out with considerable beauty
of detail, but it certainly has not much to recommend
it in point of taste.   It may be noticed, however, that
it was comparatively unobjectionable in the earlier
editions.   There Damon is a Stoic and a scorner of
beauty, and no particular obligation compels him to
give warning of his presence to the three beauties who
are under his observation.   The indelicacy of the
discovery does not occur, nor Musidora's rather shame-
less acceptance of the situation.   We are told only that
Damon's harsh philosophy was put to flight, and that
he was humanised by the image of Musidora fixed in
his heart.   It may be noted also that the comparison
to the three goddesses who came before Paris for judgment is far more appropriate in this earlier version.

The summer evening comes, and with it the hour
for walking, either alone or with a friend :—

> " Which way, Amanda, shall we bend our course ?
>   The choice perplexes.   Wherefore should we choose ?
>   All is the same with thee.   Say, shall we wind
>   Along the stream, or walk the smiling mead,
>   Or court the forest glades, or wander wild
>   Among the waving harvests, or ascend,
>   While radiant Summer opens all its pride,
>   Thy hill, delightful Shene ? "

There follows a picture of the view from Richmond
Hill, extending from London on the one side to
Windsor on the other ; the goodly prospect.

> " Of hills, and dales, and woods, and lawns, and spires,
>   And glittering towns, and gilded streams,"

inspires a patriotic apostrophe of Britannia, the land
of liberty and of wealth, parent of wise and heroic
men, and of beautiful and virtuous women. Among
patriots, Alfred, More, Drake, Raleigh, Philip Sidney,
Hampden, Russell and Algernon Sidney are mentioned
by name; among philosophers and men of science,
Bacon, Shaftesbury, Boyle, Locke, and finally Newton,

> " whom God
> To mortals lent, to trace his boundless works
> From laws sublimely simple";

among poets, Shakespeare, Milton, Spenser and
Chaucer. The panegyric concludes with a strain
exactly like that of "Rule Britannia,"—

> " Island of bliss ! amid the subject seas,
>   That thunder round thy rocky coasts, set up,
>   At once the wonder, terror, and delight
>   Of distant nations,"

and with a prayer that the Almighty will send forth
"the saving virtues" to keep watch in bright patrol
about this favoured land.

The end of the day draws near. The sun ap-
proaches to his setting, and the clouds in richly
variegated pomp attend his departure. Now he has
half of his orb immersed below the horizon,

> " and now, a golden curve,
> Gives one bright glance, then total disappears."

The evening shadows gather over the earth, gradually
deepening in intensity :—

> " A fresher gale
> Begins to wave the wood and stir the stream,
> Sweeping with shadowy gust the fields of corn,
> While the quail clamours for his running mate."

The shepherd returns home merry-hearted after he has
secured his folded flock, on his way relieving the milk-
maid of her brimming pail, his love being shown as
yet only by that best language

> "Of cordial glances and obliging deeds."

Meanwhile,

> "Among the crooked lanes, on every hedge,
>   The glow-worm lights his gem ; and thro' the dark
>   A moving radiance twinkles.   Evening yields
>   The world to night."

Things of the earth become dim, while the heaven
grows bright with radiant orbs.   There perhaps a
comet blazes, the appearance of which to the ignorant
causes terror, but by the wise is greeted as a confirma-
tion of their predictions and an additional proof of the
divine love and power.   The whole concludes with the
praises of "Philosophy," that is to say, Science.

In *Autumn* there is less appearance of a systematic
plan than in the other poems, but on the whole the
natural course of the season is followed from harvest-
time to the fall of the leaf, and so to the fogs and
frosts of the later season.

The prospect of harvest suggests the theme of Industry, raiser of human kind from naked helpless-
ness to the state of comfort and civility ; and we have
a picture of the primitive condition of man, which is
curiously at variance with the ideal state suggested in
Spring, 233 ff.   Here we find something much more
nearly corresponding with the facts :—

> "And still the sad barbarian, roving, mix'd
>   With beasts of prey ; or for his acorn-meal
>   Fought the fierce tusky boar ; a shivering wretch !
>   Aghast and comfortless, when the bleak north,

> With Winter charg'd, let the mix'd tempest fly,
> Hail, rain, and snow, and bitter-breathing frost ;
> Then to the shelter of the hut he fled,
> And the wild season, sordid, pin'd away :
> For home he had not."

It was the spirit of Industry that roused the human race from this wretched condition, and unfolded its faculties, till at length every form of cultivated life was wrought into perfection. The city, which later in the same poem is denounced as the nurse of every vice, is here exalted as the mother of commerce and industrial arts, and especially, as may be supposed, the banks of the Thames are celebrated with patriotic fervour.

We return to the harvest-fields, and see the reapers at their work,

> "each by the lass he loves,
> To bear the rougher part, and mitigate
> By nameless gentle offices her toil,"

a trait which is evidently drawn by the poet from the custom of his own native land, with which we have been made familiar by Burns. The pretty episode of Lavinia and Palemon follows. Lavinia, who "once had friends," on whose birth fortune had smiled, had been early deprived

> "Of every stay, save innocence and Heaven,"

and lived with her widowed mother in

> "a cottage far retir'd
> Among the windings of a woody vale ;
> By solitude and deep surrounding shades,
> But more by bashful modesty, conceal'd."

Thus they shunned the cruel scorn to which virtue sunk to poverty is exposed ; and the maiden grew up fresher than the morning rose newly wetted with dew, and pure as the lily or the mountain snow.

> " A native grace
> Sat fair-proportion'd on her polish'd limbs,
> Veil'd in a simple robe, their best attire,
> Beyond the pomp of dress ; for loveliness
> Needs not the foreign aid of ornament,
> But is when unadorn'd adorn'd the most.
> Thoughtless of beauty, she was beauty's self,
> Recluse amid the close-embowering woods."

Several of the above-quoted lines and the succeeding
simile of the myrtle are almost certainly due to Lyttelton, in whose handwriting they appear in the interleaved copy at the British Museum, of which so much
has been heard :—

> " As in the hollow breast of Apennine,
> Beneath the shelter of encircling hills,
> A myrtle rises, far from human eye,
> And breathes its balmy fragrance o'er the wild ;
> So flourish'd blooming, and unseen by all,
> The sweet Lavinia ; till at length, compell'd
> By strong Necessity's supreme command,
> With smiling patience in her looks, she went
> To glean Palemon's fields."

Palemon saw the modest gleaner, and his heart was
moved with unconscious love. Lavinia's father had
been his friend and patron, and he seemed to distinguish in her some likeness to him. He knew that
the family had been reduced to poverty, but he had
been unable to find the place of abode of the widow and
her daughter. When on inquiry he discovered that
this was the child of his former benefactor, he poured
out his heart to her, and offered her himself and his
fortune.

> " Won by the charm
> Of goodness irresistible, and all
> In sweet disorder lost, she blush'd consent,"

and happiness resulted to all concerned. It is a grace-

ful little idyll, more simply presented than is usual
with Thomson, and certainly owing something of its
merit to the classical taste of his friend.

We have next a scene of storm in harvest-time, with
floods which carry away the result of the husbandman's
labour.   Then mention is made of various forms of
sport, and both partridge-shooting and hare-hunting
are condemned for barbarity by the poet :—

> " Poor is the triumph o'er the timid hare,
>   Scar'd from the corn, and now to some lone seat
> Retir'd, the rushy fen, the ragged furze,
> Stretch'd o'er the stony heath. . . .
> Vain is her best precaution, though she sits
> Conceal'd, with folded ears, unsleeping eyes,
> By Nature rais'd to take th' horizon in,
> And head couch'd close betwixt her hairy feet,
> In act to spring away.   The scented dew
> Betrays her early labyrinth ; and deep,
> In scatter'd sullen openings far behind,
> With every breeze she hears the coming storm."

The chase of beasts of prey is permitted, however, and
fox-hunting, the only form of this sport which Britain
affords, is not blamed for cruelty, for it is admitted
that the fox deserves to die for his depredations.
Nevertheless, even this sport is ridiculed by a mock-
heroic description of the prowess displayed ; and it
is evident that the sympathy of the poet is to a
great extent with the hunted animal, who displays
so much resource and cunning in baffling his pursuers,
and finally dies hard,

> " Without complaint, though by a hundred mouths
>   Relentless torn."

This is followed by a burlesque account of the evening
which follows, with its robust performances in the way

of eating and drinking. It would be useless, thinks
the author, to endeavour to deter the "rougher sex"
from this sport; but an earnest appeal is made to the
other to abstain from pursuing it, and to cultivate the
feminine graces and virtues.

The fruits of Autumn are next described : we have
a scene of nutting, and then a view of the orchard,
with a tribute to the poet's immediate predecessor in
the use of blank verse, the author of *Cider*. The wall-
fruit of Dodington's garden at Eastbury, and the vine-
yards of Burgundy and Champagne are successively
celebrated.

Then follow the fogs of the latter part of Autumn,
rolling about the mountain, and gradually extending
over the plain. Objects appear indistinct and larger
than they actually are, and

> "wilder'd o'er the waste
> The shepherd stalks gigantic."

The mention of these mists leads to a digression on
the rise of streams and rivers, a part of which (ll. 743-
772), where the poet states and refutes a mistaken
theory, is a happy reproduction of the style of Lucretius.
It is noticeable that in the original editions Thomson
apparently adopted the theory against which he afterwards thus effectively argued, being doubtful whether
evaporation would sufficiently account for the constant
supply of rivers :—

> " But sure 'tis no weak, variable cause,
>   That keeps at once ten thousand thousand floods
>   Wide-wandering o'er the world, so fresh, so clear,
>   For ever flowing, and for ever full."
>
> (Ed. 1730.)

The migration of birds in Autumn suggests the
subject of the birds of the Hebrides :—

> " Who can recount what transmigrations there
>   Are annual made, what nations come and go,
>   And how the living clouds on clouds arise,
>   Infinite wings ! till all the plume-dark air
>   And rude resounding shore are one wild cry."

And this leads to a view of Scotland, her airy mountains, her forests, lakes, valleys, and rivers, from the
Tweed, which is addressed as

> " pure parent stream,
> Whose pastoral banks first heard my Doric reed,
> With, silvan Jed, thy tributary brook,"

to the promontories and islands of the furthest north.
She is celebrated, with patriotic fervour, as the nurse
of a people,

> " in misfortune's school
> Train'd up to hardy deeds. . . . A manly race,
> Of unsubmitting spirit, wise and brave,"

who, impatient of their own "unequal bounds," have
gone forth to shed their blood and to lavish their
genius and their labour for the benefit of every land,

> " As from their own clear north, in radiant streams,
>   Bright over Europe bursts the Boreal morn."

An appeal is finally made for the encouragement of
agriculture and industry in Scotland, for the protection
of the fisheries from Dutch aggression, and for the
development especially of the trade and shipping of
the country, so that Britain, "in soul united as in
name," may reign undisputed mistress of the deep : and
two statesmen especially, the Duke of Argyll and
Duncan Forbes of Culloden, are singled out as capable
of these patriotic services.

Returning to his subject, the poet speaks of the
fading of the "many-coloured woods," as the season
advances, but fails here to do justice to the special

beauty to which this change gives rise. The calm of
the season and the fall of the leaf inspire the mood of
philosophic melancholy, and ideas crowd fast into the
creative mind; devotion is raised to rapture, and the
love of nature and of man, the sympathies of love and
friendship, are felt with renewed power. The mind
turns to romantic scenes :—

> " Oh ! bear me then to vast embowering shades,
>   To twilight groves and visionary vales,
>   To weeping grottos and prophetic glooms ;
>   Where angel forms athwart the solemn dusk
>   Tremendous sweep, or seem to sweep along."

Or if the spirit be less disposed to melancholy, it may
find its satisfaction in "the garden and the rural seat";
and "the fair majestic paradise of Stowe," the seat of
Lyttelton's cousin, Lord Cobham, is especially selected
for praise.

> " And there, O Pitt, thy country's early boast,
>   There let me sit beneath the shelter'd slopes, . . .
>   And with thy converse blest, catch the last smiles
>   Of Autumn beaming o'er the yellow woods."

In 1744, when this passage was inserted, Pitt was
the political associate of the "Cobham cousins," and
had been interested in Thomson, as we have already
seen, through Lyttelton. He was at Hagley also
during Thomson's visit in 1746.

Sunset on a calm autumn day is followed by clear
sky above, though the rolling fogs cluster below,

> "and swim along
>   The dusky-mantled lawn."

The full moon rises opposite to the setting sun, and
attains the height of heaven, shedding her softer light
on all things :—

> " Wide the pale deluge floats, and streaming mild
> O'er the sky'd mountain to the shadowy vale,
> While rocks and floods reflect the quivering gleam,
> The whole air whitens with a boundless tide
> Of silver radiance, trembling round the world."

At other times streams of meteors appear in the heavens :—

> " Oft in this season, silent from the north
> A blaze of meteors shoots ; ensweeping first
> The lower skies, they all at once converge
> High to the crown of heaven, and all at once
> Relapsing quick, as quickly reascend,
> And mix and thwart, extinguish and renew,
> All ether coursing in a maze of light."

The description is of a very occasional phenomenon, and is lively rather than accurate ; indeed, some of the passage which follows seems to apply more properly to the *Aurora Borealis* than to a meteor shower. Among the ignorant superstitious fears are aroused, but "the man of philosophic eye" inspects the phenomenon with scientific curiosity,

> "inquisitive to know
> The causes and materials, yet unfix'd,
> Of this appearance, beautiful and new."

Night is followed by a day of calm beauty :—

> "the morning shines
> Serene, in all her dewy beauty bright,
> Unfolding fair the last autumnal day.
> And now the mounting sun dispels the fog ;
> The rigid hoar-frost melts before his beam,
> And hung on every spray, on every blade
> Of grass, the myriad dew-drops twinkle round."

The sight of the bees, who have been robbed and murdered "Beneath the cloud of guilt-concealing night," moves the poet to another denunciation of the selfish tyranny of Man, who ruthlessly destroys the animals by whose labour he profits. But the genial splendour of the day dispels all harsher thoughts :—

> " How still the breeze ! save what the filmy threads
> Of dew evaporate brushes from the plain.
> How clear the cloudless sky ! how deeply tinged
> With a peculiar blue !   .   .   .   .   .
>   .   .   .   .   .   .   how calm below
> The gilded earth ! the harvest-treasures all
> Now gather'd in, beyond the rage of storms."

And the poem concludes with reflections upon the happiness of rural retirement, "a philosophic country life," as it is called in the Argument, and a fine invocation of Nature to enrich the poet with a knowledge of her works, and never to permit him to stray from her.

Winter is on the whole the most successful of the four poems in producing a single harmonious impression, though this was to some extent marred by the numerous additions. It is the only poem of the series in which the season is successfully personified. Spring and Autumn are hardly brought before us as personages or individual influences at all, and Summer only partially so, as represented by the Sun, but Winter is a real monarch, of whose personality we are constantly kept in mind :—

> " See, Winter comes, to rule the varied year,
> Sullen and sad, with all his rising train,
> Vapours and clouds and storms."

> " Then comes the father of the tempest forth
> Wrapt in black glooms."

> " Here Winter holds his unrejoicing court,
> And through his airy hall the loud misrule
> Of driving tempest is for ever heard."

" 'Tis done !—dread Winter spreads his latest glooms,
   And reigns tremendous o'er the conquer'd year."

And some minor personifications are also successful :—

" Ye too, ye Winds, that now begin to blow
   With boisterous sweep, I raise my voice to you.
   Where are your stores, ye powerful beings, say,
   Where your aerial magazines, reserv'd
   To swell the brooding terrors of the storm?
   In what far-distant region of the sky,
   Hush'd in deep silence, sleep ye when 'tis calm ? " [1]

Or again :—

" What art thou, Frost? and whence are thy keen stores
   Deriv'd, thou secret all-invading power,
   Whom even th' illusive fluid cannot fly ? "

The poem follows on the whole the course of the
season. After the proposition of the subject, with a
personal reference to his own boyhood spent amid the
wilder scenes of nature, the writer describes the storms
which usher in Winter, first rain, with torrent streams
and flooded fields, then wind, in a passage which contains a good many reminiscences of Virgil :—

" When from the pallid sky the sun descends,
   With many a spot, that o'er his glaring orb
   Uncertain wanders, stain'd, red fiery streaks
   Begin to flush around.   The reeling clouds
   Stagger with dizzy poise, as doubting yet
   Which master to obey ; while rising slow,
   Blank, in the leaden-colour'd east, the moon
   Wears a wan circle round her blunted horns.
        .   .   .   .   .   .

---

[1] The last two lines of this passage were happily quoted by
Voltaire, when he was pressed by Boswell for an answer to the
question what was the mode of existence of those ideas which
had passed out of our consciousness, but were afterwards to be
recollected. (Boswell, *Hypochondriacs*, cited by Dr. Birkbeck
Hill in a note to his edition of the *Life of Johnson*, i. 435.)

> Snatch'd in short eddies plays the wither'd leaf,
> And on the flood the dancing feather floats.
> With broaden'd nostrils to the sky upturn'd,
> The conscious heifer snuffs the stormy gale."

The poet describes the effect of the wind both at sea and on land :—

> " Meantime the mountain-billows, to the clouds
> In dreadful tumult swell'd, surge above surge,
> Burst into chaos with tremendous roar,
> And anchor'd navies from their station drive,
> Wild as the winds across the howling waste
> Of mighty waters : now th' inflated wave
> Straining they scale, and now impetuous shoot
> Into the secret chambers of the deep,
> The wintry Baltic thundering o'er their head.
>
> .   .   .   .
>
>   Nor less at land the loosened tempest reigns.
> The mountain thunders ; and its sturdy sons
> Stoop to the bottom of the rocks they shade. . . ."

And then follows the passage about the howling of the storm round human dwellings, which must be that referred to by Gray, when he writes in a letter of June, 1760 :—

"Did you never observe ('while rocking winds are piping loud') that pause, as the gust is recollecting itself, and rising upon the ear in a shrill and plaintive note, like the swell of an Æolian harp ? I do assure you there is nothing in the world so like the voice of a spirit. Thomson had an ear sometimes ; he was not deaf to this, and has described it gloriously, but gives it another turn. I cannot repeat the lines : it is in his *Winter*."

Then, when the commotion is at its height, and when Nature seems to be on the point of dissolution, a hush is suddenly commanded :—

> " Huge uproar lords it wide. The clouds, commix'd
> With stars, swift gliding sweep along the sky.

> All nature reels. Till Nature's King, who oft
> Amid tempestuous darkness dwells alone,
> And on the wings of the careering wind
> Walks dreadfully serene, commands a calm ;
> Then straight air, sea, and earth are hush'd at once."

The peace which succeeds at midnight suggests solemn thoughts on the vanities of life and a fervent prayer for help and guidance :—

> " Father of light and life, thou Good Supreme !
> O teach me what is good ! teach me Thyself !
> Save me from folly, vanity, and vice,
> From every low pursuit ; and feed my soul
> With knowledge, conscious peace, and virtue pure,
> Sacred, substantial, never-fading bliss ! "

The "keener tempests" of Winter are at hand. Thick clouds gather over the sky, "in whose capacious womb A vapoury deluge lies, to snow congeal'd," and the fall of snow follows, described in a justly celebrated passage, which has been partially quoted in the preceding chapter.

The pictures which follow were evidently suggested by the poet's home surroundings, first that of sheep buried in a snow-drift :—

> "from the bellowing east,
> In this dire season, oft the whirlwind's wing
> Sweeps up the burden of whole wintry plains
> In one wide waft, and o'er the hapless flocks,
> Hid in the hollow of two neighbouring hills,
> The billowy tempest whelms ; till, upward urg'd,
> The valley to a shining mountain swells,
> Tipt with a wreath high-curling in the sky."

And then of the peasant lost in the snow upon the moors, and sinking into a treacherous bog :—

> " In vain for him th' officious wife prepares
> The fire fair-blazing and the vestment warm ;

> In vain his little children, peeping out
> Into the mingling storm, demand their sire,
> With tears of artless innocence.   Alas !
> Nor wife nor children more shall he behold,
> Nor friends nor sacred home."

This suggests the idea of human suffering generally,
and introduces a tribute to the labours of the Jail
Committee in the year 1729.

Scenes of winter among the Alps and Pyrenees
follow,—the ravages of wolves, and the destruction
wrought by avalanches.   Returning to his own country,
the poet desires for himself a rural retreat, sheltered
from the storms that blow around,—

> " Where ruddy fire and beaming tapers join,
>   To cheer the gloom,"

and there proposes to himself "high converse with
the mighty dead," calling before his mind the noblest
names of Greece and Rome, of which a detailed
enumeration ensues.   After these appear the shades
of the poets, Virgil, who is placed decisively first, and
was hailed in the early editions as "Maro, the best of
poets and of men," next Homer,

>   "and equal by his side,
>   The British Muse."

It is the society of these that he would desire in this
hallowed hour of night, on which he will allow none
others to intrude,

> " Save a few chosen friends, who sometimes deign
>   To bless my humble roof with sense refin'd,
>   Learning digested well, exalted faith,
>   Unstudied wit and humour ever gay.
>   Or from the Muses' hill will Pope descend,
>   To raise the sacred hour, to bid it smile,
>   And with the social spirit warm the heart ;

> For though not sweeter his own Homer sings,
> Yet is his life the more endearing song."

The thought of his friends suggests the memory of James Hammond, the author of the *Love Elegies*, whose early death took place in 1742; and he pays a tribute to

> " that life-diffusing charm
> Of sprightly wit, that rapture for the Muse,
> That heart of friendship and that soul of joy,"

which had only been shown to the world and then snatched away.

Thus then he would spend the winter evening "with friends of pliant soul," discussing the problems of nature and of human life, and anticipating with earnest eye

> "those scenes
> Of happiness and wonder, where the mind
> In endless growth and infinite ascent,
> Rises from state to state and world to world,"

a theory of soul-development which several times appears in Thomson's work.

In the meantime the village and the city pursue their evening recreations, and among these the theatre is especially mentioned, tragedy being represented by Shakespeare and Otway, and comedy by Steele. With the social life of the city is associated the name of Chesterfield, who is hailed as "At once the guardian, ornament, and joy Of polished life," and whose patriotism, politeness, wit, and parliamentary eloquence are enthusiastically celebrated. The year in which this passage was inserted was that in which Chesterfield was associated with Pitt and Lyttelton in entering the Government.

The poet then brings us back to the natural pheno-

mena of Winter. Frost succeeds, and the bright cold
animates and invigorates the human frame and spirits,
and helps to fertilise the ploughed-up soil. The
streams are frozen :—

> " An icy gale, oft shifting, o'er the pool
>   Breathes a blue film, and in its mid career
>   Arrests the bickering stream. The loosened ice,
>   Let down the flood, and half-dissolv'd by day,
>   Rustles no more ; but to the sedgy bank
>   Fast grows, or gathers round the pointed stone,
>   A crystal pavement, by the breath of heaven
>   Cemented firm."

The hard earth rings to the tread, and distant
sounds are more clearly heard through the frosty air.
The sky at night shines with a keen intensity, dis-
closing infinite worlds to the view,

> " and, all one cope
> Of starry glitter, glows from pole to pole."

All nature is bound fast by the rigid influence, and
in the morning appears the work of the night, the
icicle, the fair frost-work figures, the hard-incrusted
snow on the hillside, sounding to the tread of the shepherd, who with anxiety seeks his pining flocks.

Pastimes on the ice are described, skating in
Holland and sledging in more northern countries.
Meantime the horizontal sun is ineffectual to thaw the
snow upon the hills, though the valleys perhaps for a
while relent,

> " Or from the forest falls the cluster'd snow,
>   Myriads of gems, that in the waving gleam
>   Gay-twinkle as they scatter."

The sportsman with his gun desolates the fields more
fatally than the season, and adds to the ruins of
the year.

But our Winter sinks into insignificance when compared with that of the Siberian wastes in which the Russian exile roams :—

> "Nought around
> Strikes his sad eye, but deserts lost in snow,
> And heavy-loaded groves, and solid floods,
> That stretch, athwart the solitary vast,
> Their icy horrors to the frozen main."

From the frozen North came those races which destroyed the effete civilisation of southern Europe ; but here also is Lapland, whose sons are content with such wealth as the reindeer supplies to them, and who, even in the depth of the polar night, by the help of dancing meteors,

> "that ceaseless shake
> A waving blaze refracted o'er the heavens,"

find a wondrous day, which is enough to guide them in the chase and upon their journeys to the fairs of Finland. From the land "Where pure Nïemi's fairy mountains rise," we pass in imagination to Iceland, with its volcano "flaming through a waste of snow," to Greenland, and to the pole itself.

Thence the Muse takes her way along the Tartar coast eastwards, the regions where Sir Hugh Willoughby perished with his crew, to the mouth of the Obi, where human nature wears its rudest form. Yet in spite of the vastness and desolation of these regions, the power of government has moulded them into a portion of one great empire, under the guidance of a monarch who performed in one lifetime the work of many generations, that matchless prince,

> "Who greatly spurn'd the slothful pomp of courts,
> And roaming every land, in every port
> His sceptre laid aside, with glorious hand

> Unwearied plying the mechanic tool,
> Gather'd the seeds of trade, of useful arts,
> Of civil wisdom and of martial skill."

Again we return to our subject, with a rather abrupt transition. The wind blows from the south, and "The frost resolves into a trickling thaw." The rivers swell and flood the plain with brown torrents, and the ice of the northern seas cracks and roars, threatening destruction to the bark which is tossed amid the floating fragments.

The fully established reign of Winter over the conquered year suggests concluding reflections upon the life of Man :—

> "See here thy pictur'd life ; pass some few years,
> Thy flowering Spring, thy Summer's ardent strength,
> Thy sober Autumn fading into age,
> And pale concluding Winter comes at last,
> And shuts the scene."

Yet the course of the seasons itself suggests the hope of immortality, and of a second birth of heaven and of earth ; and then will be revealed the purpose of the eternal scheme, and the Power and Wisdom which have so often been arraigned will at length be justified.

CHAPTER V

THE SEASONS (continued)

IT was no mere accident which determined that the poetical work which we have just analysed should be produced by a native of North Britain. Edinburgh was at a very great distance from London in those days; and it had a literary society which was to a great extent independent of the contemporary fashions in the south, though the strictly national literature of Scotland no longer survived, and classical English poetry and prose were the accepted models. The literary society of Edinburgh was never of an exclusively urban character, and Scottish poetry had to a great extent retained that traditional feeling for external nature, which had appeared, for example, in Gavin Douglas, whose Prologues to the seventh and twelfth books of his translation of the *Æneid* had set an early example of the poetical treatment of the seasons. The youthful Thomson, full of the impressions made upon his susceptible nature by the scenery and surroundings of his home, found nothing in the literary fashions of Edinburgh to discourage him in his early attempts to describe the appearances of nature in his verse. Nor was he alone in attempting such themes. We have already seen that he acknowledged obligations to a poem on Winter by his friend Riccaltoun; and we find both Mallet and Armstrong employing their poetical powers in the same direction independently of Thomson and of one another. There seems, in fact, to have been rather a singular outburst of nature poetry in blank verse among Edinburgh students of this time; and though Thomson was the most eminently successful of the school, we cannot by any means say that he was the founder of it.

Thomson was in some respects a highly original poet. He looked at nature with his own eyes and not through the medium of books, and he combined a singular keenness and accuracy of observation with the imagination of an artist. At the same time he was dependent to a great extent upon literary models for the form of his expression; and the more so because the language which he used was for him a literary and not a vernacular form of speech. We shall see how much he was under the influence of Milton as regards the versification and the diction of *The Seasons*, and meanwhile it is instructive to note the more important reminiscences in particular passages either of Milton or of other poets, with a view to appreciating the literary influences under which the principal work of our author was prepared for and actually achieved.

Shiels, in his *Life of Thomson*, remarks: " He often said that if he had anything excellent in poetry, he owed it to the inspiration he first received from reading the *Fairy Queen* in the very early part of his life." This is quite possible, and it is fully in accordance with the experience of other English poets, but we should hardly have guessed it from *The Seasons*, where it would be difficult to find any distinct reminiscences of Spenser. On the other hand, the poetical books of the Bible are a frequent source of inspiration, the poet is familiar with Milton's early poems as well as with *Paradise Lost*, and sometimes a suggestion comes from Denham, from John Philips, or from Pope. Having had a sound classical education, he knew Virgil well, and he could not fail to be especially attracted by the *Georgics*. This is a source of suggestion which must be taken into account from the first, but the importance of it is distinctly greater for the text of 1744 than for the earlier editions. Other Latin poets, as Lucretius and Horace, occasionally have influence.

Thomson's appreciation of the poetry of the Bible is testified by his youthful paraphrase of the 104th Psalm, by his reference to the Book of Job in the preface to the second edition of *Winter*, and by his tolerably frequent use of Biblical expressions, *e.g.* "still the gracious clouds Dropp'd fatness down" (*Spring*, 261), "the lucid chambers of the south" (*Winter*, 15), "And on the wings of the careering wind Walks dreadfully serene" (*ib.*, 199), "As thus we talk'd, Our hearts would burn within us" (*ib.*, 594); and the *Hymn* is modelled largely upon the 148th Psalm. To such examples as these of Biblical influence may be added the imitation of the story of Ruth and Boaz in the episode of Lavinia and Palemon.

The special debt which is due to Milton on the score of poetical diction and versification may conveniently be discussed later. As regards the literary parallels, they seem to be due for the most part less to deliberate imitation than to half-unconscious reminiscence.

The glance of departing radiance at sunset after storm (*Spring*, 189 ff.) is partly suggested by *Paradise Lost*, ii. 492 ff.

The picture of Amanda, in *Spring*, 485 ff.,—

> "Come with those downcast eyes, sedate and sweet,
>   Those looks demure, that deeply pierce the soul,"

is evidently from *Il Penseroso*; and the "villages embosom'd soft in trees," of l. 953, from *L'Allegro*. The

"haunted stream," of *Summer*, 12, is from *L'Allegro*,
130; and the ideas expressed in *Summer*, 622 ff., are
those of *Il Penseroso*, 139 ff. :—

> "There in close covert by some brook,
>   Where no profaner eye may look,
>   Hide me from day's garish eye,
>   While the bee with honied thigh," etc.,

The fine passage in *Summer*, 175 ff.,—

> "How shall I then attempt to sing of Him,
>   Who, Light Himself, in uncreated light
> Invested deep, dwells awfully retir'd," etc.,

is suggested by *Paradise Lost*, iii. 3 ff., and the succeeding lines by *Paradise Lost*, iv. 675 f.,—

> "nor think, though men were none,
> That heav'n would want spectators, God want praise."

In the lines upon the ministry of angels and spirits,
Summer, 525 ff.,—

> "Convers'd with angels and immortal forms,
>   On gracious errands bent ; to save the fall
>   Of virtue struggling on the brink of vice ;
>   In waking whispers and repeated dreams
>   To hint pure thought," etc.,

we are reminded of *Comus*, 455 ff. :—

> "A thousand liveried angels lackey her,
>   Driving far off each thing of sin and guilt,
>   And in clear dream and solemn vision
>   Tell her of things that no gross ear can hear."

And in *Summer*, 556 ff. :—

> "Here frequent at the visionary hour,
>   When musing midnight reigns, or silent noon,
>   Angelic harps are in full concert heard,
>   And voices chanting from the wood-crown'd hill,
>   The deepening dale or inmost sylvan glade,"

we have undoubtedly a reminiscence of *Paradise Lost*,
iv. 680 ff. :—

> " How often, from the steep
> Of echoing hill or thicket, have we heard
> Celestial voices to the midnight air,
> Sole, or responsive each to other's note,
> Singing their great Creator ! "

The expression in l. 949, "while the wonted roar is
up," is an echo caught from *Comus*, "The wonted roar
was up amidst the woods."

In *Autumn*, 783, "from Imaus stretch'd, Athwart
the roving Tartar's sullen bounds," the expression
is suggested by *Paradise Lost*; [1] and with *Autumn*,
1029 ff.,—

> " Oh ! bear me then to vast embowering shades,
> To twilight groves and visionary vales,"

we must compare *Il Penseroso*, 132 :—

> " me, goddess, bring
> To arched walks of twilight groves."

The description of the full moon rising, in *Autumn*,
1088 ff., originally appeared (in the early part of *Winter*)
in a form which more closely followed Milton than
the present text. The passage ran thus :—

> " The vivid Stars shine out in radiant files ;
> And boundless Ether glows, till the fair Moon
> Shows her broad Visage in the crimson'd East ;
> Now stooping seems to kiss the passing Cloud,
> Now o'er the pure Cerulean rides sublime.
> Wide the pale Deluge floats with silver waves," etc.

The author had in his mind *Paradise Lost*, iv. 604 ff. :—

> " now glow'd the firmament
> With living sapphires ; Hesperus that led
> The starry host, rode brightest, till the Moon,

---

[1] iii. 432.

> Rising in clouded majesty, at length
> Apparent queen unveil'd her peerless light,
> And o'er the dark her silver mantle threw";

and with this also *Il Penseroso*, 71 f. :—

> "And oft, as if her head she bow'd,
> Stooping through a fleecy cloud."

The lines which follow in the original edition (of *Winter*), on the appearance of the dew-drops in the morning, have a connection with *Paradise Lost*, v. 743 f., which is especially brought out in the text of the second edition of 1726, where we read :—

> "All Night abundant Dews, unnoted fall,
> That lighted by the Morning's Ray impearl
> The Face of Mother-Earth."

The description (in *Autumn*, 1115 ff.) of the apparent conflict of armies in the sky is evidently founded upon *Paradise Lost*, ii. 533 ff.

The original text of *Winter*, 154, gives us the expression, "the thin Fabric of the pillar'd air," which recalls "the fabric of the Heavens," and "the pillar'd firmament" of Milton.[1]   With *Winter*, 197 f.,—

> "till Nature's King, who oft
> Amid tempestuous darkness dwells alone,"

may be compared *Paradise Lost*, ii. 263.   In *Winter*, 297, "Then throng the busy shapes into his mind," etc., we are reminded of *Comus*, 205 ff.   The winter evening's occupations are partly suggested by Milton ; those of the student, who holds "high converse with the mighty dead," by *Il Penseroso*; and those of the village and the city by *L'Allegro*.

The pouring forth of nations from the prolific North (838 ff.) recalls *Paradise Lost*, i. 351, and the scene of

---

[1] *Paradise Lost*, viii. 76, and *Comus*, 598.

the breaking up of the ice in the northern seas (997 ff.) owes some of its features to *Paradise Lost*, i. 207 and ii. 285 ff. ; while the picture of the sea monsters,—

> " More to embroil the deep, Leviathan
> And his unwieldy train, in dreadful sport,
> Tempest the loosen'd brine,"

is evidently connected with *Paradise Lost*, vii. 410 :—

> " part, huge of bulk,
> Wallowing unwieldy, enormous in their gait,
> Tempest the ocean ; there Leviathan,
> Hugest of living creatures," etc.

The preface which was added to the second edition of *Winter* contained a special reference to Virgil, with a quotation and translation of the celebrated lines from the second book of the *Georgics*, in which the poet expresses his desire to penetrate the secrets of Nature's working in the physical world ; and if this is denied him, prays that he may at least be a lover of Nature as she appears in the fields and the woods, the valleys and the streams :—

> " Rura mihi et rigui placeant in vallibus amnes,
> Flumina amem silvasque inglorius."

Thomson felt himself entirely in sympathy both with the interest in science and the delight in natural objects which is expressed in this passage, and he was proud to acknowledge Virgil as a master. References to Virgil by name occur more than once in *The Seasons*, for example, *Spring*, 55,—

> " Such themes as these the rural Maro sung
> To wide-imperial Rome,"

and the author is indebted to the *Georgics* for a good many suggestions. The case of Virgil is different in one respect from that of the other authors from whom Thomson drew materials, for in the case of these last

K

the process of revision has sometimes eliminated or diminished the resemblance. We have seen this in the case of some of the Miltonic parallels; and we notice that several Shakespearean expressions disappear, as "the glimpses of the Moon," "Striding the stormy Blast" (*Winter*, 1st ed., 54, 113): whereas in the case of Virgil the tendency is to increase the amount of indebtedness; and in two or three places additions are made in revision, which are in effect translations from the *Georgics*.

More than one probable reason might be given for this. The Greek and Latin classical authors are common property, and to borrow from them was in the eighteenth century considered rather creditable than otherwise. Thomson therefore had no fear of being accused of plagiarism in this case; and the influence of Lyttelton, in association with whom the revision was made for the edition of 1744, would in all probability be in favour of a fuller use of the materials supplied by the *Georgics*, which were indeed in many instances very appropriate for the purpose.[1]

---

[1] Examples of the influence of Virgil are to be found in the following passages among others: *Spring*, 452:—

> "whence borne on liquid wing
> The sounding culver shoots,"

compared with *Æn.* v. 213-217 ; *Spring*, 716 ff. (the nightingale robbed of her young), compared with *Georg.* iv. 511 ff. ; *Spring*, 792 ff. (the encounter of the rival bulls with the heifer standing by), compared with *Georg.* iii. 250-254 ; *Summer*, 458 ff., compared with *Georg.* ii. 487 :—

> "O, qui me gelidis in vallibus Haemi
> Sistat, et ingenti ramorum protegat umbra?"

Autumn, 330 ff. (the flood of rain), compared with *Georg.* i. 322 ff., and the text of l. 333 as given in the first edition, "The glomerating tempest grows," reproduces the original more closely than that which we read at present. The suggested

Touches which may have been suggested by Lucretius are visible here and there, as for example in *Winter*, 311 ff., compared with

> "Iam iam non domus accipiet te laeta, neque uxor
> Optima, nec dulces occurrent oscula nati
> Praeripere et tacita pectus dulcedine tangent."[1]

The account of the life of primitive man in *Autumn*, 47-64, may probably enough have been partly founded upon that of Lucretius,[2] and the argumentative passage about the origin of rivers, *Autumn*, 755-770, which was added in 1744, is a most happy imitation of his style.

A few words may be said about other literary influences. The stag-hunt in *Autumn*, 426 ff., is certainly connected with Denham's description in *Cooper's Hill*; and the passage in *Spring*, 119-135, which deals with insect pests in the orchard and the remedies for them,

comparison of the setting of trees to the ranging of armies in the field, *Autumn*, 1072 ff., is perhaps due to *Georg.* ii. 277 ff., and the concluding lines of *Autumn* contain a fine paraphrase of the passage of Virgil quoted (with a rather lame translation) in the preface to which we have already referred. It was chiefly in *Winter* that the later additions of Virgilian passages were made. The signs of coming storm enumerated in ll. 118-143 are almost all from Virgil, and for the most part were added after the edition of 1738. Comparison should be made with *Georg.* i. 361-392 and also 433 and 454. In the first editions of the poem this influence was hardly perceptible here, but already in 1730 two Virgilian features were introduced into the passages, "The stars obtuse," and "Snatch'd in short eddies plays the fluttering straw." The description of the hunting of the deer in the snow-drifts, *Winter*, 820-826, is a tolerably close translation of *Georg.* iii. 371-375 :—

> "Hos non immissis canibus, non cassibus ullis,
> Puniceaeve agitant pavidos formidine pinnae,
> Sed frustra oppositum trudentes pectore montem
> Cominus obtruncant ferro, graviterque rudentes
> Caedunt, et magno laeti clamore reportant."

[1] *De Rerum Natura*, iii. 894 ff.   [2] v. 925 ff.

seems to be modelled upon the style of Philips,[1] the
run of whose verse also is caught in this passage,
though, as a rule, Thomson is independent of him in
this respect.   He addresses Philips in a later passage
(*Autumn*, 645) as

> "Phillips, Pomona's bard !   The second thou
> Who nobly durst, in rhyme-unfetter'd verse,
> With British freedom sing the British song";

but it is in the matter of diction rather than verse
that Philips is important with reference to *The Seasons*.
It was in fact Philips who most markedly set the
example of employing the Miltonic diction for subjects
of ordinary life, and he probably exercised a rather
unfortunate influence on Thomson in this direction.
In Philips there was always a vein of ironical humour,
not sufficient to turn his work into burlesque, but
redeeming its heroic style from absurdity ; while
Thomson, whose genius was more enthusiastically
poetical, sometimes fell into the fault of unredeemed
grandiloquence, when speaking of common things.   Of
the happy grace of Philips in dealing with the operations of the fruit-garden, the following lines will give
a fair sample, and it is easy to see how the example
thus set might be misused :—

> " When swelling buds their odorous foliage shed,
> And gently harden into fruit, the wise
> Spare not the little offsprings, if they grow
> Redundant ; but the thronging clusters thin
> By kind avulsion : else the starveling brood,
> Void of sufficient sustenance, will yield
> A slender autumn ; which the niggard soul
> Too late shall weep, and curse his thrifty hand,
> That would not timely ease the ponderous boughs.
>   It much conduces all the cares to know

---

[1] *Cider*, i. 411 ff.

> Of gardening, how to scare nocturnal thieves,
> And how the little race of birds, that hop
> From spray to spray, scooping the costliest fruit
> Insatiate, undisturb'd.   Priapus' form
> Avails but little ; rather guard each row
> With the false terrors of a breathless kite.
> This done, the timorous flock with swiftest wing
> Scud through the air ; their fancy represents
> His mortal talons, and his ravenous beak
> Destructive ; glad to shun his hostile gripe,
> They quit their thefts, and unfrequent the fields."
>
> (*Cider*, i. 384 ff.)

Some echoes of Pope have been noted in *The Seasons*,
e.g.,—

> "'Tis done !   Dread Winter has subdu'd the year,"
>
> (*Winter*, ed. 1726)

as compared with :—

> "'Tis done, and Nature's various charms decay,"

in Pope's pastoral *Winter*, l. 29 ; and the choice of
names in the passage about "the mighty dead" may
have been partly determined by Pope's *Temple of Fame*,
since there is also a resemblance in some of the epithets
attached to them.   "Unconquered Cato" appears in
both, and Pope, speaking of Virgil, says,—

> "The Mantuan there in sober triumph sate,
> .   .   .   .
> Great without pride in modest majesty" ;

while Thomson (in his first edition) describes the same
poet as appearing

> "With sober State and of majestic Mien."

We have already seen that he acknowledged obligations to a poem on Winter by his friend Riccaltoun,
and that this poem may probably be identified with
that entitled *A Winter's Day*, which was published
in Savage's Miscellany, 1726.   The piece is of some

interest, both in itself and for its association with
Thomson's work, and as it is not very easily accessible,
it is worth while to quote the opening passage as a
specimen of the style :—

> " Now, gloomy soul ! look out,—now comes thy turn ;
>   With thee behold all ravag'd nature mourn :
>   Hail the dim empire of thy darling night,
>   That spreads, slow-shadowing, o'er the vanquish'd light.
>   Look out with joy : the ruler of the day,
>   Faint as thy hopes, emits a glimmering ray ;
>   Already exil'd to the utmost sky,
>   Hither oblique he turns his clouded eye.
>   Lo, from the limits of the wintry pole
>   Mountainous clouds in rude confusion roll ;
>   In dismal pomp now hovering on their way,
>   To a sick twilight they reduce the day.
>   And hark ! imprison'd winds, broke loose, arise,
>   And roar their haughty triumph through the skies ;
>   While the driv'n clouds, o'ercharg'd with floods of rain
>   And mingled lightning, burst upon the plain."

The descriptions are not altogether unlike Thomson's ;
but the tone of the poem, which emphasises at every
turn the supposed harmony between the gloom of the
poet's soul and the darkness and desolation of winter, is
essentially different from that of *The Seasons*. Thomson's
view of natural phenomena is not for the most part a
sentimental one ; he regards Nature as a theme of
epical grandeur, and he treats it in a broadly objective
manner. If, therefore, Thomson was indebted to the
poem quoted above, it was only as regards suggestion of
the subject and the general idea of certain descriptions.

It is of interest to note that in the revision of
his first text Thomson, in several instances, adopted
ideas and expressions from some of those who are
usually regarded as his followers. With Mallet he
was in constant communication during the earlier

years of his literary career, and each sent the other
his poetical compositions in manuscript, so that it
may be difficult sometimes to determine which of the
two originated a particular thought; but it certainly
seems likely that some part of the description of the
ice in the polar seas, which was added in 1730 and
1744, was borrowed from a passage in Mallet's *Excursion*. Here, however, we must proceed with caution,
for the *Excursion* also was revised in later editions,
and in the revised text here the author has in return
borrowed from Thomson. I quote from the first
edition (1728):—

> " Where, a white Waste of Ice, the Polar Sea
>   Casts cold a cheerless Light, where Hills of Snow,
>   Pil'd up from eldest Ages, Hill on Hill,
>   In blue bleak Precipices rise to Heaven."

With this we must compare *Winter*, 904 ff., and with
that again the passage as it stands in later editions of
the *Excursion*.

It is also fairly well established that a connection
exists between the early revisions of *The Seasons* and
a blank-verse poem on winter by Armstrong,[1] which
was not published till 1770, but which Thomson saw
in manuscript. This piece appeared in the first
volume of Armstrong's *Miscellanies* with a note by
the publisher, authorised, it may be assumed, by
Armstrong himself, to the effect that it was written
many years before, "and, what is rather particular,
was just finished when Mr. Thomson's celebrated poem
on the same subject appeared." Thomson, he proceeds
to say, hearing of it, procured a copy through a common acquaintance, Armstrong being then a student at
Edinburgh, and showed it to Mallet, Hill, and Young,

---

[1] Armstrong, was, like Thomson, the son of a Roxburghshire
minister.

who expressed admiration of it. Mallet asked the
author's leave to publish it, "a request too flattering
to youthful vanity to be resisted," but he afterwards
changed his mind, and the piece remained in manuscript.

We have then evidence, which there is no reason to
doubt, that Armstrong's poem was written independently of Thomson's, and that Thomson had a copy of
it in his hands soon after the publication of the first
edition of *Winter*. There is every likelihood, therefore, that the resemblances which are to be found in
certain points between this piece and the later editions
of Thomson's *Winter*, are due to borrowing by Thomson,[1] who very soon became personally acquainted
with Armstrong, and as we have seen, accepted his help
in the *Castle of Indolence*. In the episode of the peasant
lost in the snow, added in 1730, the line,.

> "And every tempest howling o'er his head,"

is modelled on Armstrong's

> "And hear the tempest howling o'er their heads" (l. 98);

and when he wrote the passage about the bear in the
Russian pine-forest retiring to his winter's rest,

> "Slow-pac'd and sourer as the storms increase,"
>
> > (*Winter*, 830)

Thomson probably had before him Armstrong's picturesque lines,—

> "A blast so shrewd makes the tall-bodied pines
> Unsinew'd bend, and heavy-paced bears
> Sends growling to their savage tenements."

---

[1] It can hardly be maintained that the resemblances in
question are due to a later revision of Armstrong's poem, because
in that case it would be difficult to account for the fact that all
the closer parallels between this poem and *The Seasons* are concerned with passages which were added by Thomson in revision.

The description of the polar seas, which, as we have seen, owes something to Mallet, contains also echoes of Armstrong's poem, *e.g.*,

> "Miserable they,
> Who here entangled in the gathering ice," etc.,

compared with

> "Wretched they,
> That midst such rude vexation of the deep
> Guide a frail vessel." (Armstrong, l. 165.)

The literary obligations of various kinds which have been traced affect only a very small portion of Thomson's work, and ought not to be allowed to detract from his credit for essential originality. At the same time, it must be noted that Thomson was not so much the independent founder of a school of poetry, as the most eminent member of a group of young poets, who were all working in the same direction, and who exercised mutual influence upon one another. The merits of Mallet's *Excursion*, which was published in 1728, have naturally been overshadowed by those of *The Seasons*, but it is not a mere imitation of Thomson; and Armstrong's rather striking poem, which escaped the notice of the public altogether, seems to have been entirely independent. Dyer may be counted as one of this group, and there are evidences of communication between Dyer and Thomson as early as 1726, when Thomson in the postscript of a letter to Mallet says: "Dyer's address is Aberglasney, by Llandilo Bag, South Wales."

The quotations from *The Seasons* in the preceding chapter serve to illustrate Thomson's merits as a descriptive poet, and to show that the reputation which he once had was not wholly undeserved. The poems which we have analysed unquestionably afford evidence of keen-sighted observation of the various aspects of external nature, and of a vivid experience of the emotions which these may reasonably excite; while at the same time the form of the expression is essentially poetical, in spite of the faults which are to be noted in the style. The poet's observation is of light and colour rather than of form; and these more variable elements of the scene are in fact more particularly suited for poetical description. He is at his best in the representation of atmospheric effects, and of the scenery of streams and woods: the wilder aspects of nature, such, for example, as are connected with the sea and the higher mountains, were less well known to him, and he describes them less satisfactorily. So far as regards the objects with which he was himself familiar, he shows very considerable acuteness of sense perception, and an unusually well-balanced organism. Sounds are for him almost as important as sights— the roar of the forest and the murmur of the stream, the songs of birds and the voices of animals: he notes also the impressive silences of nature, as, for example, before a storm. He is keenly alive to the impression of odours—the perfume of flowers, the scent of the new-mown fields, or the fresh smell of the damp earth after rain. Especially he is sensitive to the effects of heat, and by consequence to those of coolness and shade, as we have seen in some of the passages quoted from *Summer*. Thomson's best descriptions are of common things, and these are often full of touches which testify to the fineness of his observation. "The reader of *The Seasons* wonders that he never saw before what Thomson shows him, and that he never yet has felt what Thomson impresses." Yet his imaginative intuition enabled him also very frequently to pass beyond the sphere of his own immediate experience, and to

form from the accounts of others representations which
are true to nature as well as poetical.   The whole
work produces a certain grandeur of effect from its
universality of range, and its freedom, for the most
part, from association with particular localities, a
feature which gives personal interest to the work of
Cowper, but also rather seriously narrows its scope.

In what remains of the present chapter it will be
necessary to make a further examination of the style
of the work and to point out in detail some of its more
serious faults.

The first of these is the extent to which the author
has combined what is of really high value with what
is essentially commonplace.   The descriptive vein
which appeared in the first edition of *Winter* took the
fancy of the public, and the author deliberately set to
work to swell his small poem and its successors almost to
the dimensions of an epic.   He is apparently unable to
distinguish in his own work what is first-rate from what
is merely respectable, and accordingly, side by side with
scenes of nature described with almost unequalled
felicity, he gives us his rather commonplace talk about
the virtues of primeval society, the danger of "the
wild and irregular passion of Love," the presumption
of "impious railers" who tax the wisdom of the Creator,
the happiness, fertility, and freedom of Britain and the
glories of the British race, the triumphs of industry,
the cruelties of sport, the glories and grievances of
Scotland, the merits of Pitt, Cobham and Chesterfield,
the greatness of Socrates, Solon, Lycurgus, Leonidas
and Aristides, or the success of Peter the Great in
civilising his empire.   Most of these topics are rather
irrelevant to the subject, and though not without some
interest, could have been dealt with pretty nearly as
well by Mallet or Hill.   These parts of the work show

sometimes a laudable enthusiasm for humanity, sometimes patriotism, and sometimes appreciation of genius
and worth, but they fall short, for the most part, of a
high standard of poetry.   Even where the connection
with the subject is apparently closer, as in the case of
the rural episodes in *Summer* and *Autumn*, the effect is
not always harmonious.   The human element in *The
Seasons* is satisfactorily treated just in so far as it is
brought into vital relation with the operations of
Nature, and in particular where man appears dependent
for his livelihood on these operations, as in the case of
the tiller of the soil or the shepherd.   The husbandman leaning over his bright ploughshare to remove the
obstructing clay, the reaper working in the harvest-
field by the side of his chosen mate, or making his way
home beneath the moon, the farmer deploring the ruin
of his labours, the shepherd who "stalks gigantic" in
the mist, the peasant lost in the snow and swallowed
up at last in the fatal bog, while his family watch
anxiously for his return,—all these are figures which
harmonise with the general subject and are naturally
and effectively used.   But beyond this the author
could not safely go, and the elaborately worked out
episodes, the Celadon and Amelia, the Damon and Musidora, even the Lavinia and Palemon, are essentially
artificial, idylls of the pastoral type, which correspond
to no real state of society at all ; and notwithstanding
the charm which they have in some respects, they must
be condemned as artistically out of place.

As regards the style generally, it is certainly apt to
be too diffuse, even in genuinely poetical passages.
Johnson is reported to have said on one occasion :
"Thomson had a true poetical genius, the power of
viewing everything in a poetical light.   His fault is
such a cloud of words sometimes, that the sense can

hardly peep through. Shiels . . . was one day sitting
with me. I took down Thomson, and read aloud a
large portion of him, and then asked, 'Is not this fine?'
Shiels having expressed the highest admiration, 'Well,
Sir,' said I, 'I have omitted every other line.'" If the
story is accurately reported, Shiels must have been
rather inattentive; but it is true that some short
passages of Thomson might be treated in this manner
without absolutely destroying the sense, as, for example, this:—

> " Beside the dewy border let me sit,
>   All in the freshness of the humid air :
>   There on that hollow'd rock, grotesque and wild,
>   An ample chair moss-lined, and over head
>   By flowering umbrage shaded ; where the bee
>   Strays diligent, and with th' extracted balm
>   Of fragrant woodbine loads his little thigh."

And certainly it is true in general that Thomson's style
often suffers from the disease of undue amplification.

The want of brevity is accompanied by want of
simplicity. The diction is "in the highest degree florid
and luxuriant." Milton's magnificence of diction
springs, we feel, from the mind of the poet as the
natural embodiment of the thought : Thomson's expression does not give us quite this idea of spontaneity,
and sometimes the words rather obscure than elucidate
the meaning.

As regards diction and expression, Thomson reproduces in general the highly Latinised vocabulary of
Milton, and he exaggerates certain features of Milton's
style till they become tiresome mannerisms. He gives
us, for example, a very large number of unusual words
of Latin origin, when simpler expressions would serve.
In many cases these are used by Milton on a dignified
occasion, and by Thomson are applied trivially. A

favourite word is "convolved," which is used with
characteristic looseness of meaning.   Milton says:—

> "Then Satan first knew pain
> And writh'd him to and fro convolv'd."

Thomson has

> "his sportive lambs,
> This way and that convolv'd in friskful glee,
> Their frolics play."

Or (of bees overcome by sulphur fumes),

> "the tender race
> By thousands tumble from their honey'd domes,
> Convolv'd, and agonising in the dust."

Milton has

> "See how he lies at random, carelessly diffus'd,"

with reference to his Samson.   In *The Seasons* we find

> "the love-sick shepherdess,
> On violets diffus'd."

Milton's "unessential," used of chaos in the fine
expression,

> "the void profound
> Of unessential Night,"

becomes for Thomson an ordinary epithet in the phrase
"unessential gloom."

Thomson has a distinct preference for certain kinds
of adjective formations, chiefly of Latin origin.   One
class of these may be represented by such words as
"afflictive," "amusive," "excursive," "prelusive,"
"repercussive"; another by "innumerous," "irrigu-
ous," "umbrageous," "sequacious"; and a third by
Latin participle forms, such as "clamant," "emergent,"
"turgent," or "evaporate," "incult," "submiss."   Other
somewhat unusual Latinisms of vocabulary are to be
found in expressions like the following:—

" The torpid sap *detruded* to the root,"

"and *luculent* along
The purer rivers flow ; "

" Through splendid kingdoms now *devolves* his maze ; "

" Advancing full on the *protended* spear."

" They once *relumed* the flame
Of lost mankind in polish'd slavery sunk ; "

" *Relapsing* quick, as quickly reascend."

A few of these words seem to be of his own coinage ;
but for the most part there is the authority of former
usage ; though sometimes the earlier instances have to
be looked for in out-of-the-way places, and Thomson
may not always have been acquainted with them.

A good deal of freedom is found in the use of
adjectives as verbs, *e.g.* :—

" Nor when cold winter *keens* the brightening flood,"

" To raise his being and *serene* his soul."

" whatever *greens* the Spring,
When heaven descends in showers ; "

" *Savaged* by woe, forget the tender tie ; "

and verbs are often used with a somewhat irregular
construction, as :—

" The lightnings flash a larger curve,"

" Warbling the varied heart ; "

"they lived
The rural day, and talk'd the flowing heart,"

" Awhile he stands,
Gazing th' inverted landskip, half afraid
To meditate the blue profound below."

But the most characteristic licence is the free employment of adjectives as adverbs or in apposition.   This

also is a Latinism, which is not uncommonly used
by Milton;[1] but Thomson employs the freedom with
far greater frequency than any other English poet, and
in some passages it is exercised beyond all reasonable
limits, *e.g. Autumn*, 373 ff. :—

> "the gun,
> Glanc'd just and sudden from the fowler's eye,
> O'ertakes their sounding pinions, and again
> Immediate brings them from the towering wing,
> Dead to the ground ; or drives them wide-dispers'd,
> Wounded and wheeling various, down the wind."

Certain words, as "chief," "sudden," "gradual," "in-
cessant," are more frequently used in this manner than
others, *e.g.* :—

> "But let not chief the nightingale lament
> Her ruined care,"

> "Sudden he starts,
> Shook from his tender trance,"

> "The huge dusk gradual swallows up the plain :"

> "Incessant roll'd into romantic shapes."

But the practice is a general one, as will be seen from
the following further examples :—

> "the grand ethereal bow
> Shoots up immense,"

> "Wisdom and friendly talk successive stole
> Their hours away."

> "While o'er his ample sides the rambling sprays
> Luxuriant shoot ;"

---

[1] *e.g.* "Thron'd inaccessible," Runs diverse," "Pass'd frequent," "as day and night to men Successive," "Incredible
how swift, had thither rolled Diurnal." Pope's *Iliad* will supply
numerous examples of this use—*e.g.* "Slow he gave way, the
rest tumultuous fled," "Then sudden waved his flaming falchion
round," "When fresh he rears his radiant orb to sight," etc.

> "peal on peal
> Crush'd horrible, convulsing heaven and earth."

> "the wildly-winding brook
> Falls hoarse from steep to steep."

> "till at last,
> Wreath'd dun around, in deeper circles still
> Successive closing, sits the general fog
> Unbounded o'er the world ; and mingling thick,
> A formless grey confusion covers all."

> "The city swarms intense.   The public haunt,
> Full of each theme, and warm with mixt discourse,
> Hums indistinct."

> "Far-distant flood to flood is social join'd."

> "And where He vital breathes, there must be joy."

Akin to this is the tendency, borrowed from Milton,
to place adjectives, or determinative phrases which
stand for adjectives, at the end of the sentence, often
marking this effect by throwing them into emphatic
position at the beginning of a line :—

> "Innumerous songsters in the freshening shade
> Of new-sprung leaves their modulations mix,
> Mellifluous."

Another marked feature of Thomson's style is his
use of compound words, either substantives, as "desert-
barrier," "coward-reign," "insect-lamps," "parent-
heaven," "torrent-softness"; verbs, as "wide-hover,"
"gay-twinkle," "wide-rend," or most frequently adjectives.   Of these compound adjectives we may distinguish those formed in the more usual manner by
combination of a substantive with a participle, as
"world-reviving," "tower-encircled," "heart-thrilling,"
"love-enlivened," from the class that is especially
characteristic of Thomson, namely those in which the
first element is an adjective used as an adverb.

L

Examples of this kind of compound are very numerous in *The Seasons*. To take instances only from the first of the four poems, we note that the blighting of spring foliage by untimely frost leaves a "wide-dejected waste," the cattle before rain look up "mute-imploring," the clouds after the rain are "gay-shifting" about the sun, the brook is "mossy-tinctured" and "rocky-channelled," the lake is "breezy-ruffled," the garden flowers are (in the first edition at least) "dewy-bright," the song of the nightingale is a "mazy-running" melody, the heifer stands "balmy-breathing," the breeze is "hollow-whispering" among the trees, the lover retires to "secret-winding" bowers, or is conducted to the thorny wilds of love through "flowery-tempting" paths.

In thus endeavouring to enrich the language with new compounds, Thomson was to a great extent original, and his enterprise was not altogether without success. In another matter of style he was less fortunately influenced. Partly in imitation of Milton, who, dealing with subjects of superhuman grandeur, had often avoided the use of concrete terms, and had introduced a studied vagueness into his descriptions, but more in consequence of the general debasement of taste in poetry, a system of periphrasis had been adopted in the poetical diction of the early eighteenth century, by which it was thought that dignity was given to the mention of the common things of everyday life. John Philips, in his *Blenheim*, speaks of "the brazen instruments of war" when he means cannons, Gay calls fish "the finny brood," and even Pope, who is usually more direct, gives us "the scaly breed" in *Windsor Forest*, and "the fleecy winter," as a periphrasis for snow, in the *Iliad*. Thomson, in *The Seasons*, carries this mannerism rather to an excess. He speaks of "the flowery race," "the household feathery people," "the bleating kind," "the fearful flying race," "the plumy nations," "the glittering finny swarms," when he wishes to indicate flowers, domestic fowls, sheep, birds, or fish; and a similar want of simplicity is shown in such phrases as "Ceres void of pain" for a harvest which costs no labour, "silky pride" for garments of silk, "ovarious food" for a diet of eggs: children buried in the hay "amid the kind oppression roll," the clouds bestowing rain upon the earth are said to "indulge their genial store," and when the python drives all other beasts from the water, we are told that "all other thirst appall'd Or shivering flies, or check'd at distance stands."

As regards structure of sentences, it may be noted that simplicity of expression is often sacrificed, and sometimes obscurity is produced, by an extravagant use of inversion, as when the poet writes :—

> "Peaceful, beneath primeval trees, that cast
> Their ample shade o'er Niger's yellow stream,
> And where the Ganges rolls his sacred wave,
> Or 'mid the central depth of blackening woods,
> High-raised in solemn theatre around,
> Leans the huge elephant, wisest of brutes."

And on a smaller scale this figure is a frequent characteristic of the style, *e.g.* :—

> "White thro' the neighbouring fields the sower stalks,"

> "Resounds the living surface of the ground : "

> "Hard by these shores, where scarce his freezing stream
> Rolls the wild Oby, live the last of men."

Irregularity is rather freely admitted in grammatical construction, chiefly in connection with absolute phrases, *e.g.* :—

> "The north-east spends his rage ; and now shut up
>   Within his iron cave, th' effusive south
>   Warms the wide air,"

or

> "Even present, in the very lap of love
>   Inglorious laid, while music flows around,
>   Perfumes and oils and wine and wanton hours,
>   Amid the roses fierce Repentance rears
>   Her snaky crest."

It must not be supposed that Thomson's peculiarities of style passed unnoticed in his own generation. He was recognised as, to some extent, the creator of a new poetical language, and was severely criticised even by some of his friends. The poetical epistle of Somerville upon the first edition of *The Seasons*, urging a close revision of the style of the poem, adopts a tone of frankness which is certainly unusual in occasional pieces of this kind, and which can hardly have been entirely to the taste of Thomson :—

> "So bright, so dark, upon an April day,
>   The sun darts forth or hides his various ray,
>   So high, so low, the lark aspiring sings,
>   Or drops to earth again with folded wings,
>   So smooth, so rough, the sea that laves our shores
>   Smiles in a calm, or in a tempest roars.
>   Believe me, Thomson, 'tis not thus I write,
>   Severely kind, by envy sour'd or spite,
>   Nor would I rob thy brows to grace my own ;
>   Such arts are to my honest soul unknown.
>   I read thee over as a friend should read,
>   Griev'd when you fail, o'erjoy'd when you succeed.
>   Why should thy Muse, born so divinely fair,
>   Want the reforming toilet's daily care ?
>   Dress the gay maid, improve each native grace,
>   And call forth all the glories of her face,
>   Studiously plain and elegantly clean,
>   With unaffected speech and easy mien,

The accomplish'd nymph in all her best attire
Courts shall applaud and prostrate crowds admire.

.   .   .   .   .   .

Read Philips much, consider Milton more ;
But from their dross extract the purer ore.
To coin new words, or to restore the old,
In southern lands is dangerous and bold ;
But rarely, very rarely will succeed,
When minted on the other side of Tweed."

Thomson, however, had considerable independence of judgment, and he did not yield in any essential matter to such suggestions as these. There was no lack of revision, and the quality of the work was greatly improved thereby, but the characteristics of the style were on the whole preserved. His attitude generally towards criticism is fairly expressed by his remark with regard to Aikman's friendly remonstrances :—

" His reflections on my writings are very good ; but he does not in them regard the turn of my genius enough. Should I alter my way, I would write poorly : I must choose what appears to me the most significant epithet, or I cannot with any heart proceed." [1]

The blank verse of Thomson has been both highly praised and severely criticised. Coleridge remarks that in harmony of blank verse Cowper is far superior to Thomson ; while a competent modern critic has said of Thomson's blank verse, that it must rank with that of Milton and Tennyson as one of the chief original models of the metre to be found in English poetry. The truth is that Thomson's blank verse is in many ways excellent for his own purpose. The lines are often graceful and often sonorous, the periods have a rhetorical balance which carries the metre smoothly on from line to line, and the poet's ear is sufficiently

[1] Letter to Mallet, August 11, 1726.

good to enable him to avoid harsh combinations, and usually to secure a pleasing harmony of vowel sounds. At the same time, the verse has not sufficient variety of pause and cadence, and it is wanting in some of the more subtle elements of rhythmical effect.   In particular, it has been observed by critics that there is a rather strong tendency to round off the paragraph with a line of a certain particular type, *e.g.* :—

> "And Ocean trembles for her green domain."

> "And Mecca saddens at the long delay."

> "And Thule bellows through her utmost isles."

> "Unbounded tossing in a flood of corn."

This, no doubt, is a favourite type of rhythm [1] with Thomson, but not only at the end of a paragraph.   A comparison with Milton is almost inevitable, and the difference in the matter of variety of rhythm between the blank verse of Milton and that of Thomson is certainly very great.   Certain types recur in Thomson with quite undue frequency, and (it need hardly be said) a considerable number which are represented in Milton's verse are absent from Thomson's.   Lines of the rhythm which is exemplified above will be found to occur more than twice as often, on an average, in a passage of *The Seasons*, than in one of similar length in *Paradise Lost*.   Another facile rhythm, which closely resembles this, but is not the same, is that represented by,

> "The thunder holds his black tremendous throne ; "

> "And Egypt joys beneath the spreading wave."

---

[1] Types of rhythm are regarded, for the purposes of the present discussion, as constituted by the arrangement of pauses in the verse, and the natural, as opposed to the metrical, grouping of syllables.   It is impossible to do more here than give the general results of a careful investigation.

This appears in Thomson's verse at least three times as often as in Milton's ; and nearly the same is true of such lines as :—

"From cloud to cloud the rending lightnings rage."

Other forms which recur with much greater frequency in Thomson than in Milton are those represented in the following lines :—

"Blue through the dusk the smoking currents shine ;"

"Or whirled tempestuous by the gusty wind,"

"A suffocating wind the pilgrim smites."

On the other hand, the simplest forms of metre, in which the natural absolutely corresponds with the metrical grouping, are far more common in Milton's verse than in Thomson's, both that which has the principal pause after the fourth syllable, *e.g.*,—

"Of what he was, what is, and what must be,"

or especially with pause after the sixth syllable,

"For wonderful indeed are all his works."

A good many other types, which are quite usual with Milton, are comparatively rare in *The Seasons*, and some regular Miltonic rhythms are hardly represented there at all, especially those which depend for their character upon inversion of accent, *e.g.* :—

"Compar'd with ought on earth, metal or stone ;"

"Smote on him sore besides, vaulted with fire ;"

"Warriors, the flower of heaven, once yours, now lost,"

and so with many others, not to mention forms which are really exceptional.

Thomson is alive to the importance of varying the position of the principal pause, but nevertheless he sometimes falls into the fault of repeating the same

pause and the same type of rhythm in several successive
lines, as :—

> " The fearful flocks
> Crowd near the guardian swain ; the nobler herds,
> Where, round their lordly bull, in rural ease
> They ruminating lie, with horror hear
> The coming rage."
>
> (*Summer*, 928 ff.)

> " But chief at sea, whose every flexile wave
> Obeys the blast, th' aerial tumult swells."
>
> (*Summer*, 980 f.)

He is well aware of the danger of allowing his blank
verse to fall distinctly into couplets, as Addison does
in his so-called "Imitation of Milton"; but, nevertheless, in some passages he allows himself to be
influenced by the prevailing style so far as to produce
essentially the effect of a series of couplets, with a
triplet occasionally interspersed :—

> " Now, while I taste the sweetness of the shade,
> While Nature lies around deep-lull'd in noon,
> Now come, bold Fancy, spread a daring flight,
> And view the wonders of the torrid zone :
> Climes unrelenting, with whose rage compar'd,
> Yon blaze is feeble and yon skies are cool."

The structure and balance of these lines are essentially those that belong to the couplet. The following is somewhat more varied, but it can hardly be
called good as blank verse :—

> " Behold where bound and of its robe bereft
> By needy Man, that all-depending lord,
> How meek, how patient the mild creature lies !
> What softness in its melancholy face,
> What dumb complaining innocence appears !
> Fear not, ye gentle tribes, 'tis not the knife
> Of horrid slaughter, that is o'er you wav'd ;

> No, 'tis the tender swain's well-guided shears,
> Who having now, to pay his annual care,
> Borrow'd your fleece, to you a cumbrous load,
> Will send you bounding to your hills again."

Finally, we may note that Thomson is apt to admit assonances, producing almost the effect of rhyme, at the end of lines which are either immediately connected or not widely separated, *e.g.* :—

> " Life flows afresh ; and young-eyed Health exalts
> The whole creation round.   Contentment walks
> The sunny glade, and feels an inward bliss
> Spring o'er the mind, beyond the power of kings
> To purchase.   Pure serenity apace
> Induces thought and contemplation still."

Or again,

> " there at distance hear
> The roaring floods and cataracts, that sweep
> From disembowell'd earth the virgin gold ;
> And o'er the varied landskip restless rove,
> Fervent with life of every fairer kind.
> A land of wonders, which the sun still eyes
> With ray direct, as of the lovely realm
> Enamour'd, and delighting there to dwell."

In the first of these examples the effect is bad, because the correspondence of final vowel sounds tends to encourage pauses at the ends of the lines, and this is fatal to the natural rhythm of the passage ; while in the second the pauses are so arranged that the assonances are not only unobjectionable, but greatly improve the harmony of the verse.

On the whole, we may say that Thomson's blank verse, though originally modelled upon Milton's, is in effect a creation of his own,[1] and must be judged on its

---

[1] The blank verse of Philips in his best poem, *Cider*, is far more Miltonic than Thomson's.   Indeed, except for the fact

own merits. Those merits are not the very highest, but
nevertheless they are considerable ; and though we may
justly complain of a certain want of metrical variety,
many of the more poetical passages of *The Seasons* are
quite satisfactory in their rhythmical effect.

An attempt has been made in the present chapter to
indicate the most important features of Thomson's
poetical style, as it is shown in *The Seasons*, his most
characteristic work. With regard to many of the
points to which attention has been called, it is certain
that the verdict of sound taste must be given against
the poet, and that the first and the last word on the
subject must be that he wrote "a vicious style." It is
necessary therefore to recognise the fact that there is
more to be said than merely this. There is a strong
element of originality in Thomson's style, as well as in
his matter, and this was clearly recognised by his
contemporaries. In poetical language and style he
was an adventurous pioneer, and his bold experiments
were not without good results in an age of rather
rigid conventionality. He was not, properly speaking,
an imitator, for imitation was not his object. He was
bent upon finding adequate means of expression for
the ideas which his fervent imagination supplied, and
with this object he employed all the resources that he
possessed, whether in the language of his own day, or in
that of the poets of former generations, especially Milton.
In his endeavour to express himself vividly and forcibly
he does not scruple to take liberties with the language :
he coins new words, uses old ones in unusual senses,
forms fresh compounds, turns adjectives into adverbs,

that he uses some of Milton's characteristic peculiarities of
rhythm too frequently, Philips has produced a very successful
imitation.

and forces the construction of verbs, inverts the natural order of sentences, and at times neglects their grammatical construction. The language which he has at his command is inadequate to the demands of his imagination, and he is constantly endeavouring to compel it to perform functions to which it is unequal. Such attempts often result in failure, but occasionally a success is achieved or a discovery made ; and in the matter of epithets especially, he has undoubtedly increased the wealth of the language. Many of his newly-formed compounds are expressive and beautiful. He invented the adjective "many-twinkling," which is used by him of leaves in the sunlight. "The dewy-skirted clouds," "the dew-bright earth," "the dimply pool," "the dusky-mantled lawn," "bitter-breathing" as applied to frost, "faint-gleaming" to the dawn, "rocky-channelled" and "mossy-tinctured" to the brook, and "forest-crowned" to the mountain,—these are examples of new combinations for which we may reasonably be grateful, and in some of which Thomson was the precursor of Keats. His use of the word "bicker" in the expression "Arrests the bickering stream" (*Winter*, 725) seems to be the first instance of this application of the word to running water, which has since received the sanction of Scott and Tennyson. Other examples of a similar kind might be cited ; but what has been said is enough to show that, independently of Thomson's more generally recognised merits, he made some valuable contributions to the diction of English poetry.

CHAPTER VI

LIBERTY AND MINOR POEMS

OF Thomson's *Liberty* a modern critic observes that it is "a great poem, full of learning, eloquence, imagination, and occasionally rising to altitudes of rare poetical vision; but the subject, and more especially the length at which it is treated, was a mistake. Liberty is a lyrical theme; to treat it didactically the proper form to use is prose. This, however, may be said, that given the subject and the method of treatment, no poet of his century could have done better than Thomson."[1] This praise, qualified though it may be, must be regarded as exaggerated; and Thomson's own high opinion of *Liberty* betrays an incapacity to distinguish in his own work between what was good and what was commonplace. Because he had achieved success in the presentation of natural scenes, he imagined that he was capable of writing an epic of civilisation; and whereas in *The Seasons* we have the general affairs of mankind, society and politics, dealt with only in the form of occasional digressions, here we find a theory of political and social progress, with illustrations from the history of the world, adopted as the theme of the poem, to the exclusion almost altogether of that subject which he had himself pronounced to be the most elevating, and the most ready to awaken poetical

[1] J. L. Robertson, in the Introduction to his edition of *The Seasons*.

enthusiasm. The poem was suggested by the tour on the Continent taken by the author in company with young Charles Talbot; but the fact, which he notes himself with some surprise, that no genuine poetical enthusiasm was roused in him by the scenes which he visited, ought to have been a sufficient warning against this attempt.

Johnson, who admits that he has not been able to read *Liberty* to the end, nevertheless makes some very just remarks about it :—

"Upon this great poem two years were spent, and the author congratulated himself upon it, as his noblest work ; but an author and his reader are not always of a mind. Liberty called in vain upon her votaries to read her praises and reward her encomiast ; her praises were condemned to harbour spiders and to gather dust ; none of Thomson's performances were so little regarded.

"The judgment of the public was not erroneous ; the recurrence of the same images must tire in time ; an enumeration of examples to prove a position which nobody denied, as it was from the beginning superfluous, must quickly grow disgusting."

The poem is, in fact, a tiresome dissertation on the thesis that Liberty is the source of all prosperity for nations, and that Great Britain alone is likely to prove permanently worthy of her blessings. The idea is not an original one, and it was doubtless suggested to Thomson by Addison's *Letter from Italy*, which has at least the merit of being in rhyme :—

"How has kind Heaven adorn'd the happy land,
    And scatter'd blessings with a wasteful hand !
    But what avail her unexhausted stores,
    Her blooming mountains and her sunny shores,
    With all the gifts that Heaven and Earth impart,
    The smiles of Nature and the charms of Art,

While proud oppression in her valleys reigns,
And tyranny usurps her happy plains?
The poor inhabitant beholds in vain
The reddening orange and the swelling grain:
Joyless he sees the growing oils and wines,
And in the myrtle's fragrant shade repines:
Starves, in the midst of Nature's bounty curst,
And in the loaden vineyard dies for thirst.
 O Liberty, thou goddess heavenly bright,
Profuse of bliss, and pregnant with delight!

.   .   .   .   .   .

Thou mak'st the gloomy face of Nature gay,
Giv'st beauty to the Sun and pleasure to the day.
 Thee, goddess, thee Britannia's isle adores;" etc.

The poem of *Liberty* is an expansion of this theme into three or four thousand lines of blank verse. Thomson was capable of producing an abundant supply of patriotic sentiment and cheap optimism with regard to the present state and future prospects of the nation, and the glories of Greece and Rome are introduced with a view to exalting the superior advantages of Britain.

The characteristics of style which we have noted as belonging to *The Seasons* are present here in a much less marked degree; but this is only a part of the general tameness. The faults there proceeded to a great extent from fervour of imagination, and here there is little fervour. Moreover, the blank verse is distinctly less good, and in many places the lines are apt to fall into couplets. In fact, the number of passages which have any real poetical merit is remarkably small, considering that we have to do with the work of one who was a genuine poet. Those quoted in the following pages are perhaps the most favourable specimens.

The poem is in five parts, the first having for its

subject a comparison of Ancient and Modern Italy. In the opening lines a graceful tribute of affection is paid to the memory of young Talbot, in whose company the author had travelled, and who had died shortly after their return :—

> " And does the mystic veil from mortal beam
> Involve those eyes where every virtue smil'd,
> And all thy father's candid spirit shone ?
> The light of reason, pure, without a cloud,
> Full of the generous heart, the mild regard ;
> Honour disdaining blemish, cordial faith,
> And limpid truth, that looks the very soul."

The poet then imagines himself to be in Italy, surrounded by the ruined monuments of Rome, and there the majestic form of Liberty appears to him :—

> " Not, as of old,
> Extended in her hand the cap and rod,
> Whose slave-enlarging touch gave double life ;
> But her bright temples bound with British oak,
> And naval honours nodded on her brow.
> .   .   .   .   .   .
> An island-goddess now ; and her high care,
> The Queen of Isles, the mistress of the main."

Liberty, who, with the exception of some brief intervals, is the speaker throughout, claims that the former greatness and prosperity of Italy was due to herself, and reviews the past in contrast with the present. How different was the scene when the great Republic was mistress of the world, when the land was thronged by busy millions, and plenty smiled everywhere. Villas then rose on all sides,

> " In Umbria's closing vales, or on the brow
> Of her brown hills that breathe the scented gale ;
> On Baiæ's viny coast, where peaceful seas,
> Fanned by kind zephyrs, ever kiss the shore,
> And suns unclouded shine through purest air :

> Or in the spacious neighbourhood of Rome,
>   Far-shining upward to the Sabine hills,
>   To Anio's roar and Tibur's olive shade,
>   To where Preneste lifts her airy brow ;
>   Or downward spreading to the sunny shore,
>   Where Alba breathes the freshness of the main."

From all sides aqueducts and roads converged to
Rome, whose uncorrupted Senate and noble breed of
men are held up for unqualified admiration. To
Thomson, apparently, it seemed that Rome under the
later Republic was an ideal state, in which every virtue
and every art was displayed in its utmost perfection.
Naturally the contrast seemed striking between this
attractive picture and the view of Italy as it was in
the eighteenth century ; and naturally also it was easy
to show that "Oppression," in one or other of its
various forms, had wrought the mischief. The Roman
Campagna is thus described :—

> " 'Tis all one desert, desolate and grey,
>   Graz'd by the sullen buffalo alone ;
>   And where the rank uncultivated growth
>   Of rotting ages taints the passing gale.
>   Beneath the baleful blast the city pines,
>   Or sinks enfeebled, or infected burns.
>   Beneath it mourns the solitary road,
>   Roll'd in rude mazes o'er th' abandon'd waste ;
>   While ancient ways, ingulf'd, are seen no more."

Both the aspect of the country and the life of its
inhabitants give evidence of the evils wrought by this
baneful power, and especially Rome displays a picture
of ruin and misery. This is how the poet makes
Liberty express the fact that the churches have been
partly built out of the ruins of ancient buildings :—

> " Patch'd from my fragments, in unsolid pomp,
>   Mark how the temple glares : and, artful dress'd,
>   Amusive draws the superstitious train."

What would the ancient Romans, the conquerors of
the earth, say to these scenes of desolation ?

> " Yon wild retreat, where superstition dreams,
>   Could, Tully, you your Tusculum believe ?
>   .   .   .   .
>   How chang'd, how vacant, Virgil, wide around,
>   Would now your Naples seem ? disaster'd less
>   By black Vesuvius thundering o'er the coast
>   His midnight earthquakes and his mining fires,
>   Than by despotic rage : *that* inward gnaws,
>   A native foe ; a *foreign* tears without."

Britain is warned to learn from thence the supreme
value of Liberty, seeing that even such a land as this
sinks to desolation when deprived of it. The poet is
moved to entreat the Goddess to inspire his song ; and
she indicates the Prince of Wales as the person who
will chiefly carry on her work,

> "and added give
> The touch the Graces and the Muses owe."

In the second part of the poem, called "Greece,"
the Goddess proceeds to trace her origin in human
society :—

> " First, in the dawn of time, with eastern swains,
>   In woods and tents and cottages I lived ;
>   While on from plain to plain they led their flocks,
>   In search of clearer spring and fresher field."

Naturally crime was rare in those days, and justice was
identical with reason and equity, nor (so it seems) was
capital punishment as yet practised. But as arts and
civilisation grew, the primeval peace was broken, and
war and rapine flourished. Liberty established science,
virtue, and arts in Egypt; but Superstition and
Tyranny stepped in, and then Liberty abandoned the
East and came to Greece :—

> " How many states,
> And clustering towns, and monuments of fame,
> And scenes of glorious deeds, in little bounds ;
> From the rough tract of bending mountains, beat
> By Adria's here, there by Ægean waves,
> To where the deep-adorning Cyclade Isles
> In shining prospect rise, and on the shore
> Of farthest Crete resounds the Lybian main ! "

There follows a summary account of the states of
Sparta and Athens, with special mention of Thermo-
pylæ, Marathon, and the retreat of the Ten Thousand.
Greek philosophy, eloquence, poetry, sculpture, painting, and architecture are celebrated. Thomson reserves
his more detailed account of Greek sculpture for a later
place, but he has a passage here on landscape-painting,
which, however inappropriate in an account of Greek
art, is interesting in itself :—

> " There gaily broke the sun-illumin'd cloud ;
> The lessening prospect, and the mountain blue
> Vanish'd in air ; the precipice frown'd dire ;
> White down the rock the rushing torrent dash'd ;
> The sun shone trembling o'er the distant main ;
> The tempest foam'd immense ; the driving storm
> Sadden'd the skies, and from the doubling gloom,
> On the scath'd oak the ragged lightning fell."

Thomson was not without taste in art, and it is easy
to believe that he took a special interest in landscape.

It is then shown how all the glory of virtue and of
arts had been extinguished in Greece by the loss of
Liberty, for which the way had been prepared by
corruption of public morals. The concluding lines of
this part of the poem contain an evident reference to
Walpole's system of parliamentary government.

The third part is entitled "Rome," and begins with
a reference to the Greek colonies in Italy and Sicily.

Here Pythagoras is singled out for special distinction
in an eloquent passage :—

> "His mental eye first launch'd into the deeps
>   Of boundless ether, where unnumber'd orbs,
>   Myriads on myriads, through the pathless sky
>   Unerring roll, and wind their steady way.
>   There he the full consenting choir beheld ;
>   There first discern'd the secret band of love,
>   The kind attraction that to central suns
>   Binds circling earths, and world with world unites."

The rise of the Roman power is traced, with mention
of the chief heroes of the Republic.   Then the Roman
conquests are described, and the proclamation of freedom to the states of Greece by Flaminius.   Gradually
vices and luxury crept in, and independence failed.
Civil strife grew more deadly : corruption and law-
less force alternately threatened the safety of the
Republic.   Marius and Sylla turned Rome into a
human shambles and "made deserts lovely."   Liberty
had no true upholder.   Sylla indeed resigned his
power and died in peace, "A grace which I to his
demission gave," but ambition did not die with him.
Liberty still lingered with Cicero, Cato, and Brutus,
but after Philippi she spread her wings northward.   It
is true that the first two Cæsars encouraged arts and
rewarded merit, but from Tiberius onward all were
monsters of iniquity, except an occasional Titus, Trajan,
or Antonine.   Meanwhile, Liberty has taken her flight
to Scythia and Sarmatia,

> "A sullen land of lakes and fens immense,
>   Of rocks, resounding torrents, gloomy heaths,
>   And cruel deserts black with sounding pine ;
>   Where nature frowns : though sometimes into smiles
>   She softens, and immediate, at the touch
>   Of southern gales, throws from the sudden glebe
>   Luxuriant pasture and a waste of flowers."

Yet this climate is a "nursery of nations": a race of men is found here,

> "Hard like their soil, and like their climate fierce,"

and these, roused by the Goddess Liberty, resistlessly poured over the boundaries of the empire to take vengeance for the outrages inflicted upon her.

The seeds of Freedom lay buried long in their hearts, and only pride and fierceness appeared. In this "night of time" between two worlds, Liberty abandoned the earth and took refuge in Heaven, where the King of Nature reigns amid splendour which far transcends all that we can conceive of here :—

> "But sacred be the veil, that kindly clouds
>   A light too keen for mortals ; wraps a view
> Too softening fair, for those that here in dust
> Must cheerful toil out their appointed years.
> A sense of higher life would only damp
> The schoolboy's task, and spoil his playful hours :
> Nor could the child of Reason, feeble man,
> With vigour through this infant-being drudge,
> Did brighter worlds, their unimagin'd bliss
> Disclosing, dazzle and dissolve his mind."

"Britain," the fourth part of *Liberty*, is much longer than any of the other parts. We are told how, after ages of tyranny and superstition, Liberty at length returned to earth, and lighted upon Italy again (apparently about the time of the Renaissance). Sculpture, painting, and architecture were restored from ancient models, and Greek statues came to light. The passage which describes these is perhaps the first of the kind in English poetry. The Farnese Hercules, the Meleager, and the Fighting Gladiator are spoken of, and then the Dying Gladiator :—

> "Supported on his shorten'd arm he leans
>   Prone, agonising ; with incumbent fate

> Heavy, declines his head ; yet dark beneath
> The suffering feature sullen vengeance lours,
> Shame, indignation, unaccomplish'd rage ;
> And still the cheated eye expects his fall."

Next we see the Apollo Belvidere :—

> " All conquest-flush'd from prostrate Python came
> The quiver'd God.   In graceful act he stands,
> His arm extended with the slacken'd bow :
> Light flows his easy robe, and fair displays
> A manly soften'd form."

Then the Venus de' Medici, already referred to in *The Seasons* as "the statue that enchants the world," and the Laocoön group.   Thomson suffers, naturally, by the comparison with Byron, but his descriptions are interesting, and show a genuine appreciation of Greek art.

Among modern works of sculpture, the Moses and the Christ of Michael Angelo are specially mentioned, the development of the arts of painting, architecture, and music in Italy is briefly referred to, and it is admitted that culture is not entirely confined to republics :—

> " Even bigots smil'd : to their protection took
> Arts not their own, and from them borrow'd pomp :
> For in a tyrant's garden these awhile
> May bloom, though freedom be their parent soil."

This, however, was not to be for long.   The Goddess soon left Rome, and was not much detained by the other Italian states, among which Genoa and Venice are specially mentioned as competitors for the dominion of the seas :—

> " There in white prospect from the rocky hill
> Gradual descending to the shelter'd shore,
> By me proud Genoa's marble turrets rose.
> And while my genuine spirit warm'd her sons,

> Beneath her Dorias not unworthy she
> Vied for the trident of the narrow seas,
> Ere Britain yet had open'd all the main.
>   Nor be the then triumphant state forgot,
> Where push'd from plunder'd earth a remnant still,
> Inspir'd by me, thro' the dark ages kept
> Of my old Roman flame some sparks alive :
> The seeming god-built city, which my hand
> Deep in the bosom fix'd of wondering seas.
>
> .   .   .   .
>
> To this fair queen of Adria's stormy gulf,
> The mart of nations, long obedient seas
> Roll'd all the treasure of the radiant East."

But these too sink under oppression, and are no more.
Liberty takes refuge in Switzerland for a time ; and
the poet shows in his description of the scenery, for
which the absent native pines, that he did not pass the
the Alps altogether in vain :—

> " The flitting cloud, against the summit dash'd,
> And by the sun illumin'd, pouring bright
> A gemmy shower ; hung o'er amazing rocks,
> The mountain ash and solemn-sounding pine :
> The snow-fed torrent, in white mazes toss'd
> Down to the clear ethereal lake below :
> And high o'ertopping all the broken scene,
> The mountain fading into sky ; where shines
> On winter winter shivering, and whose top
> Licks from their cloudy magazine the snows."

Passing through Germany to Scandinavia, Liberty
bestows some of her favours on the Hanse Towns and
on Sweden ; and then turning southward she makes for
Britain, encountering on the way the Genius of the
Deep, who welcomes her to the blest isle, for the
people of which is reserved the exploration of his
remotest realms :—

> " Theirs the triumph be,
> By deep Invention's keen pervading eye,
> The heart of Courage and the hand of Toil,
>
> .   .   .   .   .
>
> Round social Earth to circle fair exchange,
> And bind the nations in a golden chain."

On her arrival she meets Britannia,

> " the Goddess, whose staid eye
> Beams the dark azure of the doubtful dawn.
>
> .   .   .   .   .
>
> Of high demeanour, stately, shedding grace
> With every motion."

She appears surrounded by a bright company of the Virtues by which her happy land is especially distinguished. "These described. Animated by the presence of Liberty, they begin their operations. Their beneficent influence contrasted with the works and delusions of opposing Demons, to verse 626. Concludes with an abstract of the English history, marking the several advances of Liberty, down to her complete establishment at the Revolution." Such are the terms in which the author summarises the last seven hundred lines of this part, and not much more need be said here. If Johnson's patience held out up to this point, which is rather improbable, it must certainly have broken down under the enumeration of "the several advances of Liberty, down to her complete establishment at the Revolution." The conclusion is rather remarkably optimistic as regards the actual state of society, considering that the poet is writing in the interests of the Opposition and dedicates his poem to the Prince of Wales :—

> " And now behold ! exalted as the cope
> That swells immense o'er many-peopled earth,
> And like it free, my fabric stands complete,

> The palace of the laws. To the four heavens
> Four gates impartial thrown, unceasing crowds,
> With kings themselves the hearty peasant mix'd,
> Pour urgent in. And tho' to different ranks
> Responsive place belongs, yet equal spreads
> The sheltering roof o'er all ; while plenty flows,
> And glad contentment echoes round the whole."

And all this after fifteen years of Sir Robert
Walpole ! It is true that the inevitable warning
follows :—

> " Nought but the felon undermining hand
> Of dark Corruption can its frame dissolve,
> And lay the toil of ages in the dust."

The fifth part, entitled " The Prospect," opens with
an address by the author to the Goddess, "marking
the happiness and grandeur of Great Britain as arising
from her influence." The blessed state of the nation
is here still further emphasised :—

> " Eternal verdure crowns
> Her meads ; her gardens smile eternal spring."

Unnumbered flocks feed upon her downs ; her pastures
are the richest for cattle, and seas of plenty wave in
her autumnal fields.

> " Enlivening these, add cities, full
> Of wealth, of trade, of cheerful toiling crowds :
> Add thriving towns ; add villages and farms,
> Innumerous sow'd along the lively vale,
> Where bold unrivall'd peasants happy dwell."

(It is interesting to remember that Thomson and
Hogarth were contemporaries.)

The nation is characterised as combining the warm
and hospitable Cambrian, the high-souled Scot,

> " To hardship tam'd, active in arts and arms,
> Fired with a restless, an impatient flame,
> That leads him raptur'd where ambition calls,"

and the Englishman, who joins high fancy and judicious
thought with a generous heart and the most tenacious
valour. The poet inquires how this mighty kingdom
shall be preserved, and Liberty replies that it can
stand by public virtue alone :—

> " Unblest by virtue, Government a league
> Becomes, a circling junto of the great,
> To rob by law. . . .
> What are without it Senates, save a face
> Of consultation deep and reason free,
> While the determin'd voice and heart are sold ?
> What boasted freedom, save a sounding name,
> And what election, but a market vile
> Of slaves self-barter'd ? "

British freedom must be sustained by the three
virtues of independence, integrity in office, and a
passion for the common welfare. Independence, the
chief of these, is shown to be closely connected with
simplicity of life, as corrupt subservience is with luxury
and tasteless extravagance, which are denounced at some
length. An appeal is made to Britons to resist the fatal
influence of corruption. Liberty is loth to believe that
any want of integrity in office can be found among her
sons ; and accordingly she proceeds to speak of the
third virtue, namely enthusiasm for the public good,
which is made the text of another discourse upon the
evils of corruption, and the necessity, if the worst
should happen, of throwing aside the nonsense of
parties, and joining to promote the public welfare.
Turning now to a "softer prospect," the Goddess
proceeds to deal with the state of science, arts and
public works in her chosen realm, and finds it not
altogether satisfactory. France, under an absolute
monarchy, is actually, strange as it may seem,
in advance of Britain in these matters, and

especially in the means of communication by land
and water,

> " the shining road,
> The flood-compelling arch, the long canal
> Thro' mountains piercing and uniting seas."

Her institutions of public charity, her social refine-
ment, her freedom from duelling, the peaceful civilisation of her cities, the honour paid to arts and science,
"by despotic bounty bless'd," her development of
literature, and especially of the drama, her schools of
painting and of sculpture, her palaces and gardens, her
mechanical arts and manufactures, are referred to with
admiration. It is the same theme which was afterwards
developed by Burke :—

> " When I consider the face of the kingdom of France ; the
> multitude and opulence of her cities ; the useful magnificence
> of her spacious high-roads and bridges ; the opportunity of her
> artificial canals and navigations, opening the convenience of
> maritime communication through a solid continent of so
> immense an extent ; . . . when I reflect on the excellence of
> her manufactures and fabrics, second to none but ours, and
> in some particulars not second ; when I contemplate the grand
> foundations of charity, public and private ; when I survey the
> state of all the arts that beautify and polish life ; when I
> reckon the men she has bred for extending her fame in war,
> her able statesmen, . . . her poets and her orators sacred and
> profane,—I behold in all this something which awes and
> commands the imagination," etc.

It is true, continues Liberty, that all these flourishing plants would have grown better in Britain, " by the
potent juice Of freedom swell'd," and that the favour
of courts is but a transitory gleam, " A false uncertain
spring," which will be followed by a killing winter ;
whereas when imperial bounty joins with freedom (in
what precise manner she does not explain), an eternal

combination of spring and autumn is produced, which
secures both growth and fruit.

The poet is naturally impatient to see this happy
result, and asks, "When shall we call these ancient
laurels ours?" and his eyes being touched by the hand
of the Goddess, he is enabled to view a prospect of
future times, in which Britain, by means of the wealth
accumulated by her commerce, shall vie with Rome in
grandeur and with Greece in art. He sees kings to
whom nothing is dear but Worth and Virtue, and
whose best delight is the public good; he sees a new
race of courtiers,

> "Not those vain insects fluttering in the blaze
> Of court and ball and play; those venal souls,
> Corruption's veteran, unrelenting bands,
> That, to their vices slaves, can ne'er be free."

He sees education improved, Justice purged of fraud
and oppression, social Labour lifting its head and pro-
tected from ruffian force, the "maddening bowl, A
nation's poison," dashed to the ground, a beauteous
order reigning everywhere :—

> "Manly submission, unimposing toil,
> Trade without guile, civility that marks
> From the foul herd of brutal slaves thy sons,
> And fearless peace."

Or if a just and necessary war should come,

> "Unfailing fields of freemen I behold,
> That know with their own proper arm to guard
> Their own blest isle against a leaguing world."

The dominion of the sea in the hands of Britain shall
destroy the Gallic dream of universal empire : colonies
shall spread southward, not built on rapine and servi-
tude, but firmly held together by the bonds of social
Freedom. The streets of our cities shall no longer be

horrid with want and misery, age and sickness shall no
more be left untended—(here we have a hint of the
reverse side of the picture); the poor man shall find
employment, if able-bodied; and if old or maimed, shall
demand and obtain "his miserable due"; the guiltless
infant shall no longer suffer for the sins of its parents.

> "Sweet sets the sun of stormy life, and sweet
>   The morning shines, in Mercy's dews array'd.
> Lo, how they rise, these families of Heaven!
> That, chief, (but why, ye bigots, why so late?)
> Where blooms and warbles glad a rising age:
> What smiles of praise! and while their song ascends,
> The listening seraph lays his lute aside."

(An early reference to the Foundling Hospital.)

The author sees poetry and the drama ennobled, the
fine arts encouraged in a practical manner,

> "Nurs'd by the treasure from a nation drain'd
>   Their works to purchase";

nature improved by art, as by Pope at Twickenham, by
Bathurst, or by Cobham; stately streets and squares,
solid high-roads, bridges without tolls, canals, harbours
and lighthouses. As all these varied wonders passed
before his view, suddenly the vision ceased, and on his
waking eye

> "Rush'd the still ruins of dejected Rome."

The patriotic vision has an undeniable element of
grandeur; and the author would no doubt have been
an enthusiastic admirer of the material progress of
Great Britain in the nineteenth century, and especially
of the extension of her colonies throughout the world.

Some of Thomson's occasional poems have merit,
and especially those in honour of Sir Isaac Newton
and of the Lord Chancellor Talbot, the father of his

young fellow-traveller. The former, published in 1727, shortly after Newton's death, shows both enthusiasm and intelligent appreciation. Newton is first greeted as one who, while yet living upon the earth, had fathomed the secret of the Universe ; who

> "from motion's simple laws
> Could trace the secret hand of Providence,
> Wide-working through this universal frame."

> "who sat not down and dream'd
> Romantic schemes, defended by the din
> Of specious words, and tyranny of names ;
> But, bidding his amazing mind attend,
> And with heroic patience years on years
> Deep-searching, saw at last the system dawn,
> And shine, of all his race, on him alone."

After reference to Newton's investigation of the motions of the moon and to the theory of the tides, the poet continues thus with reference to his astronomical system :—

> "Then breaking hence, he took his ardent flight
> Thro' the blue infinite ; and every star,
> Which the clear concave of a winter's night
> Pours on the eye, or astronomic tube
> Far-stretching snatches from the dark abyss,
> Or such as farther in successive skies
> To fancy shine alone, at his approach
> Blaz'd into suns, the living centre each
> Of an harmonious system : all combin'd
> And rul'd unerring by that single power,
> Which draws the stone projected to the ground.

Then the discoveries in other sciences are spoken of .—

> "Th' aerial flow of Sound was known to him,
> From whence it first in wavy circles breaks,
> Till the touch'd organ takes the message in.
> Nor could the darting beam, of speed immense,
> Escape his swift pursuit and measuring eye.

> Even Light itself, which every thing displays,
> Shone undiscover'd, till his brighter mind
> Untwisted all the shining robe of day,
> And from the whitening undistinguish'd blaze,
> Collecting every ray into his kind,
> To the charm'd eye educ'd the gorgeous train
> Of parent-colours."

The religious character of Newton is touched upon :—

> " What wonder thence that his devotion swell'd
> Responsive to his knowledge !   For could he,
> Whose piercing mental eye diffusive saw
> The finish'd university of things,
> In all its order, magnitude and parts,
> Forbear incessant to adore that Power,
> Who fills, sustains, and actuates the whole ? "

And his friends are appealed to for their testimony to
the goodness and humility of his disposition :—

> " Oh, speak the wondrous man ! how mild, how calm,
> How greatly humble, how divinely good ;
> How firm establish'd on eternal truth ;
> Fervent in doing well, with every nerve
> Still pressing on, forgetful of the past,
> And panting for perfection : far above
> Those little cares and visionary joys,
> That so perplex the fond impassion'd heart
> Of ever-cheated, ever-trusting man."

The poem concludes with an expression of patriotic
pride, and a prayer that the spirit of Newton may
preside over the studies of his country. The poem is
certainly much superior to most others of its class.

Britannia, published anonymously in 1729, is an
attempt to rouse public feeling against the peace-at-
any-price policy of Walpole. Britannia is represented

as mourning upon the shore, uncomforted even by the auspicious arrival of Frederick, Prince of Wales, because of the outrages which her merchants suffer from "the insulting Spaniard." She recalls first the defeat and destruction of the Spanish Armada, and then the victories of Blake; and denounces the feeble spirit which shrinks from maintaining that empire of the seas which the great spirits of former generations have founded. She pronounces peace to be the first of human blessings, the source and soul of social life; and calls that man supremely happy who can bestow it upon his country. But the more we value peace, the more necessary is war, when an unoffending state is attacked by "ruffian force." Britons are reminded of the vital importance to them of the sea-power, which has been placed in their hands by destiny, and upon which depends the very existence of their trade; and they are urged not to allow luxury to impair their vigour and to eat out the heart of their liberty and public spirit. The sentiments are to a great extent those which were afterwards expanded in the poem of *Liberty*, and they are expressed here with some rhetorical vigour. The most poetical passage is that which describes the fate of the Spanish Armada :—

> " When all the pride of Spain in one dread fleet
>   Swell'd o'er the labouring surge; like a whole heaven
>   Of clouds, wide-roll'd before the boundless breeze.
>   Gaily the splendid armament along
>   Exultant plough'd, reflecting a red gleam,
>   As sunk the sun, o'er all the flaming vast.
>
> . . . . . .
>
>   But soon, regardless of the cumbrous pomp,
>   My dauntless Britons came, a gloomy few,
>   With tempest black the goodly scene deform'd,
>   And laid their glory waste. The bolts of Fate
>   Resistless thunder'd thro' their yielding sides,

Fierce o'er their beauty blaz'd the lurid flame ;
And seiz'd in horrid grasp, or shatter'd wide,
Amid the mighty waters deep they sunk.
Then too from every promontory chill,
Rank fen, and cavern where the wild wave works,
I swept confederate winds, and swell'd a storm.
Round the glad isle, snatch'd by the vengeful blast,
The scatter'd remnants drove ; on the blind shelve,
And pointed rock, that marks th' indented shore,
Relentless dash'd, where loud the northern main
Howls thro' the fractur'd Caledonian isles."

Another poem in blank verse, which was published
anonymously in the same year, *To the Memory of Mr.
Congreve,* has been confidently attributed to Thomson
in recent times, though it was never included by
himself or his friends among his works. The style of
it has some slight resemblance to his : but by this
time blank verse after the model of Thomson had
become rather fashionable ; and after all, the resemblance in style is somewhat superficial. His essential
characteristics do not very markedly appear, and there
is more tendency to epigrammatic point than we are
accustomed to find in his verse. Moreover, a note
of personal satire appears in it, which is altogether
alien to Thomson's genius. It may be added that
Congreve's merits were not such as would especially
appeal to Thomson, and we do not know that Thomson
had any relations with Henrietta, Duchess of Marlborough, to whom the poem is dedicated.

Of the smaller pieces by Thomson published in
Ralph's Miscellany in 1729, the *Hymn on Solitude,* of
which the first draft had been sent in a letter to
Mallet in 1725, is distinctly the best. The following
beautiful lines, addressed to Solitude, of which the
original form was almost commonplace, afford a good

example of the author's power of improving his own work :—

> " Thine is the balmy breath of morn,
>   Just as the dew-bent rose is born ;
>   And while meridian fervours beat,
>   Thine is the woodland dumb retreat ;
>   But chief, when evening scenes decay,
>   And the faint landskip swims away,
>   Thine is the doubtful soft decline,
>   And that best hour of musing thine."

The style here reminds us strikingly of Collins. Of the other pieces the chief interest is that they are in heroic couplets, and prove that Thomson could move easily enough in this measure when he chose. The same fact is illustrated by the lines on the death of Aikman, the painter, written probably in 1731, but not published in the author's lifetime. The concluding couplets have a note of distinction :—

> " As those we love decay, we die in part,
>   String after string is sever'd from the heart :
>   Till loosen'd life at last—but breathing clay—
>   Without one pang, is glad to fall away.
>   Unhappy he who latest feels the blow,
>   Whose eyes have wept o'er every friend laid low,
>   Dragg'd lingering on from partial death to death ;
>   Till, dying, all he can resign is breath."

The poem to the memory of Lord Talbot was published in 1737, the year of his death. There is no reason to doubt the sincerity of the praise, but it is somewhat too unmeasured and indiscriminate. Talbot was a distinguished lawyer and a polished speaker, no doubt, but it can hardly be claimed with any show of reason that he had " All that can render man or great or good," or that,

> " In him Astrea to this dim abode
>   Of ever-wandering men returned again."

N

Thomson, however, justly and gracefully celebrates his skill as a pleader,—

> " While on th' enlighten'd mind with winning art
> His gentle reason so persuasive stole,
> That the charm'd hearer thought it was his own."

his judicial serenity,—

> Plac'd on the seat of justice, there he reign'd,
> In a superior sphere of cloudless day,
> A pure intelligence.   No tumult there,
> No dark emotion, no intemperate heat,
> No passion e'er disturb'd the clear serene
> That round him spread."

and his power of unravelling intricacies,—

> " As intuition quick he snatch'd the truth,
> Yet with progressive patience, step by step,
> Self-diffident, or to the slower kind,
> He thro' the maze of falsehood trac'd it on,
> Till at the last evolv'd it full appear'd,
> And even the loser own'd the just decree."

Referring to Talbot's judicious patronage of literature, the author, who had had experience of it, says:—

> "The gracious flood that cheers the letter'd world
> Is not the noisy gift of summer's noon,
> Whose sudden current from the naked root
> Washes the little soil that yet remain'd,
> And only more dejects the blushing flowers :
> No, 'tis the soft-descending dews at eve,
> The silent treasures of the vernal year,
> Indulging deep their stores the still night long ;
> Till with returning morn the freshen'd world
> Is fragrance all, all beauty, joy and song."

A tribute is paid to the virtues and the social grace of his private life ; and an opportunity is taken here to speak of the treatment accorded to Rundle, who

had first introduced Thomson to the notice of Talbot.
He had been recommended for the see of Gloucester,
but his appointment had been stopped, and he had
been shelved in an Irish bishopric,—

> " from native sunshine driven,
> Driven from your friends, the sunshine of the soul,
> By slanderous zeal and politics infirm,
> Jealous of worth."

The author imagines him mourning for his friend in
truly desolate surroundings,—

> " As on the pebbled shore you pensive stray,
> Where Derry's mountains a bleak crescent form,
> And 'mid their ample round receive the waves,
> That from the frozen pole resounding rush,
> Impetuous."

The poem concludes with a feeling reference to the
meeting after death of the young Talbot with his
father,—

> " Ah ! who is he that with a fonder eye
> Meets thine enraptur'd ?—'Tis the best of sons,
> The best of friends !—Too soon is realiz'd
> That hope which once forbad thy tears to flow ! "

and with an apology for " This fond, superfluous verse,"
in commendation of one whose praise is attested by
his deeds, and confirmed by the united assent of all
parties in a deeply-divided nation.

Of the songs which Thomson has left, several are
distinctly good, and in his lyrics he has much greater
simplicity of style and less diffuseness of expression
than in most of his other work. The song *To
Fortune,*

> " For ever, Fortune, wilt thou prove
> An unrelenting foe to Love,"

is sufficiently well known ; but the stanzas *To Her I Love*, beginning "Tell me, thou soul of her I love," are perhaps more charming. Finally, he claims the authorship of the song which may more fitly than any other be called the national anthem. "Rule Britannia" occurs, as we have seen, in the masque of *Alfred*, which was a joint composition of Thomson and Mallet, but it may with practical certainty be ascribed to Thomson. The internal evidence for this ascription is very strong. No utterance could be more characteristic of Thomson, whose strongest sentiment was patriotism, and whose patriotism was bound up, as we have seen, with an enthusiastic love of liberty and an intense belief in the sea-power of Great Britain. The ideas expressed in the song are precisely those that we find in *The Seasons* and in *Liberty*. The external evidence supports the same conclusion. The song, which became popular at once, was printed as Thomson's during the lifetime of Mallet, who appears to have made no claim to the authorship ; and Mallet was certainly not the man to allow another to enjoy credit which properly belonged to himself. Nor does it seem that any inference contrary to the opinion that Thomson was the author can be drawn from Mallet's account of his proceedings in recasting the play for production at Covent Garden in 1751. He tells us that of his friend's part he has retained only "three or four speeches and a part of one song." Now, of the six songs which originally belonged to *Alfred*, when it was produced in 1740, two are retained wholly in Mallet's new edition, two are altogether omitted, and two are partially reproduced. In the song, "From those eternal regions bright," the first six lines (out of sixteen) are retained, and in "Rule Britannia," out of six stanzas three are retained (the third with some alteration). On the authority of Mallet we know that of these two songs one was originally by Thomson, and there can be little doubt which that one must be.[1] As to the argument that "Rule Britannia" is called "An Ode," and therefore cannot be the "song" to which Mallet refers, it must surely be regarded as a quibble. If it is not improper to call it a song now, it was not improper then.

"Rule Britannia" is simple and manly in expression, and appeals irresistibly to the national sentiment, "a song which will be the political hymn of this country, so long as she maintains her political power."

[1] The internal evidence of Thomson's authorship was almost conclusively stated by Mr. Churton Collins in the *Saturday Review* of Feb. 20th, 1897.

CHAPTER VII

THE CASTLE OF INDOLENCE.

In the opinion of some critics *The Castle of Indolence* is Thomson's best work. With this verdict the present writer finds himself unable to agree; but it may be admitted that the author has here freed himself from many of his rather exasperating faults of style, shows greater delicacy of rhythm and a finer appreciation of musical effects, and selects his vocabulary with a more unexceptionable taste. He has given us therefore a poem which in particular passages is altogether charming; but there is very great inequality, and the effect of the whole is marred by the faults of the general plan, by the absurd management of the catastrophe, and by the extent to which the moral aim is allowed to predominate over the artistic.

The improvement of style is evidently connected closely with the abandonment of blank verse and the adoption of the Spenserian stanza. Milton had been a genuine source of poetical inspiration to Thomson; but the influence of the Miltonic style and diction was in many respects dangerous, and had encouraged some of his worst natural tendencies. In turning now to Spenser, who had been a favourite of his boyhood, he gained both in simplicity and in sweetness. It must be remembered that the two styles, different as they are, must have been used simultaneously; for *The Castle of Indolence* was in hand for many years before

the final completion of *The Seasons.* To those who are
intolerant of the particular vices of style which char-
acterise *The Seasons,* it may seem that the many
beautiful stanzas of *The Castle of Indolence,* which can
be separately enjoyed, compensate for its radical faults
of construction, and its rather commonplace moralising;
but taken in the mass, *The Seasons* will justify the
popular verdict in its favour. It is a work which can
better dispense with regularity of plan, and can better
afford an occasional lapse into commonplace, than the
elaborately finished cantos which set forth the moral
allegory of Indolence and Industry. In *The Seasons*
Thomson is working more in accordance with the bent
of his genius, and there is a native vigour and a
poetical enthusiasm, which justify us in overlooking to
some extent the faults of style. Here there is more art
and a finer choice of expression, but the total effect, after
all, is less satisfactory. The author has hardly made
up his mind whether he is producing a *jeu d'esprit* or a
serious piece of morality.

Johnson bestowed high praise on the first canto
when he said that it "opens a scene of lazy luxury
that fills the imagination." The description with which
the poem begins, of the situation and surroundings of
the Castle of Indolence, is justly celebrated :—

> " Was nought around but images of rest :
>   Sleep-soothing groves, and quiet lawns between,
>   And flowery beds, that slumbrous influence kest,
>   From poppies breath'd ; and beds of pleasant green,
>   Where never yet was creeping creature seen.
>   Meantime unnumber'd glittering streamlets play'd,
>   And hurled everywhere their waters sheen ;
>   That as they bicker'd through the sunny glade,
> Though restless still themselves, a lulling murmur made.

Full in the passage of the vale above,
A sable, silent, solemn forest stood ;
Where nought but shadowy forms was seen to move,
As Idless fancied in her dreaming mood :
And up the hills on either side a wood
Of blackening pines, ay waving to and fro,
Sent forth a sleepy horror through the blood ;
And where this valley winded out below,
The murmuring main was heard, and scarcely heard, to
    flow.

A pleasing land of drowsy-hed it was,
Of dreams that wave before the half-shut eye ;
And of gay castles in the clouds that pass,
For ever flushing round a summer sky ;" etc.

In this delicious spot the powerful wizard Indolence
had his castle,

    "'mid embowering trees,
That half shut out the beams of Phœbus bright,
And made a kind of checker'd day and night."

Here at the gate he sat, and to the music of his lute
complained of the cruel fate of labour, which oppressed
the race of man. Pilgrims who passed by along the
roads of earth were drawn by freshness of this valley
to descend from the neighbouring hills and listen to
his siren melody, which set forth first how all creatures
on earth except man enjoyed their life without inces-
sant toil :—

"Behold the merry minstrels of the morn,
The swarming songsters of the careless grove,
Ten thousand throats, that, from the flowering thorn,
Hymn their good God, and carol sweet of love ;
Such grateful, kindly raptures them emove :
They neither plough nor sow ; ne fit for flail,
E'er to the barn the nodden [1] sheaves they drove ;

---

[1] Most modern editors read "nodding"; but if Thomson had
meant this, he would have written it, as in Canto ii. st. 26.

> Yet theirs each harvest dancing in the gale,
> Whatever crowns the hill, or smiles along the vale."

Man alone, the "outcast of Nature," is consumed by the savage thirst of gain, and is the thrall of the vices which proceed from it. He laboriously pushes the cumbrous load of life up hill; but when he thinks that he has almost gained the summit,

> "Down thunders back the stone with mighty sweep,"

and his labours are for ever in vain. The enchanter invites all those who are weary of this unending toil to dwell with him and lead a life from which all lying, cheating, and flattering are banished, and in which nothing is admitted which can disturb tranquillity. And after all,

> "What, what is virtue, but repose of mind?
> A pure ethereal calm, that knows no storm;
> Above the reach of wild ambition's wind,
> Above those passions that this world deform,
> And torture man, a proud malignant worm!"

Exercise is not forbidden here if it be needed to supply zest for ease:—

> "Amid the groves you may indulge the muse,
> Or tend the blooms, and deck the vernal year;
> Or softly stealing with your watery gear
> Along the brooks, the crimson-spotted fry
> You may delude: the whilst, amus'd, you hear
> Now the hoarse stream, and now the zephyr's sigh,
> Attuned to the birds and woodland melody."

A grievous folly it is to heap up worldly estate, which will pass into the hands of those who mock you, when you are gone. It is the most vain of vanities

> "To toil for what you here untoiling may obtain."

Multitudes were induced to enter by the charm of the wizard's song:—

> " Heaps pour'd on heaps, and yet they slipt along
>   In silent ease ; as when beneath the beam
> Of summer-moons, the distant woods among,
>   Or by some flood all silver'd with the gleam,
> The soft-embodied fays through airy portal stream."

They were received by a porter, new-waked from
sleep, whose aspect breathed repose ; and by him they
were supplied with a loose-fitting garb, and ushered
into a court where a fountain threw up

> " A stream, high-spouting from its liquid bed,
>   And falling back again in drizzly dew,"

whence each drew deep draughts of Nepenthe, which
gave him oblivion of earthly cares, gladsome thoughts,
and joyous dreams.   Thence all wandered forth by
different ways, and of these endless numbers,

> " swarming round,
> As thick as idle motes in sunny ray,"

not one was to be seen : solitude and perfect silence
reigned :—

> " As when a shepherd of the Hebrid Isles,
>   Plac'd far amid the melancholy main,
>   (Whether it be lone fancy him beguiles,
>   Or that aerial beings sometimes deign
>   To stand embodied, to our senses plain),
> Sees on the naked hill or valley low,
>   The whilst in ocean Phœbus dips his wain,
>   A vast assembly moving to and fro :
> Then all at once in air dissolves the wondrous show."

Descriptions follow of the furnishing of the rooms
of the castle, the supply of banquets at a wish by
unseen hands, the tapestry with its scenes of pastoral
tranquillity and of the life of the patriarchs, the
paintings showing various scenes of nature :—

> " Sometimes the pencil, in cool airy halls,
>   Bade the gay bloom of vernal landskips rise,

> Or Autumn's varied shades imbrown the walls :
> Now the black tempest strikes the astonish'd eyes ;
> Now down the steep the flashing torrent flies ;
> The trembling sun now plays o'er ocean blue,
> And now rude mountains frown amid the skies ;
> Whate'er Lorrain light-touch'd with softening hue,
> Or savage Rosa dash'd, or learned Poussin drew."

(A stanza which may be compared with the lines on landscape-painting which have already been quoted from the second part of *Liberty*.)

Music of the Æolian harp here lulled the pensive mind, and near the pavilions where they slept, waters ran and breezes sighed; while sometimes storms swelled round, by the working of the wizard, and the demons of the tempest seemed to threaten at doors and windows with their fierce growling, but found no entrance,

> " Whence sweeter grew our sleep, secure in massy hall."

Their slumbers are visited by dreams of beauty,

> "Raising a world of gayer tinct and grace,
> O'er which were shadowy cast Elysian gleams,
> That play'd in waving lights from place to place,
> And shed a roseate smile on Nature's face."

These fair illusions, "guileful angel-seeming sprights," were such as no poetical colours can paint ; and meanwhile all the horrors of sleep were banished :—

> " But for those fiends, whom blood and broils delight ;
> Who hurl the wretch, as if to hell outright,
> Down, down black gulfs, where sullen waters sleep,
> Or hold him clambering all the fearful night
> On beetling cliffs, or pent in ruins deep ;
> They, till due time should serve, were bid far hence to
>   keep."

The principal amusement of this household was a magic crystal globe, called the Mirror of Vanity, in

which "all things that do pass Upon this ant-hill
earth" might be seen by the curious gazer: men
running after pleasure which eludes them, or gain
which they will not enjoy; authors striving for fame,
which will not come to them until after their death;
all the idle bustle of society, the intrigues of political
parties, and the wars by which nothing is achieved.

A series of portraits follow of some of the inmates
of the castle, which in all probability represents the
"detached stanzas, in the way of raillery on himself
and on some of his friends," which we are told that
the author took as the basis of his work. We have
here first "a man of special grave remark," richly
endowed as a poet, but unwilling to give forth any of
those stores which he received from nature or from art;
who at noon-tide was to be found by the side of the
purling brook, and towards sunset basking amid the
broom,

"Where the wild thyme and camomile are found;"

and then sauntered home through the twilight shadows.

"So had he passed many a day.

Yet not in thoughtless slumber were they past:
For oft the heavenly fire, that lay conceal'd
Beneath the sleeping embers, mounted fast,
And all its native light anew reveal'd:
Oft as he travers'd the cerulean field,
And markt the clouds that drove before the wind,
Ten thousand glorious systems would he build,
Ten thousand great ideas fill'd his mind;
But with the clouds they fled, and left no trace behind."

This has been supposed to be Paterson, solely on the
ground that the author declares, as we have seen, that
he has given him a place in the poem. There has been,
however, a natural disposition to find in this interesting

and rather elaborate appreciation, a description of some
one who proved himself to have true poetical genius,
and the name of Collins has been suggested.   It is true
that Thomson had been acquainted with Collins during
the year preceding the publication of *The Castle of
Indolence* ; but there is no indication that they became
intimate friends, and the description, in fact, does not
altogether apply to Collins.   It is expressly stated
that the talents of the poet in question were completely
buried :—

> " Of the fine stores he nothing would impart,
>   Which or boon Nature gave, or nature-painting Art."

Now the case of Collins was different.   He was only
twenty-six years old when *The Castle of Indolence* was
published, and he had already produced his *Persian
Eclogues*, his *Epistle to Sir T. Hanmer*, and his *Odes*, in
fact nearly the whole of his poetical work.   The
depression of spirits which put an end to his literary
activity came on later.

The silent companion of this first-mentioned inmate
may be Armstrong, but there is not much evidence,
except the expression "stung by spleen," compared
with the remark in Thomson's letter to Paterson :
"Though the Doctor increases in business, he does not
decrease in spleen."   The description is as follows :—

> " With him was sometimes join'd in silent walk
>   (Profoundly silent, for they never spoke)
>   One shyer still, who quite detested talk.
>   Oft, stung by spleen, at once away he broke
>   To groves of pine and broad o'ershadowing oak ;
>   There, inly thrill'd, he wander'd all alone,
>   And on himself his pensive fury wroke,
>   Nor ever utter'd word, save when first shone
> The glittering star of eve—'Thank Heaven ! the day is
>   done.'"

The "joyous youth," who for a time kept the castle "in a gay uproar,"

> "Turning the night to day and day to night,"

must be John Forbes, son of the Lord President Duncan Forbes of Culloden, who is mentioned in one of Thomson's letters as "the dearest, truest, heartiest youth that treads on Scottish ground." The description would not suit Hammond so well; and, moreover, Hammond, being dead, would probably have been referred to in a rather different tone.

The next character is that of Lyttelton, who is represented as an occasional visitor only, refusing to be detained long in the castle :—

> "Serene yet warm, humane yet firm his mind,
>   As little touch'd as any man's with bad :
>   Him through their inmost walks the Muses lad,
>   To him the sacred love of Nature lent,
>   And sometimes would he make our valley glad ;"

but care for the public good called him away, and when he departed, "the better sort" sent him a friendly message offering to rear for him a lodge in Hagley Park, when he should at last retire from his thankless labours to the study of nature and of books.

For a time too, Quin, "th' Esopus of the age," dwelt here, until

> "A noble pride restor'd him to the stage,
>   And rous'd him like a giant from his sleep" ;

the fact being that Quin had for a time been almost driven off the stage by the success of his younger rival, Garrick.

After a stanza, describing the author himself, with a first line written by Thomson,—

> "A bard here dwelt, more fat than bard beseems,"

and the rest contributed by a friend, we come finally
to Murdoch :—

> " Full oft by holy feet our ground was trod ;
>   Of clerks good plenty here you mote espy.
>   A little, round, fat, oily man of God,
>   Was one I chiefly mark'd among the fry :
>   He had a roguish twinkle in his eye,
>   And shone all glittering with ungodly dew,
>   If a tight damsel chaunc'd to trippen by ;
>   Which when observ'd, he shrunk into his mew,
>   And straight would recollect his piety anew.' [1]

One company sat in the Hall of Smoke, and when
the sun-burnt Mocha had cleared their inward eye,
delivered oracles as mysterious as those of old.
Another consisted of ladies, whose only labour was
to kill the time, and for whom even a listless saunter
was too rude an exertion.

But though nothing was apparent except scenes of
repose and delight, the castle had its horrors, as some
of its inhabitants too late discovered. There was a
place " deep, dreary, under ground," into which were
privily thrown such of the inmates as had grown un-
pleasing from disease ; and there they languished far
from the light of heaven, and untended except by
" fierce fiends and hags of hell." The first canto concludes with four stanzas contributed by Armstrong,
which describe under the form of personification the

---

[1] Patrick Murdoch, called Peter by his friends, had come
up to London as tutor to young John Forbes. He took orders
in the Church of England, and became vicar successively of
several parishes in Suffolk, acting in an interval as tutor to the
son of Admiral Vernon. His memoir of Thomson was written
for the fine edition of his works which was published in 1762,
and is one of our most trustworthy authorities. Thomson
several times refers to him in his letters in terms somewhat
similar to those used in the descriptive stanza.

diseases to which indolence and intemperate indulgence give rise—Lethargy, Dropsy, Hypochondria,
Ague, Gout, and Apoplexy. The passage is vigorous
and realistic, but quite out of keeping with the rest of
the canto.

In the second canto the author has to sing of the
end of all these pleasures, and of the escape of himself
and some of his fellows from the fatal castle, though
with a regretful remembrance still of its delights. He
takes occasion to complain first that every other labour
has its appointed wage, but that of the poet has none,
and the laws do not give it their due protection,—

> "Ne for the Muses other meed decree,
> They praisèd are alone, and starve right merrily."

For himself, he claims in a noble stanza to be independent of fortune :—

> "I care not, Fortune, what you me deny :
> You cannot rob me of free Nature's grace ;
> You cannot shut the windows of the sky,
> Through which Aurora shows her brightening face ;
> You cannot bar my constant feet to trace
> The woods and lawns, by living stream, at eve :
> Let health my nerves and finer fibres brace,
> And I their toys to the great children leave :
> Of fancy, reason, virtue, nought can me bereave."

He proceeds then to tell us of the birth and education of one who was destined to bring to an end the
power of the dire enchanter. Selvaggio was his father,
who neither sowed nor reaped, but spent all his days
hunting in the forest, and Poverty his mother. He
was reared in the woods, and his name was The Knight
of Arts and Industry. His education was a happy
combination of outdoor exercise with the study of
arts and sciences ; and he joined practice to theory in
a remarkable manner, for he was by turns an agricul-

turist, an artisan, and a sailor, solacing his leisure at
the same time with painting, sculpture, music, and
poetry. He then went forth bent on civilising a bar-
barous world. Setting out from the East he proceeded
to put down rapine and fraud everywhere and to
establish arts and virtue. He passed successively
through Egypt, Greece, and Rome, and at last came
to Britain, where the natives led a sylvan life,

> " In the brown shades and green-wood forest lost,
>   All careless, rambling where it lik'd them most."

With this land he was especially taken :—

> " He lik'd the soil, he liked the clement skies,
> He lik'd the verdant hills and flowery plains.
> ' Be this my great, my chosen isle ! (he cries)
> This—whilst my labours liberty sustains—
> This queen of ocean all assault disdains.'
> Nor lik'd he less the genius of the land,
> To freedom apt and persevering pains,
> Mild to obey, and generous to command,
> Temper'd by forming Heaven with kindest firmest hand."

In this isle he erected his master-work : he
quickened its towns by mechanic arts, extended its
commerce to every clime, and

> " Bade tyrants tremble on remotest shores,
> While o'er th' encircling deep Britannia's thunder roars."

The Muses which he brought from the East he established upon the Isis and the Cam, but he left literature
and the fine arts in an unfinished state, and poets had
no satisfactory livelihood assured to them.

When the knight had framed a model government
in this favoured land, he retired from the scene of his
labours to a farm in Deva's vale,

> " Where his long alleys peep'd upon the main,"

and here he lived in peace and joy like a patriarch of old, superintending his flocks and his harvests, and improving his estate :—

> " Witness, ye lowing herds, who lent him milk ;
> Witness, ye flocks, whose woolly vestments far
> Exceed soft India's cotton, or her silk ;
> Witness, with Autumn charg'd, the nodding car,
> That homeward came beneath sweet evening's star,
> Or of September-moons the radiance mild."

But meanwhile the influence of the soul-enfeebling wizard Indolence had spread far and wide, the sense of public virtue was dulled, and the vices of luxury extended themselves everywhere. These tidings reached the quiet hall where the knight lived retired, and there was a general cry to him for help. He called his page, ordered his horse, his bard, and "the net of fate" to be brought to him. The bard was Philomelus, a Druid of withered aspect :—

> " In russet brown bedight,
> As is his sister of the copses green,
> He crept along, unpromising of mien.
> Gross he who judges so. His soul was fair,
> Bright as the children of yon azure sheen ! "

They went forth together, the knight on a bay horse with a white star on his forehead, and the bard on a milk-white palfrey, "an honest sober beast, that did not mar His meditations." On the way they talked of virtue and human happiness, till at length the fatal valley dawned upon their view, at the sight of which Philomelus was inclined to say that those frail good men who had been deluded to live here, ought to be forgiven. The knight agrees that mercy shall be extended to such as repent, but penance must be inflicted on the rest.

They find the wizard at his usual occupation, and he

eyes them with some anxiety, but makes room for them
and resumes his song :—

> " With magic dust their eyne he tries to blind,
>   And virtue's tender airs o'er weakness flings.
> What pity base his song who so divinely sings ! "

The charmed crowd press in towards the gate, and
the wizard endeavours to lay hands on the knight, who
starts back, and then with the skill of a retiarius in
the amphitheatre throws the net over his head and
involves him hopelessly.

The inferior demons of the place raise hideous yells ;
a wailing "As of infernal sprights in cavern bound" is
heard from beneath ; lightnings flash, and crowds pour
out in alarm from the castle. Sir Industry calls to
Philomelus, and bids him raise a strain which shall
touch the souls of those who are not altogether
poisoned by the enchantments; and the bard, taking
his harp, sings to the listening throng a hymn in praise
of activity and industry, which corresponds to that of
the wizard in praise of indolence. All Nature, he
sings, bears witness to the effect of a never-resting
activity of Almighty Power, and a regular gradation
produced by this activity from lower to higher forms
of existence.

> " Up from unfeeling mould
> To seraphs burning round the Almighty's throne,
> Life rising still on life, in higher tone,
> Perfection forms, and with perfection bliss."

All human progress has been obtained by exertion,
and without this no art or literature could have existed, and all records of virtue would have been lost.
If pleasure be the object, then we must learn that no
true pleasure is to be enjoyed without action : the
toiling husbandman has keener enjoyments of his
simple fare than the slothful man or the glutton can

experience in their self-indulgence. Nothing avails if
health and spirits go amiss, and exercise is the vital
principle of health. The sluggard is swallowed up in
the sad abyss of disease, while he who has been braced
by toil or exercise has his limbs light and his thoughts
clear :—

> "Oh, who can speak the vigorous joys of health !
>   Unclogg'd the body, unobscur'd the mind :
>   The morning rises gay, with pleasing stealth,
>   The temperate evening falls serene and kind.
>   In health the wiser brutes true gladness find :
>   See, how the younglings frisk along the meads,
>   As May comes on, and wakes the balmy wind ;
>   Rampant with life, their joy all joy exceeds :
> Yet what save high-strung health this dancing pleas-
>   aunce breeds ?"

Here, on the other hand, every ill is fostered which
the distempered mind or body knows. Come, therefore,
the bard exclaims, and follow this good knight, who
will direct you to the places where you may exercise
your abilities. Some who listen to my lay sigh for
virtue, but despair of attainment, and therefore they
cannot get free from the grasp of sloth. Resolve to be
men, control desire, and let reason speak from her
sovereign throne the commanding words "*I will*":—

> "Heirs of eternity, yborn to rise
>   Through endless states of being, still more near
>   To bliss approaching and perfection clear ;
>   Can you renounce a fortune so sublime,
>   Such glorious hopes, your backward steps to steer,
>   And roll, with vilest brutes, thro' mud and slime ?"

The better sort listen to those exhortations and
separate themselves from the more ignoble :—

> "As when, amid the lifeless summits proud
>   Of Alpine cliffs, where, to the gelid sky,
>   Snows pil'd on snows in wintry torpor lie,
>   The rays divine of vernal Phœbus play,

Th' awaken'd heaps, in streamlets from on high,
  Rous'd into action, lively leap away,
Glad-warbling through the vales, in their new being gay."

But the greater number are moved with rage, and
mutter dire curses on those who have destroyed their
peaceful seat; upon which the knight waves a wand
which has power to destroy the illusions of magic
falsehood, and the landscape suddenly changes to a
foul wilderness, the streams become marshy puddles,
the trees are blackened, and adders and toads crawl
over the ground. Here and there are the bodies of
suicides, hanging from lightning-blasted trees or wel-
tering in their blood upon the ground, or else rolled
down by a gloomy torrent.

There was a moving scene when the lazar-house displayed its horrors, and the wretches who had lain
there, tossing in misery, once more saw the light of
day. The knight urged them to purify their souls by
patient endurance of suffering, and to learn wisdom by
past misconduct. Meanwhile he sent to their assistance the Charities, a glorious angel-train, who attended
them day and night with tender ministry. The knight,
followed by a company of those whom he had rescued,
returned to his hall again, not without some tears of
pity for the wretches who remained impenitent, pur-
sued over a joyless expanse of wastes and bogs by
cruel fiends,—

"Gaunt Beggary and Scorn, with many hell-hounds moe."

Just so a herd of swine is driven "through Brentford
town, a town of mud," grunting and squeaking and
plunging into the mire :—

"But aye the ruthless driver goads them on,
  And aye of barking dogs the bitter throng
  Makes them renew their unmelodious moan,
Ne ever find they rest from their unresting fone.'

It will readily be gathered from this analysis of the poem that the first canto is greatly superior to the second. The prominence of the moral element in the second canto is injurious to the poetical effect, and though we cannot doubt that the author was sincere in his appreciation of the blessings conferred by industry, we feel nevertheless that the delights of indolence appealed more seductively to his temperament, and that the exclamation of regret,

"Ah ! where shall I so sweet a dwelling find ? "

expressed his own feelings better than the exhortations which he has put in the mouth of his bard. The first canto is admirable in its description of the castle and its surroundings, and especially perhaps in the song of the wizard Indolence : there is little in this part of the poem to find fault with except the conclusion. The description of the lazar-house, however, ought certainly to have been reserved for a later stage. It might well have come in as a climax to the bard's persuasions. The somewhat similar discovery in the first book of the *Faerie Queene* leads at once to the departure of the Red-Cross Knight from the House of Pride ; but here the life of the inmates of the Castle does not seem to be affected.

In the second canto the account of the education and pursuits of the Knight of Industry is a mere accumulation of incongruous activities ; his passage through Egypt, Greece, and Rome to Britain is a repetition of a theme of which we have already had too much in *Liberty*, and the patriotic enthusiasm, winding up with "Britannia's thunder," is here out of place. The scene of the capture of the wizard in the net of fate is absurdly managed, and though the bard's hymn in praise of industry has some merit, it must be admitted that it is rather tiresome on the whole. Add finally that the grotesque simile of the pigs driven through Brentford, with which the poem concludes, strikes altogether a wrong note at the conclusion of a serious piece of work.

The faults of the plan are grave, but the merits of the execution are considerable, as will have already appeared from the quotations given. The adoption of the Spenserian stanza was not a novelty: on the contrary, as is observed in the Advertisement prefixed to the poem by the author, this form, and a certain flavour of archaism which went together with it, were regarded as proper for all allegorical poems in English; and in fact the stanza had been used in the eighteenth century by a considerable number of persons before Thomson. We are told by his biographer that he was not averse to rhyme in general, but only to the rhymed couplet, which, as it seemed to him, unduly fettered the expression of the poet; whereas in the Spenserian stanza it was possible to secure a sufficient space for the expression of the thought or image, and to combine the advantage of rhyme with a harmonious variety. This particular form of verse was, in fact, peculiarly suited to Thomson's genius, which needed space, but was apt to expand into diffuseness when left to the freedom of blank verse; and he has employed it on the whole with admirable effect. In particular, we may remark the rhythmical beauty in many instances of the concluding alexandrine, though the rhythm is not quite that of Spenser, and in particular Thomson uses very sparingly the Spenserian liberty of cæsura. In many of these lines it will be noted that the melody is connected with an actual representation of sounds; and this is, in fact, one of the features of *The Castle of Indolence*. The metrical effects generally are managed

with a delicacy which perhaps we should hardly have
expected from the author of *The Seasons*.

In this matter he has learnt something from
Spenser; but his imitation of Spenser is not slavish,
and he does not often allow it to degenerate into
mannerism. For the most part he does not reproduce
the faults and artifices of Spenser's style, and he avoids
in particular the euphuistic balance and antithesis,
such as,

"My chearefull day is turn'd to cheareless night,"
or
"Whose need had end, but no end coveitise,
Whose welth was want, whose plenty made him pore."

Alliteration is used by Thomson far less frequently
and obviously than by Spenser, but it is often very
effectively employed to produce subtle effects of
rhythm. The archaisms are very slight and occasional, and many passages of considerable length are
without them altogether. The forms used are not
much more incorrect than those of Spenser.[1] The
most serious fault in connection with the imitation of
Spenser is the introduction of the grotesque element.
It was inevitable, perhaps, that this should come in,
being supposed in the eighteenth century to be a leading characteristic of Spenser's style, and there is not,
in fact, very much of it in *The Castle of Indolence*; but
the detached simile at the conclusion is an unfortu-
nately prominent example.

The style is, naturally, very different from that of
The Seasons, the diction and form of expression being
here comparatively simple. The more violent Latinisms
which are characteristic of the vocabulary of *The Seasons*

[1] In a few places Thomson has made mistakes of his own.
He uses "depeinten" twice as a past participle, and says "I
passen by" and "he casten forth"; also "ligged" for "lay."

are almost entirely absent; "detrude," "turgent,"
"effusive," and the rest are banished; the favourite
"amusive" is replaced here by "amusing." Examples
of the use of adjectives as adverbs, instead of being
obvious on every page, are here only occasionally
found, but still they occur ; *e.g.* :—

> "That drowsy rustled to the sighing gale,"

> "O'er which were shadowy cast Elysian gleams."

> "Then Egypt, Greece and Rome their golden times
>   Successive had."

Compound verbs and adjectives also are less common
than in *The Seasons*, and for the most part judiciously
formed. Examples are afforded by the expressions :
"sleep-soothing groves," "soft-embodied fays," "what-
e'er Lorrain light-touched," "angel-seeming sprights,"
"O leaden-hearted men," "Dire-mutter'd curses." The
naming of common things by periphrasis is not found
here, and such stilted affectations as we have in the
line,

> "But how shall I attempt such arduous string ?"

occur very seldom. Awkward inversions, however, are
still too frequent :—

> "And his alluring baits suspected han."

> "At doors and windows threatening seem'd to call
>   The demons of the tempest,"

> "That whirl of active day the rapid car,"

and there is one intolerable mixture of stiffness with
vulgar colloquialism,—

> "So that to think you dreamt, you almost was constrain'd,"

a line which is immediately followed, it is curious to
remark, by what is perhaps the most beautiful and
poetical stanza in the whole poem.

Finally, among features of style we may note a rather graceful and original form of expression, which is found also in *The Seasons*, but here with especial frequency, namely the variation of such phrases as "from day to day," "hill o'er hill," by the introduction of an epithet, so that we have "with woody hill o'er hill encompass'd round," "Imbitter'd more from peevish day to day," "And pastur'd on from verdant stage to stage." From *The Seasons* we may quote as examples of this, *Summer*, 603, "And falling fast from gradual slope to slope," and 761, "From jasmine grove to grove."

When *The Castle of Indolence* was first published in 1748, Gray remarked in a letter to a friend: "There is a poem by Thomson, 'The Castle of Indolence,' with some good stanzas." The praise is too faint, but it is true, nevertheless, that the poem is more to be admired in particular passages than for the effect of the whole. It has therefore been appreciated rather by those who are good judges of exquisite workmanship, than by the reader who is impressed only by broad general effects; and it was as appropriate that Wordsworth should have a pocket copy of *The Castle of Indolence*, as that *The Seasons* should be found by Coleridge lying well thumbed (and no doubt "slightly torn") in the window of the inn parlour.

CHAPTER VIII

THE DRAMAS

IT is not necessary to say very much about Thomson's dramatic works. The serious drama in England was at a very low ebb during the second quarter of the eighteenth century; and though it would be true to say that Thomson's tragedies are among the best things of the kind that were written in that period, this, after all, is not very high praise. Hardly a single one of the other authors who produced tragedies in the years between 1725 and 1750 is known by name to posterity; Frowde, Lewis, Brooke, Sturmy, Martyn, Tracy, Jeffreys, Hewitt are altogether obscure, and even the more celebrated authors, Lillo, Aaron Hill, and Mallet, are no very great lights. The most successful form of tragedy was the domestic kind, represented by Lillo's *George Barnwell* and *Fatal Curiosity* (the former in prose and the latter in verse), which were genuinely popular and frequently repeated; of the rest, to judge by the number of representations, the most successful were Mallet's *Eurydice* and *Mustapha*, Hill's *Zara*, from Voltaire, and Martyn's *Timoleon*. Of Thomson's it may be said that they achieved a decent success upon the stage, which owed something to the zeal of his friends, and much to the excellence of the acting. They are not dramatically interesting, but the style is respectable, in spite of occasional lapses, and the blank verse is fairly good. On the whole,

Johnson's criticism is sound, that "his diffusive and descriptive style produced declamation rather than dialogue."

Classical subjects were decidedly fashionable at the time when Thomson first turned his attention to the stage. *The Fall of Saguntum, Philip of Macedon, Themistocles, Timoleon, Medea, Eurydice, Periander, Philotas, Merope, Orestes,*—this is a list which includes the titles of more than half the total number of tragedies acted in the four years 1727 to 1731. Thomson chose the story of Sophonisba, which, as the prologue reminds us, had been the subject of the earliest Italian regular tragedy :—

> "When learning, after the long Gothic night,
>   Fair o'er the western world renew'd its light,
>   With arts arising Sophonisba rose ;
>   The tragic muse returning wept her woes.
>   With her th' Italian scene first learn'd to glow,
>   And the first tears for her were taught to flow."

The reference is to the *Sofonisba* of Trissino, produced about 1514. Then allusion is made to the French dramas on the same subject :—

> "Her charms the Gallic muses next inspir'd,
>   Corneille himself saw, wonder'd, and was fir'd."

There were, in fact, no fewer than four adaptations of Trissino's tragedy to the French stage before the end of the sixteenth century, and then came Mairet's *Sophonisbe* in 1629, and Corneille's in 1663. No mention is made in this prologue either of Marston or of Lee. The author of the prologue, which is said to be "by a friend,"[1] proceeds to claim the subject as especially

---

[1] Johnson reports a statement by Savage that the first part was written by Pope, who could not be persuaded to finish it, and that the concluding lines were added by Mallet.

appropriate to the British stage, because the theme is
Freedom, and he makes an appeal on behalf of "our
home-spun author" on account of his "British heart":—

> "Not to his patient touch or happy flame,
> 'Tis to his British heart he trusts for fame.
> If France excel him in one free-born thought,
> The man, as well as poet, is in fault."

The drama is constructed in accordance with the
rules of the French classical stage, notwithstanding the
expression in the prologue, "He owns their learning,
but disdains their laws"; and the author is entitled to
the praise, which he claims in the preface to the printed
edition, of unity and simplicity of design.   Corneille
had injudiciously complicated his plot by the addition
of a rival to Sophonisba for the hand of Masinissa, in
order to introduce the motive of jealousy; but Thomson has been more careful to follow the truth of
history.   Indeed, so far as construction is concerned,
Thomson's play deserves praise; the fault is that it
does not sufficiently interest us in the characters.   We
cannot much sympathise with his Masinissa, who
indulges in offensive pity for his prisoner, and utters
moral sentiments intended to indicate how far superior
he is in virtue and in self-control :—

> "Thy lost condition, Syphax,
> Is nothing to the tumult of thy breast.
> There lies the sting of evil, there the drop
> That poisons nature.—Ye mysterious powers !
> Whose ways are ever-gracious, ever-just,
> As ye think wisest, best, dispose of me :
> But whether thro' your gloomy depths I wander,
> Or on your mountains walk, give me the calm,
> The steady smiling soul, where wisdom sheds
> Eternal sunshine and eternal peace.
> Then, if Misfortune comes, she brings along
> The bravest virtues."

This kind of thing would do very well in *The Seasons*, but here it is quite out of place; and we cannot wonder at the exasperation of Syphax.

Again, we hardly know what to make of the heroine in this play. She professes to do all for the sake of her country :—

> "Bear witness, Heaven,
> This is alone for Carthage."

Yet we hear of her early passion for Masinissa, and she addresses him as

> "The same bright youth, exalted, full of soul,
> With whom in happier days I us'd to pass
> The tender hour; while dawning fair in love,
> All song and sweetness, life set joyous out;
> Ere the black tempest of ambition rose,
> And drove us different ways."

We can hardly accept her assurance that there is nothing but policy in her thoughts. Corneille says, "Je lui prête un peu d'amour, mais elle règne sur lui et ne daigne l'écouter, qu'autant qu'il peut servir a ces passions dominantes qui règnent sur elle," and we may add that the love shows itself mainly in the form of jealousy of a rival, a passion more easy to reconcile with the rest of the character than the more tender emotion; she does indeed recall the "doux lien" of her youthful days, but we do not feel that it has much hold upon her. In Corneille's Sophonisba we see mainly the politician, as in Lee's we see the devoted and passionate lover; but in Thomson's we are not quite sure how the heroine stands. On the other hand, the dramatist has traced with some skill Masinissa's inevitable lapse from heroic resolution,—

> "But never dread
> The firmness of my heart, the strong attachment
> I hold to Rome, to Scipio, and to glory,"

to wavering,

> " Oh Sophonisba ! 'tis not safe to hear thee ;
>   And I mistook my heart, to trust it thus,"

with momentary recovery,

> " The danger's o'er, I 've heard the Syren's song,
>   Yet still to virtue hold my steady course " ;

but finally an absolute surrender of his position :—

> " Quick, let me fly to her, and there forget
>   This tedious absence, war, ambition, noise,
>   Friendship itself, the vanity of fame,
>   And all but love, for love is more than all ! "

And the reflections, suggested by the impatience of
Syphax,—

> " What dreadful havoc in the human breast
>   The passions make," etc.,

have a certain effectiveness in connection with what
follows.

There is no great excess of rhetorical declamation,
except perhaps in the first scene between Masinissa
and Narva, where the anecdote of Scipio's self-control
tends to fall rather flat, and has to be supported by
some vigorous admiration ; but several passages will
bear quotation :—of young love,

> " when fancy still
> Found worlds of beauty, ever rising new
> To the transported eye : when flattering hope
> Form'd endless prospects of increasing bliss ;
> And still the credulous heart believ'd them all,
> Even more than love could promise " :

of passion triumphant,

> " No more, no more ! if this is being lost,
>   And rushing down the precipice of fate ;
>   Then down I go, far far beyond the reach
>   Of scrupulous dull precaution."

The opening of the fifth act is both poetical and appropriate :—

> " Hail to the joyous day ! with purple clouds
> The whole horizon glows.   The breezy Spring
> Stands loosely floating on the mountain-top
> And deals her sweets around."

The passage was apparently objected to as too picturesque, when the tragedy was read to the actors, but it admirably expresses the exaltation of Masinissa's feelings on the day which love and friendship have marked for him (as he thinks) with all their choicest blessings, and it has a strongly ironical significance.   Scipio's rebuke is delicately managed :—

> " But has my friend, since late we parted armies,
> Since he with Lælius acted such a brave,
> Auspicious part against the common foe,
> Has he been blameless quite ?   Has he consider'd
> How pleasure often on the youthful heart,
> Beneath the rosy soft disguise of love,
> (All sweetness, smiles, and seeming innocence),
> Steals unperceiv'd and lays the victor low ?
>
>   .   .   .   .
>
> . . . Thy silence, that dejected look,
> That honest colour flushing o'er thy cheek,
> Impart thy better soul."

There are several echoes from Corneille, as for example the remark of Lælius :—

> " She had a Roman soul ; for every one
> Who loves like her his country is a Roman."

with which compare,

> " en dépit de sa haine,
> Une telle fierté devoit naître romaine."

To Lee's play Thomson has no obligations, unless the exclamation, " O Sophonisba, oh ! " suggested the unfortunate line which every one knows.

Sophonisba, when published, was dedicated to the Queen, who was addressed as "one who commands the hearts of a people more powerful at sea than Carthage, more flourishing in commerce than those first merchants," and so on. The author's next theatrical venture, *Agamemnon*, came eight years later, when Thomson had been fairly captured by the Opposition, and is full of party clap-traps; but of the political references in this and the succeeding dramas we have already spoken sufficiently. *Agamemnon* is not a good play, as it stands at present; and apparently it was much worse when it was first produced. The death of Agamemnon originally came in the fourth act; and the fifth dragged so intolerably, that the play would have been damned, if desperate remedies had not been applied. But there are worse faults than this, which were irremediable. The character of Clytemnestra has been weakened and vulgarised, so as to be almost beyond recognition. She is merely a woman who has been seduced in her husband's absence by a lover; and when threatened by the prospect of his return, vainly tries to persuade the lover to carry her off to a place of safety :—

> "Excuse my weaker heart.   But how, Egisthus,
> How shall I bear an injur'd husband's eye ?
> The fiercest foe wears not a look so dreadful,
> As does the man we wrong."

And when the lover hints that the wrong-doing is on the side of the husband, and that she may now take vengeance, she can only exclaim :—

> "What vengeance ? say.   Touch not so wild a string :
> It wakes new discord in my jarring soul ;
> To the just gods, not us, pertaineth vengeance.

> Oh make me not beyond recovery vile,
> A horror to myself! How wretched they,
> Who feel, yet cannot save, their dying virtue ! "

And after the deed is done :—

> " Yes, traitor, turn away :
> But ere you go, give me my peace again ;
> Give me my happy family around ;
> Give me my virtue, honour," etc.

Any one has a right, if he pleases, to put a character of this kind into a play, but he has no right to call it Clytemnestra.   And yet Thomson had read Æschylus. Joseph Warton, who was a scholar, says : "Thomson was well acquainted with the Greek tragedies, on which I heard him talk learnedly when I was introduced to him by my friend Mr. W. Collins." It is difficult to imagine how he can have accepted such a perversion of the character.

In the invention of Melisander Thomson has made a justifiable and effective addition to the plot, founded upon the account given of the proceedings of Ægisthus by Nestor in the *Odyssey*. From Homer we learn that Agamemnon left a minstrel to take charge of Clytemnestra in his absence, and that this man was carried off and left on a desert island by Ægisthus. Thomson has added the incident of his being finally rescued by the returning ships of Agamemnon. The lines in which Melisander describes the departure of those who had landed him on the island, have often been praised as genuinely pathetic :—

> " Yet believe me, Arcas,
> Such is the rooted love we bear mankind,
> All ruffians as they were, I never heard
> A sound so dismal as their parting oars."

And his account of his solitary life upon the island has

some poetical merit, though it is not very necessary to the drama.

As regards the general style of the play, it may be remarked that the verse is fairly good, and the expression is often poetical, but there are a good many slovenly vulgarisms of style, such as, "Was you not left?" "How more than usual mild!" and so on.

The most noteworthy thing about *Edward and Eleonora*, 1739, is perhaps the fact that it was prohibited under the new Licensing Act, and that the author's friends professed to be unable to discover the reason. Apart from politics, the play is rather wanting in interest. There is no dramatic development. Edward at the siege of Jaffa is wounded with a poisoned weapon by an enemy sent by Selim, the Sultan. Daraxa, an Arabian princess, beloved by Selim, who is a prisoner in the English camp and attendant upon Eleonora, suggests as the only remedy that some one should suck the poison from the wound. Eleonora is eager to do this; but Edward, hearing that it would be fatal to her, will not allow it. She finds an opportunity, however, while he sleeps; and he recovers accordingly, but is struck with the deepest grief when he learns at what price his life has been saved. Eleonora lies dying, and Daraxa sends a message bitterly reproaching Selim for his supposed treachery. He appears in the camp, disguised as a dervise, and by means of an antidote restores Eleonora, after she has been already given up as dead. He then explains that the envoy acted without authority; and finally he makes himself known to Edward and receives his beloved Daraxa from the hands of the restored Eleonora. In the meantime despatches have arrived from England, announcing the death of Henry III.; and the crusade, about which Edward already had grave doubts, is abandoned. It

will be seen that the drama is not a tragedy in its
catastrophe. Some of the scenes are imitated from
the *Alcestis* of Euripides, as has been observed by
Lessing and others; and especially the description
given by Daraxa of Eleonora's farewell to her household, and the scene in which she is herself borne out
into the open air and salutes the sun and the earth :—

> " *El.*   A little on, a little further on,
>   Bear me my friends, into the cooling air.
>   O cheerful sun !   O vital light of day !
> *Ed.*   That sun is witness of our matchless woes,
>   Is witness of our innocence.   Alas !
>   What have we done to merit this disaster ?
> *El.*   O earth !   O genial roofs !   O the dear coast
>   Of Albion's isle, which I no more shall see !
> *Ed.*   Nay, yield not to thy weakness, Eleonora !
>   Sustain thyself a little, nor desert me !
>   Th' all-ruling Goodness may relieve us still."

And so on throughout the scene, which undoubtedly
has a certain degree of pathos.

Alfred, a Masque, by Thomson and Mallet, was performed before the Prince and Princess of Wales at
Clifden in August 1740, and had no need of a licence ;
but in fact it contains nothing offensive. The per-
formers, among them Quin, were mostly from Drury
Lane, but Mrs. Horton, from Covent Garden, who had
been cast for the part of Eleonora in Thomson's last
play, appeared as Eltruda. *Alfred* is called a masque,
and it has no dramatic action. The principal character
is the Hermit, who encourages Alfred with visions of
the future greatness of his descendants, and pro-
phesies the glory of Britain. The authorship of the
song " Rule Britannia," has already been discussed.

Alfred was acted at Drury Lane, March 20th, 1745,
for the benefit of Mrs. Arne, wife of the composer. It

was afterwards rewritten by Mallet, and produced at
great expense, with Garrick as Alfred, in 1751.

Thomson's next venture on the public stage was
not till 1745, when *Tancred and Sigismunda* appeared.
It was based on the story of the Fatal Marriage,
related by Donna Elvira in *Gil Blas*, and the complica-
tions of the plot make it more interesting than most
of Thomson's plays.

Tancred, a descendant of the old line of Norman
kings of Sicily, and the next successor to the throne,
to secure his safety has been brought up by Siffredi,
Chancellor of the kingdom, in ignorance of his true
position. The king of Sicily dies, and Siffredi reveals
to Tancred the secret of his birth, urging him at the
same time to marry Constantia, the late king's sister,
who is popularly supposed to be the heir to the crown,
in order that the opposing claims may be united, and
the danger of civil war avoided. Tancred loves and
is beloved by Sigismunda, the daughter of Siffredi,
and utterly refuses the marriage with Constantia. He
professes his resolution to marry Sigismunda, and
gives her a blank paper signed by himself, to be filled
in with the marriage contract. This her father takes
from her, and fills it in with a contract of marriage to
Constantia, having first ascertained that the late king's
will has, in accordance with his advice, made this
marriage a condition of Tancred's succession. At the
same time, to make things more secure, he promises
his daughter's hand to Osmond, the High Constable, a
partisan of Constantia's claim. Siffredi produces before the assembled Senate, in presence of Tancred
himself and Constantia, both the late king's will and the
pretended marriage-contract, signed by Tancred, which
is received with universal acclamation. Tancred,
amazed and indignant, has not the presence of mind

to disown the contract at once, but vents his rage
upon Siffredi in private, and demands that he shall
disavow his action, which, in the interests of the
kingdom, he refuses to do. Meanwhile Sigismunda,
convinced that Tancred has played her false, accepts
the proposal of Osmond at the command of her father,
and is at once married to him. Immediately afterwards she receives a letter from Tancred, explaining
his position, and vowing eternal fidelity to her. In
an interview with Sigismunda he learns what has
happened, and orders the arrest of Osmond. The
latter escapes from confinement by the connivance of
the commandant of the castle, and after an interview with Siffredi, who fails to satisfy him, breaks
in upon a meeting between Tancred and Sigismunda
in her apartment, in which Tancred has vainly
endeavoured to persuade her to renounce her marriage. Osmond draws upon Tancred and is mortally
wounded: Sigismunda throws herself down by his
side and protests her fidelity; but he shortens his
sword and plunges it into her heart. Sigismunda
dies in the arms of Tancred, entreating him to live
and make his people happy, and he is prevented by
his friends from stabbing himself. Siffredi bitterly
reproaches himself for having attempted to command
by rude force passions which should have been more
gently ruled, and utters a warning against doing evil
that good may come.

There are some interesting moments in this tragedy;
and Tancred acts a very natural part, the moment of
weakness, which brings about the catastrophe, being
intelligible if we consider all the circumstances. This
is better managed than in the original story,
which attributes to the hero a duplicity that is foreign
to his character. Siffredi is a good example of one

who acts for the best, sacrificing his own private interests to what he conceives to be the good of the state, while at the same time he is wrecking the happiness of his daughter and of Tancred. His exhortation to Tancred, before revealing the secret of his birth, is characteristic of the author of *The Castle of Indolence* :—

> " Ah, my Tancred,
> Nothing so easy as in speculation,
> And at a distance seen, the course of honour,
> A fair delightful champain strew'd with flowers.
> But when the practice comes, when our fond passions,
> Pleasure and pride and self-indulgence, throw
> Their magic dust around, the prospect roughens ;
> Then dreadful passes, craggy mountains rise,
> Cliffs to be scal'd and torrents to be stemm'd :
> Then toil ensues and perseverance stern,
> And endless combats with our grosser sense,
> Oft lost and oft renew'd."

Tancred and Sigismunda has frequently been reprinted, and more than once revived on the stage.

The last of the dramas, *Coriolanus*, was produced at Covent Garden in January 1749, after the death of the author, and partly for the benefit of his sisters.

The play is independent of Shakespeare, and follows Dionysius of Halicarnassus rather than Plutarch. For example, the mother of Coriolanus is called Veturia, and his wife Volumnia. The character of Coriolanus, on which the tragedy depends in Shakespeare, is here of no great significance. He is indeed proud and self-willed ; but the characteristic arrogance is so far abated, that he can be described as "with every virtue Of civil life adorn'd." There is no excuse for the ingratitude of his countrymen ; and so good a case has he against them, that he seizes every opportunity of setting it forth, and considerably prefers rhetoric to action.

Hence, instead of refusing to receive embassies from
Rome, he arranges elaborate scenes for the benefit of
the Volscians, in which he triumphantly refutes the
arguments of Minucius and Cominius :—

> "Absurd !   What can you mean ?   To call a people,
>   Who with the last indignity have us'd me,
>   To call my foes my country !   No, Minucius," etc.

In the scene where Coriolanus is entreated by his
mother and his wife to spare his country, he is finally
prevailed upon by his mother's threat to kill herself
in his presence with a dagger which she has brought
under her robe for the purpose. A feature in the
play, which cannot be regarded as a happy invention,
is the introduction of one Galesus, a Volscian infected
with Pythagorean notions, who preaches peace and
moderation, in season and out of season, uttering
sentiments which are excellent in themselves, but much
out of place in a camp, *e.g.* :—

> "I glory, Tullus,
> To own myself an advocate for peace.
> Peace is the happy, natural state of man,
> War his corruption, his disgrace. . . .
> Why should we purchase with the blood of thousands,
> What may be gain'd by mutual just concession ?
> Why give up peace, the best of human blessings,
> For the vain cruel pride of useless conquest ?"

To which Tullus replies with some reason :—

> "These soothing dreams of philosophic quiet
> Are only fit for unfrequented shades."

The play on the whole must be regarded as a weak
one, and such success as it had, was due to the attendant circumstances, rather than to its merit. Miss
Woffington, who had "painted her beautiful face with
wrinkles" to act Veturia, appeared with her own

natural complexion to speak the epilogue. This, for which Thomson was not responsible, was in the usual flippant style, against which the author had previously protested. It concluded, however, with an irresistible appeal to the audience :—

> " It is my sovereign will,—Hear and obey,—
> That you with candour treat this Orphan Play."

Let us endeavour to treat Thomson's plays generally with "candour," in the eighteenth-century sense of the word, remembering that the age was not very favourable to the serious drama ; and let us not forget that when his dramas were published within a few years of his death in a German translation, they had the good word of the greatest critic of the age. Lessing contributed a preface to the collection, and after expressing his pleasure in introducing these masterpieces to the public, he continued thus : "No age in any country has produced a more picturesque poet. . . . I hold him also to be one of the greatest in the sphere of tragedy. Thomson follows the rules, but he does much more." In short, remarks the critic, he has the magic art of truthful representation, which cannot be taught by the rules either of Aristotle or of Corneille.

Allowance must be made for Lessing's taste for things English, and for his natural predilection in favour of a dramatist who had endeavoured to follow the Greek rather than the French models : but the fact remains that Lessing once called these dramas masterpieces, and this of itself ought to assure us that they are not quite worthless.

CHAPTER IX

CONCLUSION

HARDLY any English eighteenth-century poet, who wrote after Thomson, was quite uninfluenced by him. The use of blank verse in narrative and descriptive poetry became a fashion. Mallet's *Excursion*, in 1728, Somerville's *Chase*, 1734, Glover's *Leonidas*, 1737, Young's *Night Thoughts*, 1742, Akenside's *Pleasures of the Imagination*, and Armstrong's *Art of Preserving Health*, both in 1744, all in a certain sense owe their form of verse to Thomson's bold initiative. So great was the vogue, that Goldsmith, in 1765, sets down blank verse, in company with party spirit, as one of the almost indispensable conditions of popularity : "What reception a poem may find which has neither abuse, party, nor blank verse to support it, I cannot tell, nor am I solicitous to know."

If we wish to appreciate the poetic quality of *The Seasons*, we cannot do better than to compare Thomson's work with that of his friend Mallet, a man of considerable literary talent, who was dealing with nearly the same themes at the same time. The style, diction, and verse are very similar, a fact to be accounted for partly by their constant communication with one another, and partly by direct imitation on Mallet's part of the poems which Thomson had already published. Mallet declares that description of "some of the most remarkable appearances of Nature " is the

only intention of his work, but its inferiority in natural
description to *The Seasons* is obvious on every page.
The author is always aiming at sensational effects,
either by representation of the abnormal occurrences of
the physical world, earthquakes and volcanic eruptions,
for example, or by the agency of ghosts and churchyard horrors, which he had successfully employed in
his ballad of *William and Margaret*. His super-
naturalism is very crude compared with Thomson's;
and when he describes a natural scene of a common
kind, he does not produce the same effect of artistic
harmony. The following is a favourable example :—

> " On this hoar Hill, that climbs above the Plain
> Half-way up Heaven ambitious, pleas'd we stand,
> Respiring purer Air, whose Gale ascends
> Full-fraught with Health, from Herbs and Flowers exhal'd.
> Above, the Round of Ether without Cloud,
> Boundless Expansion, all unruffled shines.
> Beneath, the far-stretch'd Landscape, Hill and Dale ;
> The Precipice abrupt ; the distant Main ;
> The nearer Forest in wide circuit spread,
> Solemn Recess and still ! whose mazy Walks
> Fair Truth and Wisdom love ; the bordering Lawn,
> With Flocks and Herds enrich'd ; the daisied Vale ;
> The River's Azure and the Meadow's Green,
> Grateful Diversity ! allure the Eye
> Abroad to rove amidst unnumber'd Charms."

This is pretty enough in detail, but it is not very well
combined, and the same is true of most of Mallet's
other descriptions.

Savage's *Wanderer*, published in 1729, though much
less like Thomson's work, and not written in blank
verse, affords at least as remarkable an instance of the
influence of Thomson ; for Savage, though, as Johnson
tells us, he lived for some time in close personal relation with Thomson, did not, properly speaking, belong

to his school, but rather to that of Pope. Such a
description as the following was unmistakably written
under the influence of Thomson, to whom the author
had already paid a tribute in his poem :—

> " South-west behind yon hill the sloping sun
>   To Ocean's verge his fluent course has run ;
>   His parting eyes a watery radiance shed,
>   Glance through the vale and tip the mountain's head ;
>   To which oppos'd the shadowy gulfs below
>   Beauteous reflect the parti-colour'd snow."

The influence which was exerted by Thomson on the
later poetry of the century was more indirect, but none
the less real. Thomson's view of Nature was mainly
objective, while that of the romantic school is personal.
This is the really essential distinction, and it is
analogous to the distinction between epic and lyric in
other fields of poetry. Thomson presents the natural
scene for its own sake, the romantic poet cares less for
the scene than for the emotions with which the scene
is harmonised. Thomson has something of the romantic
spirit, but this is not the dominant note of his poetry,
and where the external influence most strongly moves
his soul, the lyric expression to which it gives rise
more often has for its subject the power and wisdom
of God, than a purely self-centred emotion.

> " By swift degrees the love of Nature works,
>   And warms the bosom ; till at last, sublim'd
>   To rapture and enthusiastic heat,
>   We feel the present Deity, and taste
>   The joy of God to see a happy world."

> (*Spring*, 899 ff.)

Passages may, no doubt, be quoted, in which the
spirit is attuned to its surroundings in the romantic
sense of the expression ; *e.g. Summer*, 516 ff. :—

> " Still let me pierce into the midnight depth
>   Of yonder grove, of wildest, largest growth ;
>   That forming high in air a woodland quire,
>   Nods o'er the mount beneath.   At every step,
>   Solemn and slow, the shadows blacker fall,
>   And all is awful, listening gloom around.
>   These are the haunts of Meditation, etc."

So also the influences of Autumn, as represented by the
luxuriance of the harvest, are addressed in the prayer,—

> " Breathe your still song into the reaper's heart,
>   As home he goes beneath the joyous moon."

Or under another aspect they are personified for the
poet himself as the Power of Philosophic Melancholy
(*Autumn*, 988 ff.).   Yet the principle upon which these
varying moods depend is not so much the imaginative
faculty of the individual, as a certain divinely
appointed harmony in the universe ; and this is very
clearly expressed in a passage which originally
followed that which has been quoted above from
Spring, but was afterwards displaced to make more
convenient room for the tribute to Lyttelton :—

> " 'Tis Harmony, that world-attuning power,
>   By which all beings are adjusted, each
>   To all around, impelling and impell'd
>   In endless circulation, that inspires
>   This universal smile.   Thus the glad skies,
>   The wide-rejoicing earth, the woods, the streams,
>   With every life they hold, down to the flower
>   That paints the lovely vale, or insect-wing
>   Wav'd o'er the shepherd's slumber, touch the mind
>   To nature tun'd, with a light-flying hand
>   Invisible ; quick-urging thro' the nerves
>   The glittering spirits in a flood of day."

Mr. Robertson is quite right in saying that this
anticipates the teaching of Wordsworth, but it is not

by virtue of this teaching that Wordsworth is "romantic."

Thomson has no preference for the strange and wild in scenery, though he does not altogether exclude it, and he seems to have felt to some extent the fascination of remoteness, as is shown in some of his accounts of tropical rivers and forests, and in his references to the Hebrides and St. Kilda. Perhaps, however, the nearest approach which he makes to the "romantic" spirit is in his suggestions of the supernatural in connection with the intercourse of the living with the spirits of the dead, as in *Summer*, 538 ff. :—

> "Shook sudden from the bosom of the sky,
>   A thousand shapes or glide athwart the dusk,
>   Or stalk majestic on.
>
>   .   .   .   .   .   .
>
>   Here frequent at the visionary hour,
>   When musing midnight reigns, or silent noon,
>   Angelic harps are in full concert heard,
>   And voices chanting from the wood-crown'd hill,
>   The deepening dale, or inmost sylvan glade."

Or again, *Autumn*, 1033 ff.,

> "Where angel forms athwart the solemn dusk,
>   Tremendous sweep, or seem to sweep along ;
>   And voices more than human, thro' the void
>   Deep-sounding, seize th' enthusiastic ear."
>
> (*Autumn*, 1033 ff.)

Collins, no doubt, would willingly have acknowledged a large debt to Thomson, to whom he was also personally attached ; and Gray owed him more perhaps than he was aware of. There are several phrases in Gray's poems which testify to his familiarity with *The Seasons* : he has borrowed the "listening senates" of the *Elegy* from *Autumn*, 15, the epithet "many-twinkling," in the *Progress of Poesy*, from *Spring*, 158,

"The secrets of the abyss," from *Autumn*, 778; while
the line "Deep majestic, smooth and strong," seems to
have been suggested by *Autumn*, 122. The thoughts
expressed in *Spring*, 51 ff.,—

> "Nor ye who live
> In luxury and ease, in pomp and pride,
> Think these lost themes unworthy of your ear,"

and in *Winter*, 597-603, have been reproduced in the
Elegy. The lines of *Winter*, 311 ff.,—

> "In vain for him th' officious wife prepares
> The fire fair-blazing and the vestment warm ;
> In vain his little children, peeping out
> Into the mingling storm, demand their sire,"

must have been consciously or unconsciously in his
mind when he wrote the stanza :—

> "For them no more the blazing hearth shall burn,
>   Or busy housewife ply her evening care :
> No children run to lisp their sire's return,
>   Or climb his knees the envied kiss to share."

But it must be remembered that the treatment of
landscape by Gray and Collins is essentially different
from that which we find in Thomson. For him it is
primarily an object of æsthetic appreciation, with them
it is subordinate to the lyrical emotion. The same is
true of Burns, who nevertheless was a great admirer of
"Thomson's landscape glow," and who refers to him
frequently in his letters. Meanwhile we find in Cowper
something of a return to Thomson's manner ; but the
difference is noteworthy. Whatever may be the outward form of Cowper's poetry, it is essentially personal.
His view of Nature is not universal, like Thomson's,
but confined to the particular scenes and localities
with which he himself was familiar. His portrait-
painting of Nature is wonderfully delicate and true,

but is hardly the result of an enthusiastic devotion to
the object of his art. His religion was no natural
Deism, like Thomson's, and depended not upon his
view of Nature, but upon Christian revelation. He
feels that it is only the man whom truth has already
made free, who can dare to exult in the glories of
Creation. Nature serves chiefly to divert his thoughts
from morbid introspection, and so to rescue him from
despair. Everything, therefore, has a personal note,
though in some passages this is more or less concealed, and something like Thomson's objectivity
seems to be attained. There are, however, always
some important differences between their methods.
Cowper's descriptions have much more the character
of set pictures :—

> " Here Ouse, slow winding through a level plain
>   Of spacious meads, with cattle sprinkled o'er,
>   Conducts the eye along his sinuous course
>   Delighted. There, fast rooted in their bank,
>   Stand, never overlook'd, our favourite elms,
>   That screen the herdsman's solitary hut ;
>   While far beyond, and overthwart the stream,
>   That, as with molten glass, inlays the vale,
>   The sloping land recedes into the clouds."
>
> (*The Task*, i. 163 ff.)

On this or some similar scene Sainte-Beuve justly
remarks, " On copierait ce paysage avec le pinceau,"
and again, " Les Flamands ont trouvé leur égal en
poésie." His observation, in fact, is more minute and
particular than Thomson's : he deals in details rather
than broad general effects : in a woodland scene each
separate tree is characterised. And the details are of
objects endeared by familiarity, " which daily view'd
please daily,"—" our favourite elms," the often-visited
cottage, the tower from which comes the accustomed

music of the bells, and the well-known Ouse winding through its meadows.

In many respects, nevertheless, these two poets, so different in temperament, resembled one another in feeling. For both, the interest of the scenes which they describe is deeply connected with human life and human labour, and the beauty which they appreciate is that which is connected closely with the supply of human wants. Scenes are not admired by either of them because they are desolate, or because they suggest images of danger or death, though both are capable of feeling the awe which is inspired by the manifestations of elemental power in nature. For both the family and the home are peculiarly sacred. Both are true lovers of their country, Thomson with the proud and unquestioning patriotism which might have been expected in the author of "Rule Britannia," Cowper with a more wistful, but not less genuine affection,— "England, with all thy faults, I love thee still." Both express strongly their sympathy with the sufferings of the lower animals, and both are enthusiasts for liberty. Finally, both Thomson and Cowper have strong religious feelings, though in the former of the two the religion is not distinctively Christian. For both the delight in the beauty of external nature is deeply connected with a sense of the divine power and goodness which is therein displayed.

On the relation of Thomson to Wordsworth something has been said generally in an earlier chapter. Here it is sufficient to observe that Wordsworth's early descriptive poems, and especially that entitled *An Evening Walk*, show distinct traces of familiarity with *The Seasons*, and that *The Castle of Indolence* was his pocket-companion.

The influence of Thomson upon the Continent was

an important one. Certainly no English poet before his time had obtained so much currency in France or Germany, or produced so marked an effect upon foreign literature. *The Seasons* was translated in 1759 by Mme. Bontemps into French prose, and found a number of imitators, Saint-Lambert, Léonard, whose poem *Les Saisons*, said to be "imitated from Thomson," is in fact to a great extent a translation, and finally Delille; but here again the less direct and obvious influence is the more important. Rousseau, who in *La Nouvelle Héloïse* set the example of a "romantic" treatment of scenery, undoubtedly owed something appreciable to the fashion set by Thomson.

In Germany *The Seasons* met with a still more enthusiastic reception. The metrical translation of Brockes, who was himself a poet of the picturesque school, appeared in 1744, and was followed by several prose versions. Brockes was nearly akin to Thomson in feeling, and caught the spirit of his original admirably, but adopted an almost intolerable metre for his translation. The school of descriptive poetry in Germany was profoundly influenced by Thomson, and his poetical work was enthusiastically praised by Lessing, Wieland, and Gessner. Kleist, in his *Frühling*, is mainly a follower of Thomson, though he does not seem to have known the original English text of *The Seasons*. He abandons in this poem the minute description of details, and succeeds in attaining to something of the epic breadth of the English poet. The enthusiasm for Nature, inspired to a great extent by Thomson, was a strong element here also in the transition to the emotional symbolism which we find in the later poetry of the century.

APPENDIX

THE REVISION OF *THE SEASONS*

WE have noted in Chapter v. some of the literary influences which are visible in the successive revisions of *The Seasons*; and elsewhere reference has been made to the celebrated interleaved copy of the edition of 1738, with corrections and suggestions in the handwriting of the author and of another person, many of which were adopted in the issue of 1744. It is an interesting document, no doubt, but its importance has been greatly exaggerated, chiefly owing to the suggestion that the hand which is here found in company with Thomson's is that of Pope. The idea that Pope collaborated with Thomson in the revision of *The Seasons* has proved to be an attractive one, and has been accepted by several competent critics; but it was long ago denounced as a mare's nest by Mr. Churton Collins. It is unfortunate that Mr. Tovey, whose judgment seems to be against the identification of the collaborator with Pope, should, in his critical notes, constantly speak as if this identification were certain. In any case the matter is one to be decided by comparison of handwriting : and it is not enough to show that the handwriting is not that of Pope ; it is necessary also to ascertain who this friend actually was, who was in such intimate literary association with Thomson. The present writer conceived it to be his duty to leave no doubt upon this question ; and a comparison with the original letters from Lyttelton which are to be found among the Newcastle Papers in the British Museum, established beyond a doubt that the handwriting in question was his.[1]

After all, Lyttelton is *a priori* the most probable person. He was in close communication with Thomson at the period

---

[1] See *Athenæum*, October 1, 1904, p. 446

when this revision was made; and Thomson expressly tells
him in 1743 that he is engaged in the correction of *The
Seasons*, and hopes to continue the work at Hagley in the
autumn.   We know how much interest he took in the revision
of Thomson's work; and the character of the emendations
proposed by the friendly critic is precisely what we should
expect from him.   The same thing is true of the original
contributions to the text.   The most important of these is the
well-known simile of the myrtle in the episode of Lavinia and
Palemon :—

> "As in the hollow breast of Apennine,
> Beneath the shelter of encircling hills,
> A myrtle rises, far from human eye,
> And breathes its balmy fragrance o'er the wild;
> So flourish'd blooming, and unseen by all,
> The sweet Lavinia."
>
> > (*Autumn*, 209 ff.)

This may be compared with a passage in Lyttelton's
Monody to the Memory of his Wife :—

> "So where the silent streams of Liris glide,
> In the soft bosom of Campania's vale,
> When now the wintry tempests all are fled,
> And genial Summer breathes her gentle gale,
> The verdant orange lifts its beauteous head :
> From every branch the balmy flow'rets rise,
> On every bough the golden fruits are seen;
> With odours sweet it fills the smiling skies,
> The wood-nymphs tend, and the Idalian queen.
> But in the midst of all its blooming pride
> A sudden blast from Apenninus blows,
> > Cold with perpetual snows;
> The tender, blighted plant shrinks up its leaves and dies."

This is more elaborate, no doubt, and leads up to a different
conclusion, but there is a close resemblance, nevertheless,
both of ideas and of style.

It may be taken then as established that Lyttelton contributed to the revision of a certain portion of *The Seasons* in the
year 1743.   His hand appears in suggestions (not nearly
always accepted by the author) throughout the whole of
Autumn, and occasionally in the latter part of *Summer*, and in

the earlier part of *Winter*. Incidently we may note that, at
least in the case of *Autumn*, the revision of the poem seems to
have been deliberately reserved on this occasion for the season
which it celebrates.

It is an interesting question how far Thomson's work was
improved or deteriorated on the whole by the process of
revision to which it was subjected.   Johnson remarked of *The
Seasons* :—

"These poems, with which I was acquainted at their first appearance, I have since found altered and enlarged by subsequent revisals,
as the author supposed his judgment to grow more exact, and as
books and conversation extended his knowledge and opened his
prospects. They are, I think, improved in general ; yet I know not
whether they have not lost part of what Temple calls their 'race,' a
word which, applied to wines in its primitive sense, means the
flavour of the soil."

We have already seen reason to think that the author would
have done better for his reputation, if he had limited the
poems to something like the scale of his original *Winter*, and
without attempting to survey the whole world, or to express
the current views about society and religion, had confined
himself more strictly to those themes for which he had a
special aptitude.   But, except in the case of *Winter*, this dis-
cursiveness is a fault of the original issues ; and we are not to
assume that the additions made subsequently are usually such
as the reader would willingly dispense with, or that they dis-
play on the whole less feeling for nature and less fineness of
observation than the earlier work.   In the cases of *Spring*
and *Autumn*, the latest forms are not materially longer
than the earliest : in each there is a difference in length of
about a hundred lines.   In *Spring* the addition consists
principally of two passages, 379-466, and 904-962, the former
of which contains the descriptions of trout-fishing and of the
noon-day rest, which have as much merit as any portion of the
poem, though we may reasonably desire a better connection ;
and the latter has the address to Lyttelton and the view from
Hagley Park.   At the same time some omissions were made,
of matter which can easily be spared, and one passage was
transferred to *Summer*.   This latter poem was very consider-

ably enlarged in the edition of 1744, and among the interpolations are the passage on sheep-shearing, which has as much "race" as any in *The Seasons*, the sand-storm in the desert, the tropical hurricane, the pestilence in the British squadron at Carthagena, and finally the summer evening's walk, with the view from Richmond Hill, with none of which we should be willing to part. The additions to *Autumn*, as we have said, are not considerable : they include the revised account of the sources of rivers, which has undoubted merit in its own way, a certain number of lines transferred from the beginning of the original *Winter*, and the mention of Stowe with its "last smiles Of autumn beaming o'er the yellow woods," and the personal references to Pitt and Cobham. The case of *Winter* is peculiar, and here alone we have in the first issue an essentially different poem. The contrast between wealth and poverty, the tribute to the Jail Committee, the scenes of city life with the address to Chesterfield, the descriptions of foreign climates, the Alps, Holland, Russia, Lapland and Siberia, and the reflections on the powers of government as illustrated by the work of Peter the Great, are all absent from the original edition, and the catalogue of the "mighty dead" was at first comparatively brief. It may reasonably be suspected that the theory, which is sometimes put forward, that *The Seasons* as a poem has been seriously damaged by interpolations, is based almost entirely on the case of *Winter*. Yet even in *Winter* there occur several passages among the additions which are racy of the soil, especially the pathetic scene of the peasant lost upon the moor, and the detailed account of the effects of frost, which however, both appeared as early as 1730.

But besides the addition of matter to his poems the author undertook a careful revision of their form of expression ; and this at two distinct periods : first before the earliest complete issue of *The Seasons* in 1730, and afterwards in preparation for the edition of 1744. Johnson's judgment, expressed in the passage quoted above, is probably not based on any minute collation of texts, but mainly upon the impression produced by the interpolations. It is of some interest, however, to institute a comparison between the later and the earlier issues,

as regards the detailed revision of the style, and to raise
the question how far the text is improved by the alterations,
and whether the process of polishing has been accompanied by
any loss of vigour. As the result of such an investigation we
shall probably come to the conclusion that few poets have
been so successful as Thomson in the revision of their work.
When we examine in detail the alterations introduced into
particular passages, we almost invariably feel that the revised
text is a distinct improvement; and we are impressed with the
fact that a sound critical judgment has been exercised upon
the minutest details, and that pains have been taken especially
to improve the rhythm of the verse and the harmony of the
vowel sounds. Nor do these alterations suggest the idea
that the keenness of the author's perceptions has been in any
degree blunted by his life in communication with an artificial
literary society. He remained singularly unspoilt, preserved
by a genuine poetical enthusiasm and a determination to
follow his own bent. If he accepted and expressed the
fashionable philosophy and the prevailing sentiments, humanitarian or patriotic, of the day, this was mainly because they
were entirely in accordance with his own temperament; and
the fact that in a certain limited number of passages he
admitted additional suggestions from the *Georgics* of Virgil
must be taken as a special tribute to Virgil, and not as an
indication that he had ceased to keep his eye upon the object
and was depending upon books rather than upon observation.

Examples have sometimes been cited of alterations, in
which it is supposed that picturesqueness or vigour has been
sacrificed without any sufficient compensation; but in most
cases it will be found that these are concerned with exaggerated
or tasteless forms of expression, which no sound critic would
desire to preserve. Such a phrase as "the worst monster that
e'er howled the waste" may be expressive, but it is hardly
grammatical; the idea of scaling mountains rapidly is rather
absurdly expressed by the line,—

"Then snatch the mountains by their woody tops,"

and with reference to the startled hare, "Shook from the
corn" is not more expressive than "Scared from the corn,"

and it is less grammatical. When in an omitted passage of *Winter* the poet described sledging in Russia thus,—

> "While tempted vigorous o'er the marble waste,
>   On sleds reclin'd the furry Russian sits,
>   And by his reindeer drawn, behind him throws
>   A shining kingdom on a Winter's day,"

he was in the first place absurdly confusing Russians and Lapps, and secondly exaggerating enormously the rapidity of the sledge. Much the same account may be given of a supposed toning down of colour effects in revision, as to which Mr. J. L. Robertson remarks, "It was in deference to English taste that he economised his reds and yellows, and toned down those glowing tints, a love for which he had inherited from the Scottish school of poetry." Thomson inherited little from the Scottish school of poetry, and when we come to examine the instances in which vivid colouring is actually less prominent in the later than in the earlier texts, we shall find that there are excellent reasons for the changes apart from the mere question of colour. The most prominent example is, perhaps, the passage in the original edition of *Spring*,[1] where the poetical ideas of the Golden Age are developed thus on the model of Ovid :—

> "Nor had the spongy, full-expanded Fleece
>   Yet drunk the Tyrian Die.   The stately Ram
>   Shone thro' the Mead, in native Purple clad,
>   Or milder Saffron ; and the dancing Lamb
>   The vivid crimson to the Sun disclos'd."

This kind of artificial absurdity might surely be retrenched without laying the poet open to the charge of having lost the keenness of his colour-sense. Another instance is where the colours of insects are enumerated in *Summer* :—

> "Swarming they pour ; green, speckled, yellow, grey,
>   Black, azure, brown ; more than th' assisted Eye
>   Of poring Virtuoso can discern."

---

[1] I may here remark that my references to the first editions of *Winter* and *Summer* depend upon the copies in the British Museum, while for a copy of the first edition of *Spring*, which the British Museum does not now possess, I have been indebted to my own College library.

We can very well spare this catalogue, and it is judiciously replaced by,

> "Swarming they pour; of all the varied hues
> Their beauty-beaming parent can disclose."
>
> (*Summer*, 247.)

Wherever brilliant colouring is proper and effective, we find it in the later as in the earlier editions. Passages of brilliant colouring might easily be quoted from the later form of the tropical scenes in *Summer*, to compensate for some which are there lost, and the single line added in 1744 to the garden-scene (*Spring*, 533),—

> "The yellow wall-flower, stain'd with iron brown,"

will more than counterbalance any possible losses that may have been sustained elsewhere.

The corrections made in revision are in fact, for the most part, improvements, both in literary taste and in the direction of greater poetical truth. The loose talk that we sometimes hear on the subject of these changes is, no doubt, chiefly based upon Johnson's phrase about a loss of "race," which was probably not intended to apply to them at all. It seems desirable in any case that the subject should be treated with some approach to precision; and this can only be done by entering somewhat further into detail. Let us take note therefore of a few of the alterations which occur in the earlier part of *Summer*, comparing the text of 1746 with that of 1727.

The opening lines ran thus,—

> "From Southern Climes, where unremitting Day
> Burns over Head, illustrious Summer comes,"

which became later,—

> "From brightening fields of ether fair disclos'd,
> Child of the Sun, refulgent Summer comes.

A geographical statement was not in place here, even if it had been accurate, and there is both more truth and more beauty in the vaguer suggestion of the later form.

The original line,—

> "Mildly elucent in the streaky East,"

was surely much improved when it became,—

> "At first faint-gleaming in the dappled East,
> Till far o'er ether spreads the widening glow." (48 f.)

In l. 68, "springing from the bed of sloth" is better both in sound and meaning than "starting from the bed of sloth"; and four lines later :—

> "lost to all
> Our Nature's boast of noble and divine,"

was far less appropriate than what we have at present,—

> "losing half
> The fleeting moments of too short a life."

Similarly, if we compare,—

> "Without whose vital and effectual Glance
> They'd be but brute, uncomfortable Mass,"

with the present text,—

> "Without whose quickening glance their cumbrous orbs
> Were brute, unlovely mass, inert and dead," (105 f.)

or

> "At thee the Ruby lights his deepening glow,
> A bleeding Radiance, grateful to the View,"

with the text of 1744,—

> "At thee the Ruby lights its deepening glow,
> And with a waving radiance inward flames," (147 f.)

or again,—

> "By thee refin'd,
> In brisker Measures the reluctent Stream
> Frisks o'er the Mead."

with the later,—

> "By thee refin'd
> In brighter mazes the reluctent stream
> Plays o'er the mead." (161 ff.)

in every case we must be struck with the improvement of the style. So in l. 200, "Melts into limpid air" is an improvement on "Attenuates to air," and in l. 282,

> "Nor undelightful is the ceaseless hum,"

is obviously better than what was first written,—

> "Nor undelightful is the humming sound."

These examples are selected from the first three hundred lines of *Summer*. Those that follow are from the earlier part of *Spring*.

In l. 16, "livid torrents," for "sudden torrents," gives an added touch of colour. The present ll. 54-66 have been re-written, the changes being all improvements either as regards the expression or the balance of clauses, except the conclusion, which was intended to make the passage more precisely applicable to the politics of the day; in l. 67, "cultivate" is altered to "venerate," thus avoiding a very unfortunate Latinism; in l. 71, "domain," for "extent," gives better sound and better sense; in l. 104, the substitution of "trembling" for "lucid" adds a picturesque touch; in l. 115, "humid wings" is better than "foggy wings"; and in the next line, "clammy" is more appropriate than "bitter"; in l. 177 (originally, "'Tis scarce to patter heard, the stealing shower"), the inversion is made decidedly less violent; and a tasteless Latinism has been got rid of in l. 183. Further examination serves only to confirm the impression : in l. 524, for example, where the author wrote originally,—

"The forest running round, the rising spire,"

the change by which we get, instead of this,—

"The forest darkening round, the glittering spire,"

makes at once a picture out of what was at first a rather commonplace enumeration of details; and in a somewhat later passage the insertion of the lines,—

"On utmost Kilda's shore, whose lonely race
Resign the setting sun to Indian worlds," (757 f.)

adds much to the poetry of the passage.

It is seldom that we see any reason to regret a change : the alteration in *Spring*, 65 f., is no doubt unfortunate; in *Summer*, 170, we might prefer to keep "A glance extensive as the day," and probably the epithet "dewy-bright" (*Spring*, 527) will be thought better than the more commonplace "bright with dew"; but such cases are quite exceptional. In general there can be no doubt that the alterations are for the better; and the critical judgment of which we see the results is clearly that of the author himself for the most part, though some of Lyttelton's suggestions are accepted (assuming that those which appear in his handwriting are due to him). The essential characteristics of the style are fully preserved, and we know what havoc Lyttelton would have made with them, if he had had his way. Thomson was not the man to "write by the judgment of another." As regards literary models, the later revision shows distinctly more independence than the original text, notwithstanding the additions from the *Georgics*. The suggestion of a modern critic that the author endeavoured in this revision to overlay his text with a "Virgilian veneer," must be regarded as a somewhat unfortunate one, whether it be intended to express the detailed or the general effect of the alterations which were made.

INDEX

A

Addison, 88, 168, 173.
Agamemnon, by Thomson, 30 *n.*
(42), 44, 46-49, 225-227.
Aikman, painter, 10, 31, 35 *n.*, 165,
193.
Akenside, M., 234.
Alcestis of Euripides, 228.
Alfred, a Masque, 51 f., 196, 228.
Alfred the Great, 121.
L'Allegro, 141 f., 144.
Alpen, by Haller, 97.
Alps, scenes of, 134, 182, 212.
"Amanda," *see* Young, Miss Eliza-
beth.
Amelia, Fielding's, 26.
Amyntor and Theodora, by Mallet,
62.
Ancrum, 9, 14.
angling, 5, 8, 110 f.
Anson, Admiral, 63.
Apollo Belvidere, 181.
Arbuthnot, Dr., 31; Pope's
"Epistle to Arbuthnot," 33 *n.*
Argyll, Duke of, 31, 127.
Arminius, by Paterson, 60.
Armstrong, Dr. John, 45, 69 f., 72,
139, 151 ff., 205, 207, 234.
Arne, Mrs., 228.
Art of Preserving Health, 234.
Ashdown Park, 35.
"Athenian Society," 7.
Augusta, Princess, 45.
Aurora Borealis, 127, 129, 137.
authors and publishers, 86 f.
Autumn, 30 f., 59, 75, 106, 122-130,
244-246.

B

Bacon, 121.
Baillie, Lady Grizel, 9, 12.

Barnet, 12, 13.
bathing, 5, 119.
Bathurst, Lord, 31, 188.
Bell, Mr., 64.
Bennett, Sir William, 4, 31.
Berry, Miss, 54.
Bible, influence on Thomson, 140 f.
Binning, Lord, 12, 13, 21 f.
birds, courtship and nesting, 112 f.
Blake, Admiral, 191.
Blenheim, by J. Philips, 162.
Blount, Mrs. Martha, 31.
Boileau, 92.
Bolingbroke, Lord, 31, 33 *n.*, 95.
Bontemps, Mme., 242.
Booth, actor, 10.
Boswell, James, 64, 131 *n.*
Boyle, 121.
Bridgewater, Duchess of, 63.
Britain, glories of, 121, 182-185,
187 f., 209.
Britannia, 183.
Britannia, by Thomson, 25, 26, 30,
190-192.
Brockes, 242.
Brooke, Henry, 49, 51 *n.*
Brutus, by Voltaire, 32.
Burke, 186.
Burlington, Earl of, 31.
Burns, 239.
Bute, Earl of, 31.

C

calm in autumn, 130; at midnight
in winter, 133.
Campbell, Admiral, 53.
Caroline, Queen, 27, 48.
Carter Fell, 2.
Carthagena, expedition to, 59, 118,
246.
cascade described, 117.

Printed by T. and A. CONSTABLE, Printers to His Majesty
at the Edinburgh University Press

S